BEGGARS AND CHOOSERS

HOW THE POLITICS OF CHOICE SHAPES

ADOPTION, ABORTION, AND WELFARE

IN THE UNITED STATES

———

RICKIE SOLINGER

———

HILL AND WANG

A DIVISION OF FARRAR, STRAUS AND GIROUX

NEW YORK

Hill and Wang
A division of Farrar, Straus and Giroux
19 Union Square West, New York 10003

Library of Congress Cataloging-in-Publication Data
Solinger, Rickie, 1947–
    Beggars and choosers : how the politics of choice shapes adoption, abortion, and
welfare in the United States / Rickie Solinger.— 1st ed.
        p.   cm.
    Includes bibliographical references and index.
    ISBN 0-8090-9702-8 (hc : alk. paper)
    1. Pro-choice movement—United States.   2. Abortion—Social aspects—
United States.   3. Women's rights—United States.   4. Women—United States—
Social conditions—20th century.   I. Title.

HQ767.5.U5 S73265 2001
363.46—dc21

                                                                    2001016652

Designed by Jonathan D. Lippincott

FOR ZACHARY AND NELL

CONTENTS

ACKNOWLEDGMENTS

———

Having worked on *Beggars and Choosers* for a long time, I am surprised to read some of the sentences I now find in the book, although I am certain that I wrote them. I am also certain that Jim Geiser's support has been crucial, unfailing, and completely generous. Even though Jim is a mathematician, he has an excellent understanding of the historical enterprise, which makes me very lucky. (Equally important, Jim has kept me connected to matters beyond the politics of motherhood. He read and, as we took our morning walks up Mt. Sanitas, told me the stories of nineteen Trollope novels, as well as numerous Balzacs, Gissings, and Galsworthys.)

I have also been lucky with research assistance. Erika Lichter showed up just when I began to realize how many things I needed to learn in order to think about this project, and she helped in all areas. Liza Butler was as conscientious and orderly an assistant as a historian could hope for. I continue to draw on the trove of materials Jon Birnbaum sent me. And my spectacular daughter, Nell Geiser, has several times helped me out in her usual simply brilliant way. My spectacular son, Zachary Leeds, has lived far away during my work on this project, but has always allowed me—even invited me—to tell him about my ideas for the book over the phone, even when this involved graciously tolerating repetition.

I am very grateful to the members of Concerned United Birthparents and to the unaffiliated birthmothers who sent me letters, e-mails, and audio- and videotapes, and sat for interviews, as I investigated the aftermath of coerced adoption. I particularly want to thank Carole Anderson, Janet Fenton, Bonnie Bis, Mary Redenius, and Pat Taylor, all of whom spent a long weekend with me in Nebraska answering my questions, posing their own, and gamely summoning up the painful and the activist past. They also kindly gave me brochures, essays, and other documents from CUB's early days. Lee Campbell was extremely generous, lending me her manuscript "Hello Again" when I needed to understand the origins of the organization she and others founded to assert the rights of birthmothers.

Several scholars read the entire manuscript and sent wonderful critiques, including comments that both set me straight and encouraged me a lot. I am very pleased to thank Gwendolyn Mink, Amy Kesselman, Lisa Brush, and Lauri Umansky for helping me in this way. I first tested ideas for this project in an essay, "Poisonous Choice," that I wrote for *Bad Mothers*, the volume edited by Lauri Umansky and Molly Ladd-Taylor; both editors were extremely helpful then. I laid further groundwork in an essay, "Dependency and Choice: The Two Faces of Eve," solicited by Gwendolyn Mink for an issue of *Social Justice* (which transmuted into a volume entitled *Whose Welfare?*). Wendy's acute reading of "Dependency and Choice" stayed with me throughout the project. Thanks also to the American Council of Learned Societies, which supported this book when I thought of it as "Who Is a Mother? And Who Decides?"

The most concrete and thoroughgoing help I got was from Lauren Osborne. I sought out Lauren because of her sterling reputation as an engaged, highly skilled editor who pays close attention to language and structure. Lauren lived up to her reputation. Her suggestions were bold and subtle, imaginative and basic, insistent and gentle. In all cases, Lauren's work on my work was smart and ameliorative. I am very grateful that she took me on.

Finally, I want to return to the subject of Zachary and Nell. These two made me a mother—a grand, rich status indeed. Even as they grow up completely and move on, I spend quite a lot of time loving their faces, their ethical relations to the world, their impressive minds, their humor, their music, and their countless other charms. But beyond all this, having these children has taught me how fortunate I was *to get to make* the choices I made about pregnancy and motherhood.

Becoming a mother in 1976 and again in 1984 meant that I could make choices because of the historical moment in which I was fertile, because of my age, my class status, my race and nationality. This is crucial: even after *Roe v. Wade* I had to meet lots of conditions for the society I live in to treat me like a valid choice maker and mother. In the United

States, many girls and women have not been—and today still are not—considered legitimate choice makers because, for reasons beyond their control, they do not meet enough of those conditions. When they have abortions or children, these girls and women are often said to have made bad choices. And yet the right to reproduce or not may be the most bedrock right of humans.

My investigations of the problems with "choice" lead me inexorably to this question: How can "choice" express the reproductive rights of all fertile females in this country while so many Americans reserve the status of proper choice maker for those who have "adequate" resources?

Being a mother has convinced me that you do not have to have a particular demographic profile to want and love your children. I am convinced that women with inadequate resources generally love their children in the same way that I love Zachary and Nell. I wrote *Beggars and Choosers* partly to insist on this: women who do not meet the conditions many Americans claim are requisite for exercising choice must nevertheless have *the right to determine for themselves whether or not to be mothers.* Zachary and Nell have made this clear to me, and so I thank them deeply for shaping my intellectual and political commitments.

CONFUSING THE RIGHT TO *CHOOSE* WITH THE RIGHT TO *SHOES*, HE CAMPAIGNED ONLY IN HIS PUMPS, SAYING, "IT'S MY BODY AND MY DECISION."

—KENNETH COLE SHOE AD, 1996

BEGGARS AND CHOOSERS

that *Roe* was "a declaration of human liberty." She remembered that as she read the text of Justice Harry Blackmun's opinion, she "rejoiced that the decision was seven-to-two [and] that it was strong and clear." She also remembered taking a phone call that day from a woman who had an urgent suggestion: "that January 22nd be declared a national holiday for women."

Roe v. Wade generated so much hope and excitement partly because it seemed so clearly to be responding to the dilemma of *all* women. Many proponents of legal abortion believed *Roe* was a symbol and a vehicle of women's liberation. A Vermont law student described the *Roe* decision as a response "to the rallying of women across the nation—a rejection of women as reproductive machines and an acceptance of women as individuals capable of choice."[5] The Court had not distinguished among groups of women by age, race, income, or level of education. *Roe v. Wade* was for everyone.

This sense of triumph was not surprising. After all, abortion rights activists and many ordinary women had talked for years about the deeply degrading impact of anti-abortion statutes and the importance of achieving reproductive freedom. The founders of an early abortion rights organization, the Society for Humane Abortion, described state laws forbidding abortion as a form of sex discrimination.[6] Many involved in the women's rights movement defined abortion rights as having tremendous political and practical significance. One second wave feminist put it this way:

> When we talk about women's rights, we can get all the rights in the world—the right to vote, the right to go to school—and none of them means a doggone thing if we don't own the flesh we stand in . . . if the whole course of our lives can be changed by somebody else that can get us pregnant by accident, or by deceit, or by force. So I consider the right to elective abortion . . . the cornerstone of the women's movement . . . Without that right, we'd have about as many rights as a cow in the pasture that's taken to the bull once a year . . . [I]f you can't control your body you can't control your future.[7]

During the late 1960s and early 1970s, advocates of legal abortion mostly used the term "rights," not "choice," to refer to what they were

1

CHOICE IS A MOVING TARGET

Although we strongly believe in the private and responsible nature of our own choices to have children, we simply do not see the choices of women in poverty in the same way.   —Thomas Ross, *Just Stories*[1]

January 22, 1973, was a remarkable day in United States history. That afternoon Lyndon Baines Johnson died. At nearly the same time, the U.S. Supreme Court announced one of its most ambitious decisions ever, *Roe v. Wade*. On the evening news, the former president's death eclipsed the announcement that abortion was now legal in all fifty states.[2] In the years since the *Roe* decision, however, the political struggle over the role of abortion in U.S. society has fiercely resisted eclipse. The meaning of the *Roe* decision, especially the meaning of the "choice" it promised women, has never stopped evolving.

After the Court's announcement, commentators called *Roe v. Wade* "one of the boldest, most sweeping decisions of the . . . era," "an astonishing decision," "extraordinary."[3] Later, after the complexities of *Roe* had become more apparent, some observers still referred to it as "a total victory" and an "expansive decision."[4] Sarah Weddington, the young Texas lawyer who argued the case before the Court, wrote in her memoir after. Still, the term "choice" did crop up. The National Abortion Rights Action League's (NARAL) first national action in 1969—a Mother's Day demonstration held in conjunction with press conferences in eleven cities—was called "Children by Choice."[8] And Dr. Alan Guttmacher, the prominent birth control advocate and important convert to the cause of legalized abortion, proclaimed January 22, 1973, "a great day for freedom of choice."[9] But until *Roe*, most activists claimed that "the *right* to control whether you're pregnant or not [was] indivisible from the right to self-determination."[10]

The rights language, however, did not last very long. Justice Black-mun referred to abortion as "this choice" a number of times in his *Roe* majority ruling. And the determination of abortion rights advocates to develop a respectable, nonconfrontational movement after *Roe* encouraged many proponents to adopt the term "choice." In a country weary of rights claims, choice became *the* way liberal and mainstream feminists could talk about abortion without mentioning the "A-word."[11] Many people believed that "choice"—a term that evoked women shoppers selecting among options in the marketplace—would be an easier sell; it offered "rights lite," a package less threatening or disturbing than unadulterated rights.

At first, people who used the term "choice" didn't talk much about what it would take for a woman to exercise her new reproductive lati-tude. The law had made choice legal for everyone, and that was that. A women's health care provider observed in 1973, "What has been hap-pening . . . is that if you can afford it, you get an abortion, and if you can't, you have the child and go on welfare."[12] Now, she indicated, the playing field would be much more level. A woman could choose whether or not to get an abortion and whether or not to become a mother, no matter how much money she had in her wallet.

This early, optimistic sense of how *Roe v. Wade* would affect women's reproductive lives reflected the utopian egalitarianism of many in the women's movement at the time. In the struggle to win reproductive free-dom, many activists didn't think about the fact that pregnancy and childbearing have historically and dramatically separated women by race and class in this country. For centuries, enslaved African-American women had endured coerced pregnancies and the human-selling prac-tices of slave owners. White urban immigrant mothers had seen their children targeted and taken away from them by "child rescue" charities in the nineteenth and early twentieth centuries. After World War II, white unmarried mothers were roughly pressed to relinquish their "illegitimate" babies, while in the same period Black unmarried mothers were stereotyped as excessively fertile welfare cheats.[13] Which women, under which circumstances, were legitimately pregnant or legitimate mothers, and which were not, had always involved race and/or class distinctions in America. The pregnancies and childbearing of women of color and resourceless women had often deepened the vulnerability of these women, and deepened distinctions between them and middle-class white women who had resources and *choices*, long before *Roe v. Wade*. In the late 1960s and early 1970s, this history—much of which was still buried or too fresh to look at historically—could have tempered optimism about "choice" as a powerful equalizer.

This book is about the complexities of "choice" in the United States after *Roe v. Wade*. What happens when the special guarantee for all women—the promise that women can decide for themselves whether and when to be mothers—is expressed by the individualistic, marketplace term "choice"? How can users of such a term avoid distinguishing, in consumer-culture fashion, between a woman who can and a woman who can't afford to make a choice? What aspects of "rights" were masked or lost when the language of choice replaced the language of rights at the heart of women's special guarantee?

I use the term "rights" to refer to the privileges or benefits of being a human and specifically a woman in the United States, privileges or benefits that one can exercise *without access to any special resources*, such as money. For example, women and minorities in the United States have struggled for and won "voting rights," that is, the right of all citizens over a certain age to vote, even if they have no money, no property, and no other resources. By contrast, choice, including the popular and problematic form "the right to choose," has come to be intimately connected to the possession of resources. Many Americans have developed faith in the idea that women who exercise choice are supposed to be legitimate consumers, women with money. This is true even when the choices they exercise, such as the choice to become a mother or the choice to end a pregnancy, might be considered a very fundamental issue of rights.

Like the copywriter in the Kenneth Cole shoe ad that is the epigraph for this book, I find the slogan "the right to choose" fairly ridiculous. It impossibly mixes "right," a privilege to which one is justly entitled, and "choice," the privilege to exercise discrimination in the marketplace among several options, *if* one has the wherewithal to enter the marketplace to begin with. Our Constitution does not, of course, guarantee anyone the *right* to enter the marketplace of reproductive (or any other) options. As I discuss later in this chapter, the Supreme Court's decisions regarding the legitimacy of the Hyde Amendment (an act of Congress denying federal funding for the abortions of poor women) have proved that.

Historical distinctions between women of color and white women, between poor and middle-class women, have been reproduced and institutionalized in the "era of choice," in part by defining some groups of women as good choice makers, some as bad. During a time when babies—and pregnancy itself—became ever more commodified, some women were defined as having a legitimate relationship to babies and motherhood status, while others were defined as illegitimate consumers. These distinctions and definitions emerged quickly in the era of choice and solidified across the last quarter of the twentieth century. I will examine how choice-driven distinctions undermined the possibility, so vibrant in the early celebrations of *Roe*, that all women would be equally empowered by legal abortion.

I am also concerned with two additional aspects of choice, issues that are rarely confronted in discussions about pregnancy and abortion, childbearing, adoption, and related subjects. First, given popular definitions of good choice makers and bad, I believe it is crucial to consider the degree to which one woman's possession of reproductive choice may actually depend on or deepen another woman's reproductive vulnerability. Parts of the book will explore this dynamic, interactive quality of choice.

Second, and perhaps most important of all, I am devoted here to making the argument that simple "choice" actually underlies the very popular (though much denied) idea that motherhood should be a class privilege in the United States—a privilege appropriate only for women who can afford it. I am convinced that choice is a remarkably unstable, undependable foundation for guaranteeing women's control over their own bodies, their reproductive lives, their motherhood, and ultimately their status as full citizens.

I consider the problem of choice by investigating its role in the ways Americans have talked about abortion, adoption, and welfare over the past generation. I am also interested in how "choice" figured in creating public policies to govern women's behavior in these areas. I start off by looking at two immediate post-*Roe* developments—the denial of federal funding to pay for the abortions of poor women and the emergence of the foreign adoption market. Together these developments at the dawn of the era of choice facilitated a crucially consequential shift in the claims associated with the Supreme Court's bold ruling: from women's right to consumer privilege.

THE MEDICAID CASES: HOW CONSUMER PRIVILEGE TRUMPED REPRODUCTIVE RIGHTS

At the very moment when the era of choice was born, Supreme Court Justices William Rehnquist and Byron White excoriated "choice" and the women who would exercise it. In their dissenting opinion in *Roe v. Wade*, Rehnquist and White defined "the power of choice" as based on a woman's "convenience," "whim," "caprice," on women willing to "exterminate" their pregnancies "for no reason at all," or because of their "dislike of children."[14] The dissenters clearly and early associated "choice" with bad women making bad choices. In this way they provided a harbinger of the future.

The dissenters' language is a reminder of the historical moment in which "choices" were granted to women. For about a hundred years, the law had denied women reproductive choices, including, for much of that time, access to effective methods of birth control. Women who tried to control their reproductive lives were first criminals and later, in the twentieth century, diagnosed as mentally ill.[15] In addition the country was just emerging from a generation of widespread cultural hostility to white, broadly middle-class mothers who "chose" to work outside of the home for wages. Such women were frequently and prominently tagged as having made poor, selfish, and damaging choices. A 1955 article in the popular women's magazine *McCall's*, "Is a Working Mother a Threat to the Home?" was typical. The article featured a male psychiatrist's assessment of working mothers as bad choice makers: "Until children are at least six, motherhood is a twenty-four hour job and one that no one can do for you. A mother who runs out on her children to work—except in cases of absolute necessity—betrays a deep dissatisfaction with motherhood or with her marriage. Chances are, she is driven by sick, competitive feelings toward men, or some other personality problem."[16]

When, in 1973, *Roe* granted what both the majority and dissenting opinions in *Roe v. Wade* called "choice," this represented, on top of everything else, a major cultural shift in mainstream Americans' view of women. Yet another male psychiatrist-expert, this one quoted in the issue of *Time* magazine that reported the *Roe v. Wade* decision, guided Americans toward a new, post-*Roe* view of choice-making women this way: "For the woman who let her life wash over her, who has let her life be directed by forces outside of herself, to make a decision to take charge of her life can be an extremely liberating, positive experience. For the first time in her life, she is the master of her destiny."[17] Indeed, American womanhood had been redefined.

"Women" were supposed to be alienated from reproductive and employment choice making in the middle decades of the twentieth century, but race definitely created divisions and distinctions among women. For one thing, African-American women had always worked; since the end of slavery, they had typically worked outside of their homes for wages.[18] In recent times, these same women had been provided with publicly sponsored access to birth control long before other women, an opportunity that poor, minority women were pressed to accept as a duty. A pre-*Roe* study of birth control distribution and race found that counties "in which family planning services were available as of 1969 were likely to have a higher percentage of Blacks than those counties in which services were not available." This same pattern, the study found, "appeared in most regions of the country—in poor counties, in rich counties, in rural and urban counties."[19] (Human rights activist Loretta Ross quotes a Louisianan in this era to explain some white support for such a pattern: "The best way to hate a nigger is to hate him before he is born.")[20]

African-American women and other women of color were pressed early and often in the years before *Roe* to avail themselves of "family planning" services as an antipoverty and population-control duty. The number one reason that the federal government increased expenditures for birth control (mostly targeting women of color) between 1967

($4.5 million) and 1971 ($24 million) was to diminish poverty and "prevent, reduce, or eliminate dependency."[21] Reproductive autonomy, or a woman's right to control her own body and her destiny—her right to make choices—was way down on the list of reasons.

In the period immediately following *Roe v. Wade*, unofficial, extralegislative public policy continued to target poor women of color in ways that clarified dramatically the limits of the Court's ruling. Sociologist Elena Rebecca Gutierrez has described how the fertility of a Mexican immigrant woman in California—one of many[22]—was targeted in this era:

> While under general anesthesia in preparation for her Cesarean section delivery, Jovila Rivera was approached by a doctor who told her that she should have her "tubes tied" because her children were a burden on the government. Ironically, Ms. Rivera was not receiving public assistance, nor were any of the other plaintiffs in the *Madrigal* case [a class action suit brought by Mexican-origin women sterilized against their will]. However, it was the doctors' perception of these women as poor welfare recipients that deemed them necessitating sterilization.[23]

It became impossible to claim that *Roe* could grant all women equal protection, reproductively, after the U.S. District Court for the District of Columbia noted in 1974 the existence of "uncontroverted evidence that poor people, particularly pregnant women whose deliveries would be paid for under Title XIX [of the Social Security Act], had been coerced into accepting sterilization under the threat of losing welfare benefits."[24] News of coerced sterilizations of poor African-American women in Alabama and South Carolina received national attention between 1973 and 1975.[25] Two women, Virgil Walker and Shirley Brown, dealt with a South Carolina obstetrician who made public policy on his own: he refused to accept as patients any welfare recipients who already had a certain number of children unless they agreed to be sterilized.[26] In the spring of 1974, having been presented with some of the "incontrovertible evidence," federal judge Gerhard Gessell ordered the government to redraft its sterilization regulations regarding welfare patients.[27] And in the summer of 1975, the government officially acknowledged that some health and welfare professionals were exerting this kind of pressure

against poor pregnant women when it adopted an anticoercion amendment aimed at government employees and anyone who managed or received federal funds. These personnel were enjoined from coercing or
endeavoring "to coerce any person to undergo an abortion or sterilization."[28]

Despite the ugliness publicly associated with sterilization, however,
the federal Department of Health, Education, and Welfare decided at the
end of 1974 (seven months before Congress passed legislation to stop
sterilization abuse of poor women) to develop an attractive federal funding scheme for reimbursing the states for sterilizing poor women. The
funding scheme allowed for much less generous reimbursement for abortions.[29] For many poor women after *Roe*, perhaps especially for poor
women of color, reproductive choice came to mean deciding between an
abortion they didn't have the money to pay for and a sterilization they
also did not have the money for, but for which the federal government
would pick up the tab. Many poor women and their advocates interpreted this 1974 policy as an official expression of the government's
desire and determination to curtail certain women's childbearing permanently.[30] For some women, choice was, early on, a hollowed-out
promise.

In the early 1970s the federal government was crafting ways to reduce
the childbearing of poor and minority women. But studies showed that
these women were, on their own, seeking and often obtaining abortions
at rates much higher than those of white middle-class women. A New
York City study conducted between 1972 and 1973 (New York State legalized abortion in 1970) found that there were twice as many white
women of childbearing age as Black in the city. But Black women were
getting more abortions. Of the 69,776 abortions performed during this
period, 47.6 percent were obtained by Black women, 39 percent by
white.[31] Several years later, a national study indicated that "the poor"
obtained about three times more abortions than "the non-poor."[32]

In the middle 1970s, however, negative attitudes toward poor, minority, childbearing women became much more powerful and relevant to
many Americans than factual information about how many children or
abortions these women actually had. As I will make plain in Chapter 5,
these years saw the emergence of widespread hostility toward such
women—often called ghetto matriarchs, and then "welfare queens." At

the same time, the anti–abortion rights movement was coalescing and developing its tactical agenda. When these two strains of hostility entangled, the result was a political program that fatally attacked the idea of abortion rights and seriously diminished the citizenship status of poor women in the United States. In these years, federal-level politicians and others devised and promoted restrictions on abortion access to crack down on poor women as choice makers. They also drew on the unpopular specter of poor women making choices to establish the sturdiest anti-abortion beachhead they could. These accomplishments were completed in 1980, before Ronald Reagan became president. Sarah Weddington reflected on the developments that followed *Roe* when she wrote years later, "I felt—and still feel—a chill when I think about [those] years."[33]

Almost immediately after *Roe v. Wade*, state departments of social services began to craft rules to limit the use of public funds to pay for the abortions of poor women. In Utah, for example, the rule said that a woman seeking an abortion must submit an application to the department of social services and the department must approve the abortion as therapeutic, that is, "necessary to save the mother's life or to prevent serious and permanent harm to her health." Like a number of early state efforts of this kind, Utah's attempt to restrict public funding was invalidated by a federal appeals court that decided "this broad abortion policy is intended to limit abortion on moral grounds." Such a policy, the court found, "constitutes invidious discrimination and cannot be upheld."[34]

In the first years after *Roe*, most federal courts agreed that it would be unconstitutional for a state to refuse to pay for a poor woman's elective abortion while agreeing to pay for other pregnancy-related medical treatment through its Medicaid program.[35] Similarly, the Bartlett Amendment of 1974, an early, unsuccessful congressional effort to restrict public funding, was condemned by the Congressional Research Service because "the courts have declared that all such . . . actions represent illegitimate interference with the reproductive freedom acknowledged in *Roe*."

Senator Edward Brooke of Massachusetts, one of a number of Republican senators who vigorously championed abortion rights in the 1970s, spoke aggressively on the Senate floor in 1975 in an effort to preserve reproductive rights for poor women. He pointed to the fact that federal courts had repeatedly ruled that "under the Fourteenth Amendment, once a state makes medical services available to poor women, it cannot discriminate against those women who choose to terminate their pregnancy during the first trimester."[36] Brooke emphasized that neither state laws nor the Bartlett Amendment would outlaw abortion, but that all of these efforts would "put an economic test on the questions of abortion." Brooke, an African-American, spoke boldly about how anti-abortion strategists were willing to use poor women to create class-privileged access to abortion in order to further their cause. "What they really wanted to do," he said, "was to get a constitutional amendment and failing to get this constitutional amendment, they targeted on the most vulnerable sector of our society; namely, poor women who could not afford to have an abortion . . . At the same time, other women who could afford it could make that decision and go to a safe, legal clinic and have an abortion." Senator Jacob Javits of New York made the same point more bluntly, pointing to the "essence" of the matter: "The poor use coat hangers and the wealthy go to clinics."[37]

Federal court rulings and politicians' bold statements between 1973 and 1975 insisted on the intentions of *Roe* to provide equal protection for all women. But a group of 1976 Supreme Court cases dashed the hopes of those concerned about protecting the reproductive rights of poor women. One legal scholar called these cases "a surprising and severe setback for those favoring unhindered access to abortion" because they upheld state regulations denying Medicaid funding for all nontherapeutic (elective) abortions.[38] At roughly the same time that the Supreme Court acted, Congress too affirmed its willingness—by adopting the Hyde Amendment—to forbid the use of Medicaid to pay for the abortions of poor women.[39]

The *Roe v. Wade* decision had, it seemed, made constitutionally impermissible the public policy view that abortion in and of itself was morally objectionable.[40] But these new developments, spearheaded by anti-abortion advocates, trumped *Roe*. They represented a major victory for religiously inspired anti-abortion policy makers. One observer explained, "[A]ny literate adult living in the United States since 1975 who has paid attention to politics knows that the exclusion of abortion services from Medicaid is motivated by opposition to abortion."[41] Representative Henry Hyde of Illinois, the author of the amendment, was anything but shy about admitting his intentions and his strategy. In June 1977 Hyde described his agenda this way: "I certainly would like to prevent, if I could legally, anybody having an abortion, a rich woman, a middle-class woman, or a poor woman. Unfortunately, the only vehicle available is the HEW Medicaid bill."[42]

Henry Hyde's efforts to restrict government support for poor women's abortions were so successful because by 1976 a critical mass of anti-abortion members of Congress had been elected—and the anti-abortion movement itself had emerged and grown strong.[43] Also, a critical mass of Americans did not approve of associating the sexual behavior of poor women, particularly minorities, with "choice." Many Americans, taking cues from the media treatment of poor women, questioned why their tax dollars should go for cleaning up the mistakes of careless, oversexed women.[44] Paradoxically, many of the same people believed that poor women should have fewer children and participated in stigmatizing "welfare mothers." And many believed that this paradox could be resolved only by constraining the choices that poor women could make. (This is what, for many, made sterilization such an attractive policy option.) Jacob Javits pointed out at the time that the effort to deny federal funds for poor women's abortions "eliminates all decision-making and exercise of choice on the part of women who are poor, thereby infringing upon their civil rights and personal freedom."[45] Supreme Court Justice William Brennan emphasized that the rulings restricting funding embodied a "distressing insensitivity to the plight of impoverished pregnant women" and forced such women to "feel they have no choice."[46] In 1980, the majority of the Supreme Court, in *Harris v. McRae*, upheld the Hyde Amendment and justified denying federal funds for the *medically necessary* abortions of poor women. Here Brennan and the other dissenters declared, "the reality of the situation is that [these policies] . . . effectively removed . . . choice from the indigent woman's hands."[47]

It is worth noting here that die-hard anti-abortion congressmen in the mid-1970s used House debates about restricting funds and choices for poor women as opportunities to mount discussions about *all women* as bad choice makers. The issue whether federal funds should be available for rape victims provided such an opportunity. Representative Richard Schweiker of Pennsylvania spoke vehemently against funding for rape victims because, he said, "There can be no question that a rape or incest provision would invite fraud and compound the problems of law enforcement since one sure way to obtain an abortion is to charge rape."[48]

Oklahoma Senator Dewey Bartlett, whose unsuccessful no-funding amendment preceded Hyde's, agreed with this perspective. Bartlett pointed out, "The person who is raped very fortunately in the first place very seldom becomes pregnant." Bartlett even went so far as to suggest that the very rare woman who becomes pregnant as the result of a rape has herself to blame. A responsible person, he said, would go "immediately to a doctor for a D&C and in that way presumably would not become pregnant."

In the mid to late-1970s, the abortion-funding cases suited the purposes of many politicians and policy makers for at least three important, choice-related reasons. First, the cases could be used as vehicles for dissolving the relationship between federal funding and "extermination." Second, the cases provided a way to end poor women's "inappropriate" and "unearned" relationship to choice. And third, the funding cases gave many politicians and others a way to dissociate the government from the "tyranny" of rights claims and from financial responsibility for guaranteeing rights. Dewey Barlett offered an analogy to show the gist of this last, important appeal of the funding cases: "Hopefully," the senator said, "we are not at the point that because we have a right to read our morning newspaper, the Government has an obligation to provide all of us home delivery."[49]

The abortion-funding cases gave many politicians and jurists the opportunity to express their dislike of incessant rights claims and their determination to halt government expenditures in the name of these rights. In the context of the funding cases, anti-funders first of all disavowed the association of abortion rights and "women's rights" that Roe v. Wade had foisted on them. Time magazine noted in 1977 that the Hyde Amendment put "people who believe that abortion is every woman's right . . . in retreat."[50] Beyond this, the cases were generally considered to have dealt a serious blow to the notion of "welfare rights" as well. Legal scholar Susan Frelich Appleton observed that Harris v. McRae and the other Supreme Court decisions validating the exclusion of abortion from Medicaid funding "unequivocally confirm that governmental protection of the poor—even the provision of such essentials as necessary health care—is a matter to be resolved [not by courts or by reference to constitutional rights] but . . . in accordance with majoritarian will."[51]

Senator Robert Packwood of Oregon, another abortion rights Republican, argued that the funding cases were at their heart discriminatory and directly released the government from responsibility for enforcing *equal rights*. Packwood described the Hyde Amendment as discriminating "against the women of this country, poor women to be exact, and black women in particular—who constitute the greatest proportion of Medicaid abortion patients." Most distressing, the amendment "flies in the face of all the progress this country has made toward granting equal rights toward every American, and is the worst example of socially unjust legislation this Congress could ever hope to put into law."[52]

Finally, the funding cases strongly suggested Congress's and the courts' interest in distancing themselves from a commitment to *human rights*. All the available indicators pointed to increased medical complications and deaths as a result of curtailing public funding for abortions.[53] But Congress did not consider this information. One group of public health observers called it "remarkable" that Congress "passed the Hyde Amendment without establishing any mechanism for examining the human consequences of its actions."[54] Brenda Joyner, an African-American abortion provider, spoke some years later about a crucial "human consequence" of the amendment: "The Hyde Amendment will not pay for a $200 or $300 abortion procedure for a poor woman on Medicaid. But it will pay for a $2000 to $3000 sterilization procedure for the same poor woman."[55]

The funding cases gave politicians and jurists a chance to resist publicly the government's expanding association with rights and its expanding role in ensuring access to rights. The cases also became an opportunity to insist on reasserting the traditional functions of government, especially reminding Americans about government restraint. When the Supreme Court decided that the state of Connecticut could refuse to pay for a poor woman's elective abortion, the Court emphasized that lack of money could indeed prevent a woman from getting an abortion. Justice Lewis Powell explained for the majority, however, that the Connecticut abortion funding regulation didn't cause that woman's poverty. And the state regulation itself didn't stop the woman from obtaining an abortion. Powell wrote that the Court was sympathetic to the plight of the poor woman who wants an abortion but doesn't have the money to pay for it. But for the Court's majority, Powell explained, the main point was "the Constitution does not provide judicial remedies for every social and economic ill."[56] Three years later, writing the majority opinion in *Harris v. McRae*, Justice Potter Stewart returned to this theme, that the government is not responsible for a person's poverty or for alleviating it. The government's responsibilities, Stewart wrote, must be narrowly drawn: "[A]lthough government may not place obstacles in the path of a woman's exercise of her freedom of choice, it need not remove those not of its own creation: Indigency falls in the latter category."[57]

In these cases between 1976 and 1980, the Supreme Court backed the government away from taking responsibility for causing poverty, for alleviating poverty, and for paying the bill for poor women to access abortion—a medical service that many believed *Roe v. Wade* had established as a "right." At the same time, in Congress, a number of representatives and senators regularly offered an alternate definition of abortion and the abortion-seeking woman, a definition that would justify removing federal funds. In Congress, abortion often became just another service that a consumer could or could not purchase, depending on how much money she had. Representative Charles Grassley of Iowa made the case for treating abortion more like other "goods and services": "Some argue that the Hyde Amendment deprives poor women of something that more affluent women can pay for." Nothing, he suggested, is the matter with that, since in all other matters that is the natural course of things.[58] While Grassley tried to normalize abortion as just another consumer service, Senator Orrin Hatch of Utah aimed to normalize the poor woman affected by restricted abortion funding. He cast her as a consumer, like any another woman. Imagine the abortion-seeking woman as a potential spender who could, if careful, stash away a "five" or a "ten" every couple of days, Hatch said. "[T]here is nothing to prevent [a poor woman] . . . from either exercising increased self-restraint, or from sacrificing on some item or other for a month or two to afford [her] own abortion."[59]

Those who insisted that abortion was just another consumer service and the unwillingly pregnant woman just another consumer ignored, of course, that unlike the typical consumer, the woman here—even if she had the resources—did not have the time to save. Public health officials were clear about facts that some politicians chose to obscure, "that the risk of death [from abortion], though small, increases by almost 30 percent with each week of gestation over eight weeks, and the risk of other major complications increases by about 20 percent with each additional week past the eighth."[60] Not surprisingly, the poor woman's access to resources was just as compromised as her access to time. When the Hyde Amendment became law, the average cost of an abortion in the United States was $280, forty-two dollars more than the average AFDC, or welfare, check for an entire family for a whole month. Researchers at the time found that poor women could pay for their own abortions only by sacrificing (to use Orrin Hatch's term) the basics—"food and shelter for themselves or their families."[61]

While a growing number of politicians pressed hard to transform abortion from a "rights" issue into a consumer-type issue—an issue for which the government had little responsibility—some politicians continued to insist that *Roe v. Wade had* established abortion as a constitutional right under the right of privacy. William Hathaway of Maine sternly reminded his fellow senators that "we do not have the right to deny constitutional rights to people because they are poor." He reminded the Senate that in the United States, the government allocated money in many cases to help poor people exercise their constitutional rights. He cited public support for public defenders who helped "people avail themselves of their civil rights . . . so that people will not be denied equal protection under the laws." Hathaway insisted that "the money being spent [before Hyde] for an abortion achieve[d] a similar purpose, because it . . . allow[ed] a poor person to avail herself of her constitutional right." Robert Packwood pointed out that to a certain extent even in the absence of a constitutional right or guarantee to education, health care, and housing, the government looked after the poor in these areas. Wasn't it ironic, Packwood asked his colleagues, that in the case of abortion, the Supreme Court had "guaranteed that every woman in this country, rich or poor, can make a choice as to whether or not [she] wants an abortion. Only we effectively deny it to the poor [woman if she] cannot pay for it."[62]

When abortion rights proponents pointed out this unequal denial of access based on poverty, or asked why the government supported policies that priced abortions out of reach of the poor, anti–abortion rights politicians responded in ways that elevated the causes of limited government and consumerism.[63] These responses pointedly eclipsed the causes of the 1960s and early 1970s: racial equality, economic justice, women's rights, and abortion rights. In 1976, Representative Jim Santini of Nevada explained his position in these terms: "There are a host of services and facilities that are not realistically available to the poor but enjoyed by those in better economic status because of that economic status. Does this constitute economic discrimination? If so, then only a completely socialistic state would ever eradicate such a prejudice."[64] Senator Hatch argued this point in a way that melded consumerism and conscience. He asked why Americans should be forced to pay for something they abhor.[65]

Perhaps President Jimmy Carter expressed the political philosophy of the opponents of abortion funding most richly during an interview with NBC news reporter Judy Woodruff in 1977. Carter managed to weave the rights-denying, the small-government, the consumerist, and the anti-abortion arguments together elegantly enough to be memorable. Woodruff asked Carter, "Mr. President, how fair do you believe it is then, that women who can afford to get an abortion can go ahead and have one, and women who cannot afford to are precluded?" The president responded, "Well, as you know, there are many things in life that are not fair, that wealthy people can afford and poor people can't. But I don't believe that the Federal government should take action to try to make these opportunities exactly equal, particularly when there is a moral factor involved."[66]

In 1980, the majority of the Supreme Court announced that it agreed with serial majorities in Congress that had approved and reaffirmed the Hyde Amendment. The Supreme Court ruled in *Harris v. McRae* that *Roe* had not established a constitutional right to abortion. It had merely promised women protection from "unduly burdensome interference with [their] freedom to decide" to terminate a pregnancy.[67] In other words, the government would not criminalize abortion, but neither would the government pay for it, no matter where that left a poor woman. These majorities, and the Americans whose attitudes they represented, muscled a market perspective right past racial equality and other human rights claims regarding reproductive rights.[68] The abortion-funding cases became a platform from which various constituencies could express what one observer called at the time their "growing annoyance with abortion rights."[69] The cases also provided, not for the first or the last time, an opportunity for the government to raise censoriously the subject of the sex and reproductive lives of poor minority women—and to use this subject as an argument for restricting the size and scope of government and government expenditures.

The Congress, the Supreme Court, and the president all endorsed abortion-funding restrictions for poor women but did not investigate the impact of the restrictions. Others did, though.[70] Among the findings was information that clearly established poor women as deeply alienated from consumerism, despite the funding cases' mandate to define abortion as a consumer service. A federal district court judge cited evidence that "many indigent women who were able to raise the money for their abortions [did] so only by not paying rent or utility bills, pawning household goods, diverting food and clothes money, or journeying to another state to obtain lower rates or fraudulently using a relative's insurance policy."[71] These findings applied generally to a substantial number of women. The Alan Guttmacher Institute found that just before the Hyde Amendment went into effect, 295,000 poor women a year had abortions paid for by Medicaid. Just following the enforcement of the amendment, the number declined to about 2,000 yearly.[72]

Horror stories began to crop up in the late 1970s, stories that attached faces and other details to these statistics. One story from Ohio, a state where the impact of the abortion-funding decisions was harsh, captured the full tragedy of transforming abortion from a woman's right into a consumer's privilege in the years immediately following *Roe v. Wade*. A teenage mother, eligible for Medicaid but ineligible for abortion coverage, by no definition in the world an empowered consumer, shot herself in the stomach after having been told by a public hospital "that she could not have an abortion unless she paid $600 in cash."[73]

FOREIGN ADOPTION: THE RELATIONSHIP BETWEEN CHOICE AND CHOICELESSNESS

When abortion rights advocates began to call their cause "choice" and imply that now all American women had "choice" and that the great crusade was to preserve "choice," the poor Ohio teenager—and other poor women struggling to establish *both* their right to have children and their right to abortion—were not, generally, part of this discussion. In fact, many fertile women living in the United States at this same time, the 1970s, lacked the means to control their fertility, and many of these women were poor. Thousands of women in these groups lost their children to adoption or foster care, a subject I will take up in Chapter 6. But it is worth noting here that while many women had won a significant degree of reproductive liberty in the 1970s, many others had not. LeRoy Wilder, a member of the Karuk Indian tribe in California and an attorney for the Association on American Indian Affairs, reported in 1978 on "a frightening, pervasive pattern of the destruction of Indian families in every part of this country." Available figures at the time documented, for example, that one out of eight Indian children in Minnesota was adopted. In the state of Washington, the Indian adoption rate was nineteen times higher than the rate for white children. This pattern held across the country. A Choctaw chief decried the disrespect Indian families continued to encounter, especially the willingness of non-Indian social agencies to challenge their "parental capacities."[74]

Poor mothers caught in situations such as these did not have "choice" and "privacy." These terms, which seem to create an elegantly personal space where the individual woman could make a life-defining decision, severely distorted the reality of many women. Legal scholar Dorothy Roberts explains, "The traditional concept of privacy makes the false presumption that the right to choose is contained entirely within the individual and not circumscribed by the material conditions of the individual's life."[75]

When Americans began to refer to reproductive liberty by the simple name "choice," they obscured the fact that millions of women in the United States—and abroad—lived in conditions of poverty and oppression that precluded many of the kinds of choices that middle-class American women thought of as a matter of personal decision making. Then and now, many Americans have glossed over this: poor and/or culturally oppressed women in the United States and abroad may lack the money to "choose" abortion. They may live where abortion is inaccessible, illegal, or life-threatening. They may lack the resources to feed the children they have, much less a new baby. They may want to be mothers but lack the resources to escape stigma, punishment, or death for having a baby under the wrong conditions. They may lack the resources to avoid pregnancy from sexual violence. Can women in any of these circumstances be described as in a position to make a choice, a private, personal choice in the way that middle-class Americans generally use that term? When American women get lulled into believing that reproductive liberty is simply a matter of choice, for themselves, for all of us, that is short-sighted. The attitude of many Americans toward foreign adoption is an example of one cost of that shortsightedness.

In fact, the way the "adoption market" took form after *Roe v. Wade* is a case study of how some women's choices depend on exploiting the rel-ative choicelessness of other women. In presenting this view of inter-country adoption (ICA), I focus tightly on the plight of poor mothers. This group is most often effaced in the process of evaluating the quality and quantity of available babies and the new relationships American adopters form with infants from abroad.[76] The inability of poor mothers in Romania, Russia, and elsewhere to take care of their children is not the only important aspect of ICA. But neither should this aspect be ig-nored. In drawing attention to the tragic circumstances under which many poor mothers abroad lose their children, I do not mean to suggest that ICA is simply evil and that "child rescue" should never be under-taken. I mean, rather, to highlight the dynamics of this form of *child transfer*, and to underscore how such transfers almost always depend on extremely poor and/or culturally oppressed mothers who utterly lack choices.[77]

The adoption of babies from abroad took off in 1973. One study showed a 33 percent increase in the number of foreign children admitted to the United States for adoption between 1972 and 1973.[78] This was not, of course, an arbitrary moment. It was precisely the moment when American women won the right to decide whether or not to carry a par-ticular pregnancy to term. Once abortion was legal, many pregnancies that might have yielded adoptable babies were terminated. An unex-pected corollary of *Roe v. Wade* was that once a woman had the right to decide whether or not to stay pregnant, many women also determined that they had the right to decide whether or not to be the mother of the children they bore. As I show in Chapter 4, unmarried women at this time began to refuse to let various authorities redistribute their babies to adopting couples. The legalization of abortion, in other words, had a lot to do with the rise of single mother–headed families. Many women in the United States who got legal abortions or became single mothers in the 1970s felt that their newly won ability to control their fertility gave them a degree of independence and dignity. Dignity and independence are, in fact, the life-enhancing ingredients that tend to be incompatible with relinquishing a child.[79]

These newly enhanced aspects of life for many women in the United States were not so life-enhancing for women in poor countries. Beginning in the early 1970s, reports rolled in regarding children put up for adoption in countries where women were desperate. The operative principle in all of these cases seemed to be that desperation had created a baby supply for the new baby consumers: wealthy choice makers from the United States, Canada, and Western Europe. In the middle 1970s, for example, in the aftermath of a gruesome war, a U.S. State Department employee observed that while adoption was "not a common Vietnamese phenomenon," now the country and many Vietnamese families were without "any social fabric at all," and so, in thousands of cases, parents were unable to "find the resources" to keep their children.[80] For many years after the Korean War, "the children of the poor" in South Korea remained the most commonly adopted foreigners.[81] (When economic conditions in South Korea improved, the number of available babies, predictably, declined.)[82] There are multiple studies, reports, and journalistic treatments that charge that parents (usually mothers) in third world countries were pressed by their desperation to give up their babies.[83] In the early 1990s, following the fall of Romanian dictator Nicolae Ceaușescu, Americans and other Westerners flocked to that country looking for babies born into social and political chaos. There were babies and older children whose parents couldn't feed them or otherwise provide for them.[84] More recently, a baby-smuggling ring was uncovered in Agua Prieta, Mexico, where, according to news reports, "Social workers . . . say they counsel dozens of mothers . . . who are in such dire economic and social distress that they broker their children for money or shelter." A former journalist living on the Mexico-Arizona border commented on the baby smuggling: "It's like things have gotten really bad if women are offering to sell their babies."[85] Referring to the current situation in China, where national policies limit childbearing, the cultural preference is for male children, and massive economic chaos prevails, one close observer wrote, "Behind all too many goods made in China, I now know for certain, are exploited workers, most of them women, any one of whom could be the mother of a child who winds up 'lost.' "[86]

Some observers have remarked that adopters are not, these days, primarily moved by "humanitarian" intentions when they arrive in Ecuador or Mexico looking for babies. Rather, they travel to poor countries because of the "acute shortage of white children" at home, what some analysts have called the "White Baby Famine."[87] Observers have also pointed out that all the traffic goes in one direction—babies from the third world transferred to developed countries: "the more powerful nations . . . 'robbing' [poor] countries of their children."[88] Proponents of this perspective have said that wealthy couples in the United States are perpetrators of "a new kind of rather patronising colonialism."[89] Some have even accused the richer countries of an interest in making sure that child welfare services in the target countries remain undeveloped "so as to ensure a continued supply of babies for the childless rich."[90] An early critic of the surge in international adoption tied the transfer of babies from poor to rich countries directly to the historical, imperialist pursuits of the West: "[H]omeless and orphaned children in Bangladesh, Vietnam and Cambodia had been brought to this condition by the imperialist apportionment of resources to the rich, developed countries . . . by wars in these countries fostered by imperialist powers."[91]

The transfer of babies from poor to rich countries is often discussed in marketplace terms, using tropes that emphasize how children in desperately poor situations have been transformed into commodities.[92] In the late 1970s, stories about where to get babies were passed around, such as the one about a facility near Tijuana where "couples could pick out a child from a room full of babies, sort of like a supermarket."[93] On a 1991 *Sixty Minutes* segment called "Babies for Sale," one American was quoted using an oil-field metaphor: "Don't you understand, Buddy," this American baby broker said to a representative of the Romanian government, "this is the last reservoir of Caucasian babies in the world."[94]

Vietnam, Romania, and other countries in crisis have been desperate to develop desirable, exportable commodities. Unfortunately, as one U.S. politician put it, sometimes that commodity is "babies instead of . . . widgets."[95] In the 1970s, impoverished Latin American countries generated a supply of babies to export. The number of Colombian babies adopted by foreigners was six times higher in 1980 than in 1977.[96] Between 1979 and 1989, South Korea placed about 4,400 babies in the United States each year, a tally that reportedly caused some commentators at the 1988 Olympic Games to observe wryly that "Korea's chief export was still babies." This claim deeply embarrassed the nation and stimulated efforts to slow down adoption.[97] By the 1980s, 70 percent of all babies brought into the United States for adoption came from four countries: South Korea, Colombia, India, and Mexico, all countries with large, desperately poor populations. The rest came from El Salvador, the Philippines, Honduras, Sri Lanka, and Guatemala.

Reports from the front seemed to highlight the process of baby commodification. Sometimes reports indicated that inter-country adoptions didn't always yield the highest-quality babies, and passed on "consumer protection" advice, such as this nugget from a 1983 Ms. article: "Those in the adoption network with the strongest track records for good, untroubled adoptions are often the safest people to work with . . . Pragmatically, if they place children who are seriously ill or retarded, word quickly gets around in adoption circles, and their business could dry up overnight."[98] Reports also—wittingly or unwittingly—featured "shopping" metaphors so often that consumerist intentions completely overwhelmed any sense of inter-country adoption as a child-rescue mission. One international observer of the adoption scene told about running into the director of a large California adoption agency, who, "it was obvious," was "in Asia shopping for children . . . Later, when I saw [this director] in the Philippines, he told me triumphantly that he had found an orphanage there that would supply him with babies."[99]

Americans who rushed to participate in the Romanian "adoption frenzy" in 1991 widely characterized their baby searches as marketing expeditions.[100] One woman told an American reporter: "This is so bizarre . . . It's a little weird—like going around shopping." Another said, "Sometimes I feel sort of guilty, like the babies are being sold . . . But," she added, with a nod toward comparison pricing and child rescue, "then when you think about open adoption in the States, and all the costs of that, that's like buying a baby. Besides, look at the conditions of these children's homes."[101] One American, who went to Romania determined to help out in the orphanages and improve the conditions there for many children before he'd "pick out one or two" to bring home, ended up quite disillusioned. Instead of helping out, he said, "you find out you're driving around villages, basically asking what's the price per pound for babies?"[102] *New York Times* writer Anthony Lewis described how some Vietnamese resented the transfer of babies from that war-torn country to the United States in 1975. He quoted a South Vietnamese lieutenant in Saigon: "It is nice to see you Americans taking home souvenirs of our country as you leave—China elephants and orphans."[103]

Perhaps many of these crude expressions have survived because journalists and others have aimed to expose the abuses of international adoption. But whatever intentions were involved, reports from the adoption fronts consistently demonstrated that the commodification of babies generally required one thing: the potential adopter needed to imagine the child as a product entirely separate from a mother, even when a mother was involved with her baby and nearby, even if there was no hard evidence that the baby was, indeed, an orphan. In 1975, for example, the deputy commissioner of the U.S. Immigration and Naturalization Service (INS) acknowledged that among the Cambodian and Vietnamese children brought to the United States as part of Operation Baby Lift following the collapse of the South Vietnamese government, there were many children for whom the INS had been "unable . . . to develop persuasive evidence" that they were "in fact orphans or . . . abandoned by their parents."[104] Similarly, in the Romanian situation, Gene McNary, commissioner of the INS, acknowledged at a 1991 congressional hearing that "if orphan investigations were actually conducted probably 30% of all approved foreign adoptions would be questionable."[105]

Kathleen Hunt, who wrote about the Romanian adoption "frenzy" for the *New York Times*, reported that among children "in orphanages and hospitals [there], very few are bona fide orphans. Nor have they ever been technically abandoned."[106] INS commissioner McNary explained how it could happen that desperate Romanian parents in the midst of social chaos tried to look out for but lost their children: "We have . . . [sent] . . . an investigator out to talk to natural parents, where the parents had not intended to give the child up, had instead thought that the child would come to the United States, . . . [the biological parents would stay in touch with the child] . . . and after the child was old enough to be returned to Romania . . . the child would be returned. I'm sure," the commissioner added, "that's not an abandonment."[107]

Some years earlier, Martin Russo, a congressman from Illinois, described the anguish of a Vietnamese who complained about the means Americans used to obtain children in other countries for adoption. This woman described American strategies as "terrible procedures" for a number of reasons, but especially because they made it impossible for actual relatives to step in and become parent figures when necessary. Now that Americans had become involved, she said, too much money was required to adopt a child, even one who was a relative.[108]

Parents and relatives in poor countries lost children because demand for babies in the West exceeded supply. According to two experts on transracial and inter-country adoption, when this situation exists, there is a lot of potential "for finding alternative means of obtaining the scarce item."[109] Indeed, stories about bribes and pressure surfaced wherever wealthy potential adopters showed up. An American television news reporter described the "unbelievable scene" in Romania in 1991, and captured a "baby broker" on camera explaining the distribution of money that facilitated adoption there: "Bribes, a lot of bribes, nurses, mother of the child, judges, attorneys, crown judges, people that complete the home study, everybody. Everybody wants some."[110] A newspaper reporter formed a similar impression: "Thousands of people who could afford the plane tickets packed their suitcases with cash (to bribe doctors and orphanage officials and judges and translators and government bureaucrats), nail polish, candy bars and disposable razors (to pass out to nurses and women who may or may not be birthmothers) and flew to Romania to buy a baby."[111]

The most distressing aspects of these accounts are the parts that tell about middlemen "earning huge profits," for example "by persuading women to give up children for small sums and then producing forged papers for potential adoption." In the 1980s, experts reported these kinds of activities in China, Colombia, Brazil, Sri Lanka, the Philippines, "and possibly elsewhere."[112] Again, these stories have been corroborated around the world, featuring "baby brokers eager to capitalize on . . . confusion" and poverty, brokers who "exert undue pressure upon biological mothers, usually young, poor and unmarried, to get them to relinquish their offspring for adoption."[113]

Some observers have pointed out that rich Americans have thrown their weight—as well as their money—around when they have found inconvenient rules and regulations blocking foreign adoption. When, for example, reports of abuse in Romania surfaced and consular staff "began applying a strict interpretation of [various visa and other] regulations," potential adopters complained bitterly to their congressional representatives back home. Melanie Barnes, an adoptive mother, was bitter when she spoke before Congress. She lauded Americans who adopted "needy children" from poor countries and was shocked that these people should be "subjected to rude and inhumane treatment by our own Embassy," a bureaucracy, its employees claimed, that was only trying to follow the rules. These complaints were quickly effective. Politicians began to speak out about the need to grant "humanitarian waivers" to couples having trouble securing a child. In 1991 Congressman William Broomfield urged a new, less "rigid" definition of abandonment so that more children could be obtained for adoption. He made the case for bringing babies out of Romania this way: "Many American couples are desperately searching for a child they can love and raise as a member of their families. I would hope that America's laws would do everything possible to promote that spirit of generosity."[114] When we consider how completely Broomfield's "spirit of generosity" depends on effacing the biological mother (or parents) of the baby-to-be-freed, we can get a glimpse of the relationship between a relatively wealthy American woman's choices and the choicelessness of a desperate, poor woman, a mother living in a faraway country.

In fact, Americans who have portrayed ICA as primarily a child rescue mission have tended to define the situation in ways that insist that the biological mother doesn't really count. This strategy, often unwitting I think, shares a lot with a strategy of the anti–abortion rights movement. Some anti–abortion rights activists and groups have waved pictures by photographer Lennart Nilsson, or others like them, as their iconic banners. These are photos of fetuses in utero, floating alone and magical in what looks like "outer space." There is no woman, no mother, in these pictures.[115] It is not uncommon for those who characterize their mission—whether as adopters or as proponents of "fetal rights"—as one of child rescue to erase the interests and even the person of that woman in order to strengthen their own argument.[116]

For example, one of the strongest, most articulate, and most sophisticated spokespersons for ICA is Harvard law professor Elizabeth Bartholet, a person who successfully adopted two boys from Peru. Here is how

Bartholet expresses her support for foreign adoption: "My current vision [of adoption] seems to me so clearly right that I find myself impatient with the society that apparently sees things so differently. Adoption works, and works well, both for children in need of homes and for the infertile who want to parent."[117] Bartholet does not consider here or elsewhere whether adoption works well for the mostly desperately poor women whose children "are in need of homes." Nor did Gene McNary, INS commissioner in 1991, who believed that "every orphan" who arrived in the United States "represents a dream fulfilled, a family enriched, and the successful conclusion of a process involving the adopting parents, a state or licensed child welfare agency, three federal agencies, and a foreign government." One might well consider, who is missing in this picture? Whose dream has not been recorded, much less fulfilled? The biological mother is not mentioned as one of the "involved" parties.[118]

Americans who have gone abroad to adopt and have later written about the experience have typically had little to say about the moral dimensions of the situation, or more precisely, the moral aspects of using their status and resources as consumers to take children from choiceless "surrendering" mothers. One woman reported that "on my fourteen-hour trip to Santiago . . . to pick up my adopted Chilean child, I thought a lot about government policies that push large numbers of poor people into giving up children out of desperation. Should I have allowed my political conflicts," this woman muses, "to keep me from getting a child I deeply wanted?"[119] Having raised the question, the author moves on and does not return to this matter. Elizabeth Bartholet acknowledges that during her adoption expeditions in Peru, she "did not get to know any birthparents." She acknowledges that "most of these women [who relinquish babies] have no good options," but highlights the "stories" she's heard "of the pleasure that some women seem to take in the life they are giving their children, as they look at him or her cradled in the arms of eager parents from the faraway mythical land of opportunity."

It appears that Bartholet can believe in this "pleasure" experienced by relinquishing mothers because she believes that poor Peruvian women are profoundly different from herself. I say this because of Bartholet's description of her own quick and fierce bonding with the boys she adopted, a bonding that made the specter of separation unbearable for her. She writes that getting through the bureaucratic moments of uncertainty in

Peru "without somehow cracking" were among the most challenging experiences of her life. The Harvard professor adds, "The worst aspect by far was my terror that the child I had come to think of as my own shortly after he came home to live with me would be taken from me."

Bartholet writes, without any apparent sense of irony, that her friends would probably not understand "what it is like to have other people be in a position to take away for any or no reason the child you think of as your own." She acknowledges that the child in question had been in her life for only one week, so her friends would have a particularly hard time understanding "why this child would feel uniquely mine."[120] Bartholet and other inter-country adopters use terms like "pleasure" and "brave and courageous" to describe the experiences of poor third world mothers when their children are taken by foreigners.[121] When inter-country adopters imagine their own potential loss of a child they've just acquired, the terms are typically much more dramatic. One American woman having trouble leaving Brazil with a baby she was trying to adopt said, "Without my child, I prefer to die."[122]

During a congressional hearing on the out-of-control Romanian adoption situation, Representative Lamar S. Smith of Texas asked a woman who had just adopted a child in that country, "So, you're not disturbed by the fact . . . in some foreign countries you may have a living parent still exerting some control over that child, and you're not concerned about that parent being forced to give up their child or feeling any pressure to do so?"[123] This woman and others who testified at the hearing explained that the adoptions were justified because these children would otherwise live in terrible poverty.[124] One woman asked, "Can't we give these children a chance to live in America where . . . [we] are able to provide for them?"[125] Others have claimed that not adopting children out of impoverished families, communities, and countries is "grossly immoral."[126]

Often, however, the justifications for foreign adoption focus clearly and forthrightly on the needs of Americans. U.S. Representative Christopher Smith of New Jersey argued in 1991 that because of foreign adoption, "many families have become more complete and much love has been shared as a result of these adoptions." Smith's colleague, Bob McEwen of Ohio, used even stronger terms to explain why an American couple's infertility justifies transferring babies across national borders: "A death in a family cannot have a greater strain on a relationship than the inability to have a family . . . [M]ost people do not . . . fully appreciate the tremendous, tremendous strain that is on a potential mother, a potential father, a loving family that wishes to become a family."[127] Again, the argument here relies on the premise that Americans have the reasons and the resources to transfer babies; they have primacy as legitimate consumers of children and parenthood.

Elizabeth Bartholet (and many others) cite a "side benefit" of these adoptions: "the enrichment of our understanding of the meaning of family and community." Families "built across lines of racial and cultural difference," she feels, are "families whose members must learn to appreciate one another's differences while experiencing their humanity."[128] This may be a particularly obtuse and even cruel "side benefit," since the American's choice to celebrate cultural diversity and difference through adoption depends on the immiseration of a woman from a "different" culture and on her presumably profound loss of a child: on her choicelessness. Here the American woman's wealth allows her to be a legitimate consumer of multiple cultures, at a cost that she need neither acknowledge nor pay.

At one point Bartholet writes: "I can see [my adoptive son] now, standing proudly behind a table strewn with our Peruvian treasures, describing them . . . handing them to an eager friend to be passed around the class, telling his classmates about how the Spanish invaded and how they stole the golden artworks of the Inca rulers and boiled them down."[129] A critic of ICA might identify Bartholet's acquisition of "Peruvian treasures"—the boys she adopted—with the depredations of European invaders.

Finally, and perhaps most forthrightly, some Westerners have justified ICA as "the safer way." One expert explained, "[A]s own-country adoption becomes more open, more couples may of course turn to intercountry adoption in the expectation that they will not have to concern themselves too much with issues about parental access and possible interference.[130] Here we get a glimpse of the relatively wealthy intercountry adopter's determination to maneuver unimpeded in the "free market" and to insist, as the privileged consumer, that child acquisition have no strings attached. This argument for ICA wants to entirely efface the biological mother in order to make things easier for the consumer.

This discussion is not meant to constitute a brief against foreign or inter-country adoption. It is meant to suggest what happens when choice *entitles* Americans to acquire poor children in other countries. It is meant to demonstrate that Americans may too easily define poor women as illegitimate mothers because they are poor. A way to think about how Americans' sense of consumer-related entitlement applies to motherhood is to consider why child-rescue adopters speak so rarely about methods of child rescue other than acquisition by adoption. For instance, Americans might participate in programs that support specific Peruvian or Korean or Indian families in their own countries. That way children could be "rescued" and could stay with their families.

Americans could also target their support to already-existing programs in poor countries that aim to keep families together. During the worst period in Romania, for example, the director of an "orphanage" worked hard to rehabilitate a group of children, providing good nutrition, education, and training in motor skill and language development, so that the parents of these children could afford "to take back their [healthy] children." The program was successful, reporting in March 1991 that it had facilitated sixty reunions, which included a number of children who would have otherwise been bound for American adoption.[131] And, of course, Americans who deplore child poverty abroad could be powerful advocates for foreign aid.

Since *Roe v. Wade* dramatically tightened the supply of adoptable babies, the market has demanded a new, dependable supply. Not surprisingly, the only way to re-create an adequate supply of babies was to find the children of the most resourceless, choiceless women in the United States and abroad and "rescue" these children from their disqualified mothers and other relations. As one legal scholar observed soon after *Roe* in an essay considering choice and motherhood: "Poverty is an alterable characteristic, bearing at least some relationship to merit."[132] The reestablishment of a baby supply after *Roe* has depended on this maxim and its suggestion that poverty and maternity are an illegitimate mix.

CHOICE IS A MOVING TARGET

I have argued that the selection of "choice" as women's special guarantee underlay—or was deeply compatible with—the transition from abortion as a woman's right to abortion as a consumer privilege. I also understand "choice" as an invitation to focus on individual desires and to ignore the relationship between some women's resource-full choice making and other women's choicelessness. The meaning of choice has expanded, and mostly contracted, in many ways since the early 1970s, and not all of these ways are included in this book. For example, the courts and legislatures have redefined "choice" many times since 1973, with age qualifications for making the abortion choice, parental notification rules for teenagers, mandated waiting periods, counseling sessions, education/propaganda requirements, ever-tighter restrictions on public funding, bribe programs that give women money if they get sterilized, and federal contests to reward states with low abortion rates. These and other non-"undue burdens"[133] that now constitute and bind "choice" are a far cry from the simple image of "the woman and her responsible physician" sitting in consultation alone, "free of interference by the State," that was envisioned in *Roe*.[134]

Beyond legislatures and the courts, "choice" has been redefined again and again since the early 1970s, by technology and by popular opinion. Reproductive technologies to treat infertility—some aspects of which I discuss in Chapter 6—have pressed new meaning into "choice" and who gets to be a choice maker. Also, methods using drugs to induce "medical abortion" (the term used to refer to abortion using methotrexate and mifepristone, or RU 486, instead of traditional, surgical abortion) have lent additional meaning to choice. One study that investigated physicians' attitudes toward medical abortion found that in order to satisfy medical protocols, the counselor or physician had to evaluate the "prospective candidate" as a choice maker: is she "responsible enough to return for the necessary visits . . . to report complications?" and so forth. Sometimes, the study's author reports, health care providers "encounter ambiguous cases where the patient meets all the formal criteria but 'seems' unreliable. In such instances, said one administrator, you find a way to 'talk her out of it.' "[135] Medical protocols used to track the efficacy of early-abortion methods may involve weeding out questionable choice makers.

The new methods can also create an elite of "superior" choice makers. In fall 1999 I interviewed several abortion providers about the impact of medical abortion and "morning-after pills" on the meaning of choice. These physicians acknowledged that the growing availability of abortion before six weeks may have the effect of creating a hierarchy of choice makers. Girls and women who take care of unwanted pregnancies early may be, in time, considered more knowledgeable, efficient, and responsible. Abortion seekers who wait too long for medical abortions and must get "old-fashioned" later surgical abortions may be viewed as less capable persons or bad choice makers. Over time, the core judgmental question—the typical question that has defined girls and women as bad choice makers—has mutated. We used to ask, especially in the case of an unwillingly pregnant poor woman, why did she have sex? Then we asked, why did she have unprotected sex? Then, why didn't she get an abortion?[136] Next, will we define bad choice makers with a question like this: What's the matter with her that she couldn't get an early, medical abortion? Here the shifting meaning of choice may threaten any fertile female, without reference to race or class. Anyone who waited just a day "too long" could be placed into the reviled category of bad choice maker.

The interacting arenas of professional, political, and public opinion have a crucial impact on defining and redefining good choice makers and bad, on legitimizing and variously demonizing serial meanings of choice. Psychologists Sharon Gold-Steinberg and Abigail Stewart studied and compared the experience of obtaining an abortion "under four sets of political-legal circumstances: illegal abortion, therapeutic abortion, legal abortion in the 1970s and early 1980s, and legal abortions in the context of protest, harassment and threats of violence."[137] They found that the experience of being stigmatized was powerful for women who sought abortions during three of those four periods: "Women who had illegal abortions may have felt stigmatized by having to go outside of the law to secure reproductive freedom. Women who sought therapeutic abortions all too frequently were humiliated by members of medical boards. In the current political climate," Stewart and Gold-Steinberg wrote in the late 1990s, "women are vulnerable to being stigmatized by those who construe the choice to have a legal abortion as being morally wrong."[138] Under all the circumstances—except the period immediately following legalization, when the association of abortion and rights was the strongest—women making the abortion choice were threatened as bad choice makers.

Would these women and others whose lives I've considered in writing this book have had different experiences if the law empowered them, as full citizens, to have the right to control their own bodies, *and* if the culture facilitated this legal empowerment? "Rights" may have their own problems as a "special guarantee." I have come to believe, though, and try to show in this book, that if there is a hierarchy of special guarantees, surely choice must be at the bottom, the lowliest and weakest of all "guarantees." The chapters that follow aim to make a case for the proposition that, in a political and cultural context shaped by racism and sexism, the embrace of choice was deeply problematic. "Choice" turned out to be a term and an idea that reflected and foreshadowed the commodification of reproduction and a new, hard set of financial qualifications for motherhood.

2

JUSTIFYING CHOICE

THE BACK ALLEY BUTCHER AS SPECTRAL ICON

If you were very, very lucky, you didn't get infected by dirty hands or catheters, your uterus wasn't perforated. —Brett Harvey, *The Fifties*[1]

[I]n those days, I thought the solution was to jail the abortionist. It took me another twenty years to fully understand that . . . the system, and especially the lawmakers who left her no choice, killed her. —Patricia Miller, *The Worst of Times*[2]

Since the legalization of abortion in 1973, Planned Parenthood and NARAL have made their most passionate arguments for preserving *Roe v. Wade* by invoking the specter of the Back Alley Butcher. In fact, the old, iconic butcher turns up surprisingly often. *New York Times* columnist Bob Herbert, for example, recently wrote in defense of *Roe* by summoning up the danger he knew his readers would credit: "The vast majority of women and girls who wanted an abortion [during the criminal era] had no alternative but to roll the dice on a criminal procedure that might be performed in some wretched undercover location by some inept practitioner using unsanitary and often unscientific methods."[3] A generation after legalization, the Back Alley Butcher remains a vibrant cultural icon—and perhaps the most widely accepted justification for granting women reproductive choice. In this chapter I explore historical problems with the back alley icon. I am especially interested in what happens when this figure, not women's rights, underlies legal abortion.

DANGEROUS LAW

The criminal abortionist, it turns out, was far from the main source of danger for girls and women determined to control their fertility when abortion was a crime. Focusing on the Back Alley Butcher has allowed us to overlook the most profound and most certain source of danger to women in the criminal era: *the law*. Statutes enacted mostly in the second half of the nineteenth century mandated women's alienation from information, from supportive medical advice and service. The laws simply granted control over women's bodies and their fertility to husbands, doctors, lawmakers, and law enforcers. Women who tried to exercise control over their own bodies had to associate with criminals to do so; they had to become criminals themselves. By the mid-twentieth century, of course, women were resisting abortion laws in astounding numbers and pressing others to help them break the laws. But both the letter of the law and its spirit continued to structure and enforce extreme danger for women nonetheless.

During the roughly one hundred years that abortion was illegal in the United States, the law proscribed choices for women and robbed women of the sense of self-determination that goes with having choices and making them. Nancy Howell Lee's 1969 study, *The Search for an Abortionist*, found that less than a third of the women in her sample felt they could choose an abortionist on reasonable grounds such as competence or because the practitioner was recommended. Lee found that few women could compare alternatives and choose. For many, the law placed the most logical alternative—a doctor—out of the question.[4] One woman explained, "I never even tried to find a doctor to help me. I was too afraid that the doctor would report me to the police."[5] In Lee's study, about a quarter of the women who sustained complications did not seek or find competent medical care because they "feared prosecution from a physician or a hospital."[6] Under the law, the medical community could well become the enemy.

Ironically, anti-abortion statutes were originally championed by "regular" physicians in the nineteenth century looking to raise and stabilize the status of the medical profession, solidify physicians' relationships with and control over pregnant and parturient women, and snuff out the relationships between childbearing women and midwives and other medical "irregulars." But one powerful effect of the statutes was to stimulate and cement relationships between unwillingly pregnant, abortion-seeking women and whoever would perform abortions. The law ended up creating opportunities for all kinds of people—qualified and unqualified. As Dr. Theodore Lidz of Yale University argued in the 1950s, the legal abortion restriction itself "foments crime."[7]

There is no question that actual "underworld" types did see abortion as a lucrative opportunity in the postwar decades. One rather sensational account of the illegal abortion arena described the criminal fit between gangsters and practitioners:

> Abortion rings are often controlled by the crime syndicate. In the 1950s, one of America's most notorious gangsters was called to New York to testify about his racketeering activities. Among the many shocking confessions revealed at the hearing was one dealing with abortion. The gangster, under constant questioning, admitted that he had close to 347 trained and skilled abortionists operating throughout the country . . . Each abortionist (many were midwives, but thoroughly trained and experienced in inducing miscarriages) was compelled to pay fifteen per cent of his earnings to the local gang chief.[8]

According to this account, abortionists were placed in areas known to be "fruitful," such as the "wide open towns" where gambling, prostitution, and abortion all "flourished" and police payoffs were routine.[9] Women whose only "choice" was to get mixed up with lawbreakers were well aware that the law forced them into commerce with these types. As one put it, "You know when something is illegal, you have to go through all this subterfuge to get it, you really feel like a criminal." Another said, "You felt very dirty. You felt like a criminal. It was incredibly humiliating."[10]

When women were pushed into the space the law allocated for abortion, they were often burdened by the dehumanizing consequences of the law: fear and degradation. "Eleanor" described herself as "terrified" when she sought out a woman she knew nothing about except that the woman was willing to help her. "I had never seen this woman before. I had heard horror stories about back-alley abortions, and I really had no idea what to expect. If she had brought out a knife, it would not have surprised me."

"Marie's" experience similarly suggests that the law actually forced ordinary, generally law-abiding women to confront their death: "I was beyond fear—truly beyond it. I was so terrified I couldn't move or speak or even think. I just huddled there in the front seat. I didn't know where I was going or what was going to be done to me . . . was someone going to cut my head off or cut my belly open? Either was equally possible in my mind."

One woman speaks vividly about the impact of fear then: "I don't remember the doctor washing his hands or anything like that, but I was so frightened I might not have noticed." This woman's memory might have been an artifact of her fear, or it might have been true; working on the wrong side of the law has never been an antiseptic business. One of the physician-respondents in lawyer Patricia Miller's oral history of the criminal era, *The Worst of Times*, explains, "The problem was that even if you were a competent doctor, the whole illegality thing meant that you were doing it in your office under dangerous conditions."[11]

Stories that women have told about their illegal abortions reveal a great deal of terror, far more terror than medical mayhem. And it is important to imagine the sources of that terror. As Lawrence Lader, a journalist and prominent early abortion rights activist, wrote, the media carried "scare propaganda," stories suggesting that an abortionist's office was "where you went to be killed."[12] Terror was surely induced by the fact that abortion was a crime, a sex-related crime. A great deal of terror must have been stimulated by the sheer degradation of being forced into shameful, shady, criminal activity because one had had shameful sex, because one was willing to mess with what was defined then as female destiny.

And, of course, the legally mandated danger didn't stop when the operation was over. In a typical show of the practitioner's fear of the law—and how that fear structured her practice—one woman said to her patient lying on the abortion table, "If there are any problems, don't call me." Worse still, another practitioner forbade her abortion patient from getting any help at all if there were postoperative complications: "She insisted that no matter what happened, under no conditions was I to go to a hospital, under no conditions was I to call the police, under no conditions was I to give out her name."[13] Here it is very plain that the law created massive danger for unwillingly pregnant women and those who helped them.[14]

To press this point a bit further, it is important to recognize that when the "overly restrictive law sentenced women to a barbaric, primitive underworld"—or what one woman called "the underbelly" where abortions could be had—most women were fully aware of the range of dangers they faced beyond the notorious physical threat.[15] Danger was involved, for example, when the law made women financially vulnerable. Nancy Howell Lee calculated that the mean cost of abortion in the late 1960s was around $300 (equivalent to more than $3,000 today), with some procedures costing as much as $1,000 and more. The total cost including travel was typically as high as $500. Lee found that nearly one-half of her sample had to borrow to meet such prices.[16] Sociologist Ed Schur asserted in his influential study *Crimes Without Victims* that "the woman is prepared to do almost anything to achieve her purpose and as a result she is open to various types of exploitation."[17] Interestingly, Schur seems to identify the source of the woman's danger here as her own strength of purpose, rather than the law. He also names the practitioner as dangerous, liable to prevail sexually or with threats and cruelty, even though Schur himself was an early and outspoken proponent of decriminalization who recognized that the law was harmful and counterproductive in this arena.

Law enforcement agents and others associated with the legal system were often directly responsible for the danger women encountered when they attempted to control their reproductive lives. When police raided abortionists' offices in the 1940s and 1950s—historian Leslie Reagan writes that raids were "the national norm then"—women unlucky enough to get caught in the wrong place at the wrong time were terrified.[18] As Reagan aptly puts it, the law "captured women and invaded their bodies as part of their investigation into illegal abortion." One woman explained, "You always hear horror stories about the dirt: dirty fingernails, instruments that were not sterilized, but I think sometimes the horror had to do with other things. I think for many people, the illegality was very frightening, not only in the sense of what the punishment might be if you were caught. It seems to me that any woman would feel a lot of fear about the possibility of the operation being stopped in the middle."[19] It wasn't unusual for a policeman to press a woman at the scene, or later at her home, for information. A San Diego policeman described how he pressed and threatened this way: "I didn't want to get tough with her. [But] abortion is a felony for her too." He told the woman, "I know as well as you do it would be mighty unpleasant for you to go into court to testify that an abortion had been performed on you."[20]

Indeed, the danger of public exposure and humiliation in the courtroom must have felt like a hideous risk, especially after World War II, when abortion trials became more common. In the courtroom, the lawyer defending the person accused of performing an abortion was typically unrestrained in attacking the alleged victim—the woman who had been dragged into court to testify against the man or woman who had been willing to help her. The defense lawyer's tactic often consisted of simply discrediting the reputation of the "victim." If the girl or woman testifying about abortion could be portrayed as a lowlife, defense lawyers figured, their clients would more likely be exonerated. Here is an excellent and typical example of how one defense lawyer characterized the woman testifying against his client: "I am not condemning this woman but . . . I think the woman, while she is a good woman, undoubtedly is neurotic and has undergone psychiatric treatment in the past. Her history shows other habits, cigarettes, two packs a day, alcohol, three or four drinks a day; she considers herself almost an alcoholic . . . she has taken Dexedrine and Phenobarbital in the past few years, partly to lose weight, partly to control her nerves." The defense lawyer went on to describe in open court an affair he said this woman had had with a married man.[21] In this situation, the law mandated dangerous exposure of the "victim" twice, first by the prosecution and then by the abortionist's defense. Typically and meaningfully, the "victim," raked over the coals in the courtroom, was the only principal with no legal representation.

It is also important, of course, to remember and catalogue the substantial dangers the law created for women who did not venture into the illegal abortion arena when they were carrying pregnancies they could not manage—but whose lack of abortion rights mandated life-changing dangers. These dangers have been recited elsewhere, but I want to underscore here that all of these fertility-related dangers were mandated by law and surely overtook hundreds of thousands of women each year in the era of criminalized abortion.

First of all, women faced everyday danger when the law assigned doctors and public policy "a stunning assemblage of powers derived from surveillance and regulation." According to one observer, these powers were based on two fundamental principles or entitlements: "mastery over women" and "punishment-centered rules." Women who tried to avoid the so-called back alley and get legal, therapeutic abortions in hospitals labored under these principles, and worse. As a ticket of admission to the hospital, thousands of women had to associate themselves with psychosis. They had to step into and depend upon the very dangerous, very misogynistic postwar arena of psychiatry in order to construct and justify their request for permission to abort. One investigator found that diagnostic categories justifying hospital abortion were often unrelated to the patient's "actual medical or psychiatric status." He found that "in 80% of all cases [in this study], 'psychosis' was cited as an indication for abortion."[22]

Among "psychotic" petitioners for therapeutic abortion were women whom desperation and the law pushed to threaten suicide. A prominent postwar gynecologist, unhappy with hospital abortion boards that regularly rejected abortions for seriously depressed patients, quoted such a woman in the early 1950s: "What must I do to prove how desperately ill I am? Must I attempt or actually commit suicide or finally be committed to a mental hospital to prove it to them?"[23]

In a related horror, the law allowed doctors to interpret its intentions with what one called "medio-religious confusion," justifying a hospital's chief of gynecology "who would permit no abortions on his service unless there was concomitant sterilization of the woman."[24] At the Chicago Lying-In Hospital, about 70 percent of women granted abortions were sterilized, usually by hysterectomy.[25] This is, of course, a ghastly figure and vastly higher than any percentage of fertility loss ever associated with Back Alley Butchers. Operating under the sanction of the law, these real doctors, arguably, did far more physical harm to women than criminal practitioners did.

Stories of women trying to handle their problem through "proper authorities"—hospital abortion boards and private physicians—are often about doctors subjecting women to evaluations of their "moral character."[26] Women seeking legal help tell stories about being threatened with "excommunication," of being so scared by medical authorities and so degraded that they were ready to renounce sexual activity forever. There are many stories of women steeped in guilt for violating "women's destiny" by seeking an abortion, of women feeling guilty about "murdering motherhood." One woman described the nightmarish message conveyed by the law she was determined to break: "You're terrible. You're a bad person. There is nothing about you that's redeemable. You are condemned to live in hell forever."[27]

Finally, among the horrifying consequences of anti-abortion laws was the development of the social practice of forcing some women (mostly those who gave birth to valuable white babies) to give their infants away.[28] Laws that forbade women from deciding for themselves whether to carry a pregnancy were consistent with, contemporaneous with, and interactive with social mores mandating that unmarried mothers could not decide for themselves whether to be mothers of the children they bore. Two sociologists in the mid-1960s described a direct link between these mandates:

> Abortionists frequently encounter clients whose pregnancies are too far advanced to be terminated safely or who are obviously ambivalent about seeking an abortion. They then offer to pay the women's confinement fees and extend personal living expenses until the birth with a promise to secure "a good home" for the newborn infant. Frequently, a bonus of $100 or so is included as a further inducement. Many homeless and impecunious young women see this package deal as an answer to their prayers.[29]

No one knows how many women gave their babies away in adoption before *Roe v. Wade*. Many adoptions were handled by agencies, but thousands were managed by doctors, lawyers, ministers, and others who kept no records. Estimates, however, do suggest numbers in the neighborhood of a couple of hundred thousand a year in the 1950s and much of the 1960s. Some commentators have argued with deep conviction that the abortion laws that interacted with and occasioned infant removal were much more dangerous and degrading to women in the postwar decade than criminal abortion and illegal abortionists ever were. Ellen Messer and Kathryn May, who edited *Back Rooms: An Oral History of the Illegal Abortion Era*, found that among the women they interviewed, the ones who had illegal operations felt relief afterward, even "exhilaration." But the ones who gave up a child described the consequences as a lifelong, psychologically wrenching burden.[30]

It is not enough to say that the law was the real source of danger to women before *Roe*. It is crucial to underscore this additional fact: like many laws, the anti-abortion statutes affected different groups (of women) differently. Specifically, they created more danger for poor women, many of whom were women of color. Jane Hodgson (and other "doctors of conscience" interviewed by Carole Joffe) reported being motivated to become an abortion practitioner in part because of what she observed about the ways that race and class structured women's opportunities, or lack of them, to get abortions.[31]

Apparently, abortions were readily available in some communities of color in the illegal era, even though, as one African-American doctor put it, "the climate was so hostile to abortion" in his Pittsburgh area. This doctor remembered, "As to early abortions in our community, we did thousands with no complications at all." Maybe in white communities, he said, "you got dishwashers and mechanics, but in the Black Community, mine and others, you got midwives who were by and large good." Nevertheless, this doctor stressed, "race makes a difference!" When a Black practitioner got in trouble with the law, he or she would simply not have been "given the benefit of the doubt in the same way that a white doctor [was]."[32]

Many studies of abortion and its consequences before *Roe* showed that legal hospital abortions were available for private patients, but not for "charity" patients. In a Buffalo hospital, for example, 293 out of 299 psychiatrically justified therapeutic abortions were done on paying customers.[33] In sixty leading hospitals in the United States in 1965, one abortion was performed for every 315 births among private patients, while one was performed for every 1,149 births among ward patients.[34] Dr. Christopher Tietze, the leading postwar expert on the public health consequences of abortion, noted in this era, "It would seem that the difference in the incidence of therapeutic abortion between private and public ward patients is not because the private patient can pay for the abortion and the ward patient cannot pay, but because the ward patient cannot pay for the psychiatrist."[35]

In Detroit, a doctor found that "nearly all" of 138 deaths from septic abortion occurred "in the medically indigent group of women living in the poorest and most rundown areas in [the] city."[36] Nancy Howell Lee's findings were consistent with this doctor's and with Jane Hodgson's: "In obtaining an illegal abortion, to use the old cliché, it is not what you know but who you know that matters . . . [C]ompetent doctors make their services discreetly available to their middle class patients, and the informal networks circulate this information among people similar in background, while poor women find only non-physicians or self-induced methods available to them."[37] Observers were aware that it also mattered whom you knew when it came to the matter of public exposure. One noted, "It is not the woman of the 'privileged group' who comes before the court [in abortion cases]."[38] In many communities, the law exposed poor women, above all, to danger.

A young man who grew up in a very poor neighborhood on the Lower East Side of Manhattan described how abortion was "pretty common" there in the 1960s. "Especially for young girls," he recalled. "What else could they do? . . . Young girls if they can't have abortions they will give it up, or else they will just get rid of it. They're frightened, they don't know what to do." He remembered one girl who was pregnant and had no options and was afraid to tell her mom. "But she did tell her after all, and her mom took care of it for her . . . I just thought it was bizarre how these people would think that they knew how to perform abortions with coat hangers and lye. I couldn't understand that."[39]

THE ENDURING BUTCHER

Despite the overwhelming power of anti-abortion laws to create a world where women were in danger, we continue to remember and name inept, perverse mercenaries as the source of women's danger. The components of this figure's villainy remain familiar and explicit. Commentators in the illegal era often framed their condemnation by referring to the man's parasitical relation to "the lucrative trade." One observer despaired that "the nefarious traffic in death continues in the hands of get-rich-quick quacks who prey on desperate women."[40] Others focused on the pathological character of criminal practitioners in this way:

> Many abortionists and their assistants seem to lead somewhat disorganized lives—numerous divorces, alcoholism, drifting from job to job and place to place. Police sometimes find pornographic literature in their possession. Sometimes abortionists have sexual re-

lations with their patients before aborting them. Like professional burglars or confidence men, abortionists tend to stay in the racket, even after being convicted. One abortionist while on trial performed an abortion during noon recess.[41]

Recalling this version of the past, a woman in the 1990s generalizes, "You were very likely to find yourself in a dim, dirty room that smelled of disinfectant, in the hands of a so-called doctor whose breath stank of bourbon, and who might cop a feel before going to work."[42]

"Detective Stan" in Pittsburgh, like many others, stressed that back alley abortionists were not professionals, not proper medical men. "All these abortionists fit the same mold," the policeman claimed. "It didn't matter whether they worked out of houses or the back seats of cars. It was the same dirty routine . . . It was just filth."[43] A New York district attorney was quoted in a 1960 exposé to this effect: "Characteristic of the illegal abortionist—whether physician, midwife, chiropractor or totally untrained layman—is the wanton disregard of the health of the victim."[44]

Whatever the specific characteristics or character of the back alley abortionist, many commentators argued, these men were willing to wreak "psychic trauma" on women. Generally, experts agreed from the 1930s onward that abortion caused "a high incidence of pathologic conditions, some of which interfere with the further possibility of reproduction."[45] Possibly worse than that, some doctors claimed that "if women know they can destroy the fetus very easily, they become lax in their sexual morals." Another commentator put the same problem another way when he posed a threatening question: "If abortions were as easy . . . as visiting a dentist, would there be a shocking increase in promiscuous activities?"[46] In these fearsome renditions, the abortionist represents medical danger and psychological destruction, and becomes the perverse agent of gender ruination. The Back Alley Butcher as villain is the wickedly responsible party, according to the standard and inherited narrative. In this story, desperate women are always victimized. They are always helpless.

One group that told this story endlessly in the criminal era was physicians, great champions of the Back Alley Butcher icon. They told the story even when they knew otherwise, and even when they regularly referred patients to good abortion practitioners. (An African-American nurse, "Fay," took abortion referrals in Pittsburgh for years from doctors and nurses who knew of her skill. Fay recalls, "It's like they all wanted me to be out there doing good abortions so they could send their patients to me, while at the same time, they didn't have to be 'involved.' " A doctor who knew Fay and the quality of her work concurred: "With a Fay out there, there was almost no reason for a doctor to take a chance to do an abortion himself.")[47] Dr. Alan Guttmacher, for years chief of obstetrics and gynecology at Mt. Sinai Hospital in New York and a force in Planned Parenthood, referred to this behavior of his colleagues in 1942 as "patent hypocrisy" about abortion. He said that most doctors had "a holier than thou attitude" concerning this subject that he found "revolting."[48]

Patricia Miller has documented the course some, possibly many, doctors followed from the late nineteenth to the mid-twentieth century, to convince women that they must eschew this outlawed activity and its practitioners: "[S]ome doctors began to denounce abortion as 'morally reprehensible' as well as medically unsafe. It was a short step from 'reprehensible' and 'disreputable' to 'damnable,' 'evil,' 'abominable,' and finally 'unnatural.' "[49] Over this period, many physicians were mouthing such sentiments while secretly tucking a few abortion patients into their weekly schedule, regularly referring desperate women to criminal practitioners, and using the hospital abortion board or some other mechanism to distance themselves from public, personal responsibility or participation in the abortion arena.[50]

Moreover, while the number of postwar-era physicians who had some kind of contact with abortion was probably growing, the community of physicians in the mid-twentieth century was still composed of doctors trained by parents, medical school faculty, and a senior profession that were closer to the generation that criminalized abortion. One doctor practicing in the 1950s described how his doctor father taught him that "abortionists had the same social status as a child molester or a rapist." His father's message was echoed by his teachers in medical school, who stressed that good doctors didn't do immoral things like abortion. This man, who admitted he had no contact with abortion or abortion practitioners in the criminal era, had easily internalized these lessons: "I had strong opinions about the scum of the earth—abortionists."

Another doctor who had also received medical training before *Roe v.*

Wade remembers that abortion was considered "dark and dirty." She recalls that in medical school, "I was taught that abortion was not only illegal but immoral, and that no self-respecting doctor who considered herself part of the medical community would perform an abortion . . . Abortionists were 'bums,' 'murderers,' real 'lowlifes,' and very inept physicians who could not make a living any other way. They were objects of contempt and scorn."

Most doctors and nurses who did hospital duty before *Roe v. Wade* have a powerful visual memory that comports with medical school contempt for abortionists. One doctor remembers, "The septic abortion ward was sort of a separate unit off in a corner of the hospital. It was dingy and dark, and there were always a bunch of women in there, typically fifteen to twenty, and they all had septic abortions. They were real sick!"[51] Many of the medical professionals who did service in these "septic tanks" report having felt "enormous rage at the illegal abortionists who had done such inept work" to such gruesome ends.

As Carole Joffe shows in *Doctors of Conscience*, sometimes septic abortions could be traced to specific "shady, incompetent" abortionists.[52] In many other cases, however, the agent of the botched abortion was unidentified—and doctors and other observers simply lumped Back Alley Butchers and self-aborters together, as they labored to repair perforated uteruses and other disasters. One physician remembered a typical 2 a.m. arrival in the emergency room: "another victim of a hack abortionist or of self-abortion." Reflecting this tendency to blur the source of the problem, Al Blumenthal, a politician from the Upper West Side of Manhattan, reported in the late 1960s while working to liberalize New York State's abortion laws: "[I]n the last ten years, 367 women in New York City died as the result of abortion or attempted abortion, either self-inflicted or performed by an unqualified person under unsafe circumstances."[53]

THE SPECTRAL ICON

Even though the Back Alley Butcher icon was enormously vibrant in the criminal era, and especially in the period after legalization, the historical evidence we have—about how many abortions were performed in the pre-*Roe* era, how many deaths resulted, and who did abortions then—

does not support the proposition that the criminal era was characterized by practitioners of this type. First of all, nobody knows how many abortions were carried out annually before legalization in 1973. Perhaps the most commonly cited appraisal of how little even public health professionals knew in the postwar period is this expert's 1953 statement: "The size of the population of women who obtain deliberate abortions . . . is estimated as on the order of one million per year, although the true number may be as low as 200,000 or as high as two million."[54] Sexologist Alfred Kinsey's data, for a disproportionately white sample, showed that in the late 1940s and early 1950s about one in five women who had ever been married or who had had coitus had had an abortion.[55]

Exact numbers of both abortions and abortion deaths were so hard to come by and so crucial for capturing the magnitude of the problem that journalists would frequently borrow any figures they could find, as in this 1951 claim from "The Abortion Menace" in Ebony: "For each year, nearly 700,000 abortions are performed on unfortunate, desperate women by quack surgeons and disreputable physicians whose criminal and unethical methods annually claim the lives of about 8,000 victims, among them some several thousand Negro women."[56] The estimates here are almost certainly drawn from guesses provided by Frederick Taussig in his magisterial 1936 book, Abortion, Spontaneous and Induced: Medical and Social Aspects. Taussig ties his numbers to increased abortions during World War I and the Great Depression of the 1930s—conditions probably not relevant to 1951.[57] In fact, Christopher Tietze, an expert on the public health consequences of abortion, noted a "striking decline" in abortion deaths between 1927 and 1945—possibly a result of the increasing number of competent practitioners who responded to the high demand during the Depression and World War II.[58] With the advent of antibiotics in the 1940s and their use in the criminal abortion arena, death rates fell more sharply still. One study claimed in 1964 that "deaths due to abortion are now approximately one-sixth of what they were prior to 1940."[59] A recent oral history of the criminal era attaches an actual number to the incidence of abortion deaths after World War II: "By 1950, when antibiotics were widely available," Patricia Miller notes in The Worst of Times, "the number of reported abortion-related deaths in the United States was 316. Starting in the mid-to-late 1960s, the figure dropped further."[60] If we use the middle-range estimate for the postwar era—one million illegal abortions a year—this 1950 death figure represents a mortality rate of *three one-hundredths of 1 percent.*

Clearly, nobody can reliably calculate the criminal abortion rate or the death rate from abortion before *Roe v. Wade.* But we can be confident that the death rate did decline sharply—as did the death rate for all invasive medical procedures—after antibiotics became available. Yet even after the death rate plummeted, the generalized association of abortion and death and the figure of the death-dealing abortionist persisted in our national consciousness. One study conducted toward the end of the criminal era tested persistent "media claims that one to one-and-a-half-million abortions were performed a year in the United States, resulting in five-to-ten thousand deaths." The author speculated, "If Minnesota contributes one-fiftieth of the [U.S.] birthrate annually, it should also contribute one-fiftieth of the criminal abortion deaths annually. Thus, one-fiftieth of five thousand is one hundred and one fiftieth of ten thousand is two hundred." But actually, the investigator shows, there were only 1.3 criminal-abortion deaths annually in Minnesota.[61] Findings such as these did not make an impact at the time, nor in retrospect. In the early 1990s, a cultural study of the 1950s described the horrors of the illegal abortion arena using the same old claims: "By 1962, black market abortions were killing an estimated five to ten thousand women a year."[62]

If we can't find statistics showing that many women died or were harmed at the hands of back alley miscreants, we might look for the Back Alley Butcher in contemporary, serious, nonfiction descriptions of practitioners. But in the 1950s, Kinsey—who was very interested in the criminal-abortion scene—claimed that "nearly 90% of the operative abortions . . . performed today are being performed by physicians, most of whom are not recognized as abortionists." Dr. George Loutrell Timanus, a Baltimore abortion-performing physician, agreed on the high proportion of physician practitioners, estimating that he and one other medical practitioner performed 90 percent of the illegal abortions done in that city.[63] We have histories of outstanding long-term practitioners like Dr. Timanus in Baltimore, Dr. Robert Spencer in Pennsylvania, Dr. Ed Keemer in Detroit, and Ruth Barnett in Portland, Oregon—all of whom worked for decades doing hundreds of abortions a year, with very few complications and little contact with the law. We also have a wealth of anecdotal evidence and oral histories supporting the claim that upstand-

ing, respectable physicians all over the country did abortions before
Roe.[64] Again, the evidence suggests that decent, competent practitioners
performed the lion's share of abortions in the criminal era.

This claim is also borne out by attitudes toward abortion practitioners
in communities around the country in the criminal era. Postwar commentators frequently remarked that criminal abortionists were rarely
prosecuted and that most people didn't seem to mind an abortionist in
the community. As one legal observer typically described the situation in
1952, "Many citizens and public officials look upon criminal abortions
with toleration, the citizens because they don't care, and some officials
because . . . it is difficult to obtain evidence to secure convictions."[65]
These descriptions of casual indifference on the part of ordinary citizens
and law enforcers are common enough to strongly suggest that an epidemic of Back Alley Butcher–induced abortion deaths in these decades
was unlikely.

"Detective Jack" in Pittsburgh remembers when police came to arrest
Dr. King, a Black physician who worked in an African-American neighborhood, because he performed abortions. A huge crowd, including
"some real tough types," formed to protect the doctor and block the law.
It was a "wild" demonstration of community support for this man's
important, quality work.[66] In 1969, one researcher found that many
presumably competent abortionists were able to "remain in the same location for years and depend upon the loyalty and discretion of their customers to protect them from the law."[67]

In the 1940s, an investigator observed, "the greatest obstacle so far
encountered to the legal control of abortion is public indifference [to]
. . . the enormous number of abortions performed."[68] Ten years later, with
the figure of the Back Alley Butcher more vibrant than ever in the media, and the number of criminal abortions performed annually reported
to be very high, law enforcement was still quiescent, relative to the scope
of opportunity. District attorneys and police chiefs were fully aware that
most juries were simply unwilling to convict. (Taussig had remarked in
the 1930s that "the most striking evidence of the attitude of the public"
was that juries wouldn't punish abortionists.)[69] When convictions did
occur, the punishment was often a suspended sentence, a puny outcome
for trials that cost taxpayers a lot of money.[70]

A student of this syndrome, finding that "the prevalence of this criminal act is far greater than most law enforcement officials realize," observed in the postwar period, "It is doubtful if any other felonious act is so free from punishment as is criminal abortion."[71] A comment in the *Women's Home Companion* in 1955 may have explained this kind of community tolerance: "One of Detroit's leading obstetricians, asked to comment on the illegal trade, expressed the private opinion, 'that a skilled abortionist is an asset to the community.' " A similar though more sour assessment by another doctor called the criminal practitioner a "necessary evil."[72] And a former district attorney in Pittsburgh remembered how, in the criminal era, the police dealt with abortionists as public health resources. They "would know who in the community was doing abortions and who was good and who was not so good." An officer would "act as a sort of intermediary" and set up abortion appointments."[73]

Years later in Chicago, the underground abortion network, called Jane, was similarly considered a public health asset for women, a resource for doctors, and a hands-off proposition for police.[74] Rosalind Petchesky points out that "[t]he police were not interested in stopping [these women from performing abortions] . . . The police had known what they were doing and had not intervened . . . since they were providing a necessary service for policemen's wives, mistresses and daughters and for all policewomen, and did so in a manner that left women healthy and well."[75]

Policemen and ordinary citizens who recognized skilled abortionists as public health assets were probably also aware of the desperate practitioner who was, indeed, the cause of butchery and death in the criminal era: the woman herself. Dr. Regine K. Stix, in her important study of the consequences of abortion, recognized in the early 1930s that many women tried to abort themselves and were often horribly unsuccessful. In her sample of women who tried self-abortion, 76 percent ended up with significant medical complications.[76] In the same era, Taussig notes that "a considerable portion of our knowledge of poisonous drugs is derived from the human experiments made upon themselves by women desirous of abortion." Few have succeeded with their abortions, he noted, and many have been hurt by "the haphazard use of drugs and homemade appliances."[77]

Several decades later, in the late 1950s, Alfred Kinsey and a number of physicians documented the prevalence of self-induced abortions. Reports included the fact that as many as 80 percent of women seeking illegal abortions had first tried to self-induce, and the fact that 75 percent of the criminal abortions that came to the attention of law enforcement were self-induced. One Washington, D.C., physician was unequivocal when he described the situation at hospitals in that city, such as the one that admitted about fifteen septic abortion cases a month. He said, "I think the matter of self-induced is extremely important. At least, in the Washington, D.C., area, what information we have would indicate that those who get into serious trouble are self-induced." This physician was so convinced of the source of danger that he strongly recommended that anti-abortion laws not be enforced: "Any steps you [take] to suppress abortion further might conceivably raise the self-induced rate and consequently the death rate."[78]

Even now, when invoking the criminal era, it is common to foreground the butcher and all but efface the self-aborting woman. Dorothy Fadiman, in her acclaimed documentary From Danger to Dignity, reports that "most women faced the back alley," invoking that venue's association with the death-dealing, miscreant quack. But Fadiman's own material, presented immediately following the back alley claim, shows that the danger many, if not most, women faced was much closer to home. The first tragedy we hear about is a girl who died after her mother attempted to abort her. Then we learn of poor women, many of whom were Black, who didn't have the connections to get safe abortions. The consequences of this kind of isolation were horrifying self-abortions. Fadiman's informant tells about one young woman so resourceless in the criminal era that she used the wire stem of a fake flower to abort herself, with disastrous consequences. Another informant remembers, "Women were using Lysol. They would drink it or they would douche with it. Anything caustic. They would stick needles, anything that they would poke in the general direction of their uterus in an effort to dislodge this pregnancy."[79]

Like Fadiman, Patricia Miller, compiler of the oral history of the criminal era in Pittsburgh, begins her account with death. The Worst of Times starts off with "Coroner Fred," who tells how anti-abortion statutes pushed helpless women into the arms of Back Alley Butchers.[80] Notably, despite what Kinsey and others can teach us about the frequency with which women attempted to perform operations on themselves in the criminal era, Miller includes no stories or examples of self-induced abortion in her volume.

When we think back on the illegal era, who—or what—we blame for the tragedies associated with illegal abortion shapes how we define the solution. If we blame the figure of the Back Alley Butcher (even though "he" is not a historically valid actor), then the point of legalization becomes saving women from being victimized. Focusing on the Butcher stops far short of a women's rights argument. On the other hand, if we see danger and tragedy springing from anti-abortion laws, then the point of legalizing abortion is to assure women the rights (which create opportunities and choices) that enable women's sovereignty over their own bodies.

WOMEN'S POINT OF VIEW

Finally, women who went to the so-called Back Alley have told us what they found there. What stands out in the oral histories of the criminal era is that even though criminal practitioners were vilified in the media, many women knew that it was far more dangerous to self-abort than to be operated on.[81] Also, women who have spoken about these desperately scary trips have clarified a crucial point: even in the face of danger, unwillingly pregnant women were not always helpless, desperate victims in the pre-*Roe* era. I think it is important to imagine that these abortion-seeking women could be simultaneously, or alternately, awash in terrified helplessness *and* terribly focused on finding a way out, determined not to be victims of sex, of their sexual partners, of their bodies, of the law. Perhaps most relevant here, the stories make it plain that a great many women went home after the procedure unharmed and no longer pregnant.

Rosalind Petchesky has written profoundly and insightfully about the politics of abortion, in both the legal and illegal eras. Among her observations is the following: "The state attempts to accommodate, rechannel or delegitimate women's everyday practices and values around fertility; rarely is it possible to wipe them out. Thus, ordinary women play a dynamic part in determining the politics of reproduction and sexuality, through their practices and sometimes their consciously articulated ideas."[82]

Perhaps we need to reimagine the criminal era as a time when, despite the law, millions of women—and their reproductive practices—played a "dynamic part" in shaping reproductive politics, including what went on in the arena of illegal abortion. In the 1930s, Taussig boldly observed that the women's suffrage movement, the "newer economic independence of women," and women's "revolt" against male domination had brought women's need to have the "the right . . . to control their own bodies" into sharp relief.[83] Surely many women had the same recognition as they determined to end pregnancies and looked for assistance. In a time when women lacked the birth control pill, when other forms of contraception were hard to come by and were often illegal to acquire, when men generally felt entitled to be in charge of sexual relations with their wives and girlfriends, many women nonetheless played a "dynamic part" in shaping the abortion arena. As historian Leslie Reagan put it, women had a part in constructing "a system that worked well for both women seeking abortions and for physicians."[84]

In this system, many women went to the so-called Back Alley as "consumers." The criminal abortion practices with which we can be most familiar—Timanus's, Barnett's, Spencer's—have many signs of having been constructed to meet the needs and preferences of "customers." For example, these and other practices allowed "sliding-scale" fee schedules to accommodate customers' financial capabilities. When they could, practitioners created inviting surroundings. Ruth Barnett's office in Portland, Oregon, was tasteful, antiseptic, and, in the private space, luxurious. A long-time nurse who worked for Barnett described the clinic as "a gorgeous, beautiful place." According to Barnett's daughter, the abortionist designed her practice to please the women who purchased her services: "There was a hoity-toity service kind of thing. It wasn't like a hospital. It was like going up to a very nice atmosphere where people waited on you hand and foot—can I get you a cup of coffee? Can I get you a hot tea? How do you feel, dearie?"[85] Even mainstream doctors in regular hospitals shaped medical provision according to women's demands and needs regarding abortion.[86] One survey in the early 1960s found that in eighteen out of twenty-four California hospitals "therapeutic abortions" were performed illegally.[87]

Possibly the most credible, qualitative study of the abortion experience during the criminal era is Nancy Howell Lee's *The Search for an Abortionist*, published just a few years before *Roe*. Lee herself was surprised that her sample of 112 women yielded only 17 who had found the abortion practitioner they'd seen an "unpleasant" sort of person. Seventy-six women in the sample reported a straightforward "good opinion."[88] (Patricia Miller describes the old-time illegal abortionists she interviewed in the early 1990s as "surprisingly likable as they earnestly described their experiences in the underground.")[89] Given this finding, it makes sense that a great many of the stories from the pre-*Roe* days are actually quite positive.

Naturally, many women were enormously grateful when they found someone to help them. One woman wrote to the doctor who treated her, "When you agreed you would [perform the abortion], I wanted to jump up and kiss you. I felt like the prisoner about to be hung who is given a last minute reprieve."[90] Another woman wrote of her abortion doctor, "When I paid him forty dollars, I kissed his cheek."[91]

Some women remembered the sensitivity and fairness of the practitioner, as well as the skill. One woman recalled, "It was over before I knew it. I thought I was just having the examination at the time. [The doctor] even tried to make me feel not guilty by telling me that the long automobile trip had already started a spontaneous abortion. He charged me $25. That was on Friday and on Monday I was back at work. I never suffered any ill from it."[92]

Sociologist Carole Joffe's outstanding study of "doctors of conscience" captures the stories of a number of individuals who provided excellent service to presumably very grateful women.[93] Other oral histories are replete with these stories as well. The writer Elizabeth Janeway, for example, describes her criminal abortion as having been "comfortable, clean, the absolute tops." And writer Kay Boyle went to "a wonderful woman, Dr. Mary Halton, who specialized in abortions for working women." Boyle emphasized, "I had no sense at all of anything precarious taking place. Dr. Halton's mere presence reassured me."

The many women whose published stories are available include a large number who got abortions from men and women who were not doctors. This group, too, apparently received service from many high-quality practitioners. The actress Barbara Corday describes the man who helped her. "He was a tall, attractive grey-haired man, and he was very nice to me. He told me what he was going to do." Corday reports that afterward, her doctor in New York said the man had done "a very decent job."[94]

"Audrey," in Pittsburgh, went to "Flo," a nurse's aide who "knew exactly what to do." Audrey describes herself as having been "scared to death," but, she writes, "Flo had a wonderful bedside manner. She was a stout light-skinned Black woman. She had a nice home. She was very clean, and her home was clean. She was a warm, nice, caring person, and I could tell she felt bad for us—the women who were pregnant and didn't want to be, and came to her for help. I think that's why she went into it."

"Rachel" said she went for help to a man "I absolutely know . . . was not a doctor. The nurse-girlfriend [who assisted him] was as close as we got to real medical expertise. However, they were both very nice and they treated me very well. He really came highly recommended, so I was pretty confident and not as scared as you'd imagine, given that he wasn't a doctor." "Estelle" had a similar experience with a nonmedical practitioner: "[S]he told me exactly what to expect and when to expect it . . . She told me what was normal and what to worry about . . . She was very good—just like a real doctor—and everything happened just like she said it would."

"Eleanor's" description of her flamboyant abortionist, "Bertha," reminds me of Ruth Barnett, who estimated that she performed 40,000 abortions over her long career. And she never lost a patient. According to "Eleanor," "Bertha didn't look real. She had dyed red hair teased and sprayed to a stiff, towering beehive on her head. She had too much makeup and long bright-red fingernails. She had on a gaudy-print kimono-type thing and high-heeled floppy mules which were decorated with what looked like ostrich feathers." Bertha may have looked unreal, but she, too, knew what she was doing. As Eleanor put it, "Everything was fine. Bertha was skillful, and that's probably why the doctor referred me to her."[95]

What is striking is that so many of the women remembering the awful past associate their successful illegal abortion with *luck*. Having "good luck" was the only way, many women believed, and believe in retrospect, that things could have turned out okay. One woman, who got an abortion in 1964, put the matter typically: "Luckily it worked out well. Luckily I went to the kind of person I went to, rather than to someone who was going to . . . stick . . . the instrument right through my uterus. I felt very lucky."[96]

Luck is, of course, crucially important in an arena that forbids choice, autonomy, self-determination. Luck is all you have when cultural norms and the law want you helpless. When a journalist writing about illegal abortion for the *Saturday Evening Post* in 1961 considered the "cruel choices" open to a pregnant high school girl or a housewife then, he imagined, "When somebody says, 'I can get you an abortion,' that's all they want to hear. They don't give a damn about the abortionist's credentials."[97] One woman seeking an abortion at the time confirms the feeling of helpless choicelessness endemic to the situation: "I was so frightened that I really didn't pay a lot of attention to my surroundings. I had absolutely no knowledge of this woman's medical competence, but I sure wasn't going to ask . . . I didn't want to die . . . But I didn't have a choice."[98] For women who felt like that, if you lucked out and got a decent practitioner instead of a Back Alley Butcher, well, you lived.

The concept of luck in the criminal abortion arena is totally consistent with the looming figure of the Back Alley Butcher. He was the norm. If you did better than that, it was simply luck. (As Dorothy Fadiman puts it, "Some women found safe operations, but most faced the back alleys.")[99] Writer Grace Paley was among the *lucky ones* when the woman whom she asked for a referral told her nothing about the abortionist, but just said, "Call." Paley remembers, "I just assumed he was a real doctor, and he was. That may have been luck."[100] "Miriam" feels no regret about her abortion. She says, "I didn't die and I wasn't sterile. Considering what happened to a lot of women in those days, I guess I have been very lucky."[101] The writer Nora Sayre remarked about her abortion, performed in the 1950s by a distinguished feminist gynecologist, "Abortion was something other people died of; you hadn't."[102]

Of course women did tragically die in the illegal era and the incidence of death plummeted to near zero after legalization. But it was not simply *luck* that attended these and hundreds of thousands of other women in the so-called back alley each year. The fact is, an uncountable but very large number of competent practitioners performed abortions even then.

THE POWER OF THE ICON

With so much evidence about good practitioners and good results in the criminal era, why has the Back Alley Butcher remained such a vibrant symbol? It is an important question: Why does the monster (male) abortionist eclipse the law and the desperate self-aborting woman in the story we tell about the criminal era? Why do we invoke, iconically, the Back Alley Butcher to explain why we must preserve legal abortion? Even today, we prefer the story that casts the male villain and the female victim. It is a fact that we have a lot to draw on in this regard. With only occasional exceptions, postwar popularizers and commentators—our sources—tell the familiar tale and use the powerful, credible, stock figures, with emphasis on the practitioner and his villainous, fatal association with sex, money, and aborted motherhood.

The Back Alley Butcher lives on in part because the icon adapts well to changing agendas; the symbol is capacious enough to absorb and reflect meanings, one after another. Most tragically, the Back Alley Butcher lives on because some women died at the hands of unskilled people and that is enraging and unforgettable. Second, the Back Alley Butcher has always suited traditionalists disturbed by the specter of the woman who appears to challenge or violate female norms. This is the woman "who all her life has disliked being female," who is in conflict with her husband and other men, and who is "the basically immature woman who cannot accept the outstanding responsibilities of mature femininity, namely becoming a mother." Psychiatrists called this woman "abortion-prone," and described her as deeply confused and hypervulnerable. They imagined her as prey for the villain, the Back Alley Butcher.[103]

The evil icon had several functions for physicians before *Roe*. On the one hand, doctors were threatened, challenged, and enraged by the figure of the Butcher and the trail of destruction created by botched abortions. On the other hand, this figure became a useful marker against which doctors of probity could distinguish themselves.[104] As Alan Guttmacher put it in 1965, "My own value would be impaired if I did abortions. So I have to take this hypocritical attitude, stay holy and let others do the dirty work."[105] Even today, many physicians keep their distance from contemporary providers as a mark of probity.

Back Alley Butchers have also served the abortion rights movement since the late 1960s, certainly since 1973. Ever since legalization, an active, determined, sometimes murderous anti–abortion rights community has tried to block abortion practice and overturn *Roe v. Wade*. In reaction, pro–abortion rights forces have argued that legal abortion must be sustained because women must be saved from the back alley villain.[106] No less relevant here, the Back Alley Butcher has served anti-abortion folks, too, who argue that abortionists were maimers and murderers before *Roe* and are the same today. The powerful figure of the Butcher easily takes precedence over the long history of women's successful resistance against the law and their determination to control their own fertility no matter what the law mandated. The Butcher configures the woman under his hands as helpless. The figure makes a woman's attempt to manage her own body into an act of pure desperation; it constructs the woman's fate as just deserts and a lurid story—a piece of slasher erotica.

Also, the Back Alley Butcher presupposes a simple, bifurcated historical narrative: before *Roe v. Wade* abortion was deadly dangerous; afterward it was safe and legal. (Illogically, this narrative suggests that after 1973, the law qua law was very powerful, but before 1973 it was weak and the Butcher prevailed.)

THE BACK ALLEY BUTCHER, CONSUMER PROTECTION, AND ABORTION RIGHTS

The Back Alley Butcher turns out to be a much thinner icon than we have thought. This is important because—again—how we assess the source of the danger in the criminal era matters. It is also important to be clear about where the focus on the Butcher leaves women as rights-bearing persons.

To credit an oppressed population (such as women alienated from their own bodies by law) with rights—with the human status and capacity to deserve rights—it has usually been important for those in power to believe that the oppressed population is determined to have rights and even that the population in question will seize rights before they possess legal sanction, no matter what. The focus on the Back Alley Butcher before legalization and on women as helpless victims has the effect of casting doubt on women's ability to seize rights and even on whether such thoroughgoing victims deserved and could manage rights.

In fact, I believe that the focus on the Back Alley Butcher effaces the rights issue altogether. When we hear representatives of NARAL or Planned Parenthood claim that abortion must stay legal to protect women from the ghastly back alley of old, we are hearing the echo of one strain of a worn-out debate about what women need: Do women need protection or do women need equal rights? That is—and this is the crux of the matter—do women need protection from the Back Alley Butcher or do they need *the right* to control their own bodies? If we focus on the Butcher, we conjure up the powerful, destructive, overbearing male who must be neutralized, by regulation. The purpose of the law becomes protection, not the guarantee of rights. The focus on the Butcher is an indication of continuing cultural and political ambivalence about the association of women and rights—a continuing ambivalence about making laws that empower women.

As it works—and this should be obvious—the focus on the Butcher is an indication of the broad cultural and political ambivalence in the United States about abortion in general and abortion practitioners in particular. The figure of the Butcher links the past to the present in several destructive ways. It is crucial to recognize that this icon has a way of bleeding across time to infect, endanger, and even justify the murder of contemporary practitioners.

The medical profession, whose support for legalized abortion in the late 1960s and early 1970s was a factor in decriminalization, has not rallied in support of abortion doctors during the long assault they've sustained since 1973. Carole Joffe provides ample evidence of this in *Doctors of Conscience*, and contemporary abortion practitioners have infuriating, humiliating stories to tell about how they've been marginalized in their medical communities.

One doctor who performed abortions before legalization and after explained to Joffe how the stain has spread across time and affixes to all abortion practitioners, as far as other physicians are still concerned:

In attempting to establish a nonprofit abortion clinic and get local physician [support], Bennett found that his history as a provider of illegal abortion tainted his image among his would-be colleagues.

"There were some [doctors] who said they'd be willing to provide abortion service with such a set-up but they didn't want to have anything to do with me . . . It was because I was an 'abortionist.' . . . An abortionist is a despicable person. They assumed you did it for the money, you didn't have the qualifications to be a real doctor . . . you were either a drug addict, an alcoholic, a ne'er do well, you couldn't maintain a practice or you were owned by the Mafia . . . You weren't a good person and probably weren't a good doctor either. At the very least, you were an embarrassment to the medical community."

Since abortion practitioners suffer what Joffe calls the "passive toleration" of the majority of the medical profession,[107] anti-abortion forces perceive these doctors as vulnerable targets. This is not a theoretical observation. In an essay called "Life on the Front Lines," Dr. Warren Hern, a longtime abortion provider in Boulder, Colorado, and my neighbor, has described what it's like being the target of assassins on an everyday basis. Hern describes the extraordinary security precautions that were necessary for him to give a brief speech at a 1995 candlelight vigil in town to commemorate people recently gunned down by anti-abortion murderers. That evening, "[l]aw enforcement officials expected someone to attempt to assassinate me." Hern asks, "Is it possible for a physician who performs abortions in the most pro-choice community in the country to walk a few blocks from his medical office without an armed security escort to the front of the city hall to speak to a publicly announced peaceful assembly of his fellow citizens about this matter without a serious risk of being assassinated? The answer to that question is, No. Think about what that means for your country."[108]

My questions are related to Dr. Hern's: Why was there no wall, physical or symbolic, of physicians to stand up and protect this doctor who serves the women of the community and the region so well? Is it possible that the widespread contemporary reliance on the enduring figure of the Back Alley Butcher contributes mightily to the danger faced by abortion practitioners today? Before leaving the Back Alley Butcher, I want to return for a moment to the popular idea that, above all, *Roe v. Wade protects* women. When we claim that abortion must be legal so that girls and women are safe from back alley miscreants, we are, when it comes down to it, identifying—even defining—*Roe v. Wade* as a *consumer protection ruling*: a woman must be able to purchase good service when she goes out to buy an abortion. In this sense, the problem of the Back Alley Butcher is deeply consistent with the problems I've identified with "choice" in Chapter 1.

Consumer protection is, after all, fundamentally protection of the interests of the individual in the marketplace. Consumer protection empowers the individual to function safely, without exploitation, in the marketplace. In this case, imagining the role of *Roe v. Wade* as a consumer protection function can help untie the interests of one woman from the interests of all other women. When abortion access becomes a consumer issue—a matter of purchasing quality service—it is more difficult to press abortion rights as a political issue that shapes our notion of womanhood and that shapes the lives of all women, no matter which women actually climb up on the abortion doctor's table. It is certainly worth noting that the all-important contemporary status, that of consumer, refers specifically to neither women nor men. Abortion rights advocates, above all it would seem, would want to be very cautious about mixing abortion rights arguments with consumer-defined concerns.

The fact is, we have moved from an era when the law endangered women to an era in which the law—in the name of "choice"—protects women from those who may take advantage of their vulnerability. So far, women in the United States have not lived under a legal system that establishes and protects their reproductive rights. This is the kind of system we would need in order to provide all women with the basic dignity they require to live safe lives.

3

CLAIMING RIGHTS IN THE ERA OF CHOICE

PART I: AWAKENINGS

————

There were so many of us and the pain was so great. It should be recorded as part of women's history.

—Kathleen Leahy Koch[1]

WAKE UP LITTLE SUSIE REDUX

Most historians never experience the shock of having their subjects—the men and women they've unearthed in the archives and written about—come looking for them. After my book *Wake Up Little Susie: Single Pregnancy and Race before Roe v. Wade* was published in 1992, though, that is what happened to me.[2]

For months, starting in the spring of 1992, I got almost daily phone calls and letters from white women, most just about my own age, who had years before surrendered their babies for adoption. These communications came as a shock to me. I had responded sharply to archival evidence I had found of the dreadful circumstances that white, unmarried, pregnant young women faced in the 1950s and 1960s. Their humiliation, fear, anger, and defeat were captured vividly in documents prepared and saved by maternity home matrons, government workers, and psychologists, and by the young women themselves. Despite my sharp response to these papers that had sat in various repositories in Washington, D.C., Minneapolis, and New York for thirty years and more, I think it never occurred to me as I worked on *Susie* that the subjects of these documents had a real, continuing life. Both my indignation and my historical project addressed the plight of young women frozen, as it were, in the archives, at, say, the age of seventeen in 1964. In my mind, I said goodbye to them at the moment when their babies were being lifted out of their arms and transferred to other, more adult, more financially secure and independent married couples who, society judged, would be *proper parents*, in contrast to these bad teenage girls. There these girls stood in my mind.

But the women who called me and wrote to me jolted me out of my historian's dream. They called to say that I had gotten the story right, as far as I'd gone with it. Most asked why on earth had I thought to write a book about "unwed mothers" and their lost babies. (Surely, many hinted gingerly, I must be one of them.) And they wanted to tell me about their lives since the surrender. How hard they had resisted. How much they had suffered, for twenty-five, thirty-five years. Many wanted to tell me about how the experience of having been defined as not-mothers of children they had borne eventually catalyzed them to embrace an energetic feminist politics in the mid-1970s. This collective activism, they said, together with searching for and often finding their lost children, helped them regain the selfhood and even the sanity they'd lost with their babies.

Reading their letters, listening to their stories, I realized that the generation-long social experiment that involved transferring white babies from their unwed mothers to white, mostly middle-class couples, was not a phenomenon bounded by the dates I used in *Wake Up Little Susie*, approximately 1945 to 1965.[3] Furthermore, these women pressed me directly and indirectly to think more clearly and deeply about feminism in the 1970s. They both challenged what I knew about the formation of feminist consciousness in the mid-1970s and enlarged my understanding of feminist claims in that era. They also pressed me to think harder about adoption, which, despite its core role in the lives of unmarried, pregnant, and parturient white females in the postwar decades, was not really my subject in *Susie*. After many years of conversations with "former Susies," I am willing to go out on a limb with this hypothesis about adoption:

that the incidence of adoption, that is, the transfer of babies from women of one social classification to women in a higher social classification or group (within the same country or transnationally), may be a very accurate index of the vulnerable status of women in the country of the birthmothers.

Based on what I've learned about the experiences of birthmothers in the United States, I want to suggest that the conventional understanding of adoption should be turned on its head. Almost everybody believes that on some level, birthmothers *make a choice to give their babies away*. Here I argue that adoption is rarely about mothers' choices; it is, instead, about the abject choicelessness of some resourceless women.

Also, after rethinking the experiences of middle-class birthmothers in the postwar era, I've come to believe that the "success" of the social experiment that separated so many white babies from their mothers between the end of World War II and *Roe v. Wade*—forestalling the nationwide explosion of single motherhood until later in the twentieth century—may have emboldened politicians and others to believe that defining motherhood in exclusionary ways is really possible, even into our own time.

It is the case, of course, that political and cultural authorities today regularly express frustration about having lost the ability to set and control definitions of who is a mother. It seems likely to me that when Gary Bauer and Charles Murray express this frustration, they are not really yearning to return to a time when unmarried girls and women did not have babies before they were married. There was, of course, no such time. Nor is their nostalgia precisely for a time when many unmarried girls gave their babies up for adoption. Except for the postwar decades, there was no such time as this, either. And even in the postwar decades, only *some* groups of white girls were very likely to be pressed to relinquish—although the unmarried mother of any white baby then had a valuable commodity on her hands.

The nostalgia of Murray and his colleagues is rather, I think, for the time when cultural and political authorities had a great deal more control over women—over their sexuality, the circumstances of their pregnancies, their vulnerability to punishment, and the conditions of their motherhood. Welfare reform legislation, federally and in the states, is one way that the Murrayites have aimed to reconstruct lost authority, revitalize women's *lost dependency*, and in the process, redefine dependent women as bad choice makers.

Most important, in this chapter and the next one, I aim to make the case that the experience of postwar unwed mothers is not a side issue in the arena of reproductive politics and history. Nor is adoption a special case. This story captures the heart of what it means to wrap reproductive issues in the language of consumerism. This is the story of fertile women who lacked the right to control their fertility and, on top of that, lacked the right to control the basic decision about whether to be mothers of the children they gave birth to. This is a story about how thousands of young, white, middle-class mothers in the United States in our recent past lost their babies because authorities determined that these females should not be mothers. I am treating the experience of white unwed mothers as a case study that clarifies how women who lack the right to control their fertility and their motherhood status can be degraded—and how "natural" that degradation can come to seem. Many women who went through this experience have said that when women lack such fundamental controls, their lives can be ruined.

This chapter and the next show how a group of women made something heroic out of their vulnerability and loss. Many of them were inspired by the "choices" women gained with *Roe v. Wade* to become activists, but they soon determined that the choice was quite different from the right to be a mother. These women constructed a collective voice, a feminist organization and identity, and ultimately, a theory of rights to redress what they experienced as a life-defining traumatic violation.

Between approximately 1945 and 1973, unwed mothers, both Black and white, were defined as deviants. But white and Black unwed mothers were treated very differently from each other by their families and communities, by social agencies and by the government. After the war, a Black single mother typically stayed within her family and community and kept her child to raise herself, often with the help of her family. As larger numbers of these mothers (most shut out from well-paying employment opportunities) became eligible for public assistance in the late 1940s and early 1950s, and as the civil rights movement was gathering form and focus, white politicians and policy makers went to extreme lengths to portray these mothers as sexually and maternally irresponsible, interested in having babies only to increase their welfare checks. Politicians routinely promoted policies that used the out-of-wedlock child-bearing of some women of color to shore up racial segregation in general and specifically made it difficult for these mothers to get public housing, public assistance, education, and jobs.

The postwar experiences of white unwed mothers were quite different, though equally cruel. As Freudian theory seeped into the front lines of service delivery in social agencies, white single mothers were for the first time diagnosed as psychologically disturbed. Their nonmarital pregnancies were treated as evidence that they were unfit to be mothers. Treatment for these girls and women involved banishing them from their families and communities and placing them in maternity homes or other remote locations.

The new psychological explanation of white single pregnancy replaced the earlier explanation that girls and women who became pregnant while unmarried (and had no prospects that the father would make them "honest women") were products of poor environments and the weakened moral and physical fiber that resulted from growing up in urban slums, with, for example, alcoholic parents and subnormal IQs. Unwed mothers from such tainted environments were understood to produce similarly tainted babies. Before World War II, there were no hordes of childless white couples vying for selection as adoptive parents of bastard babies. The biological mothers of illegitimate babies were "fallen women," but they were still the mothers of the children they bore. These women were often consigned to live out their ruined lives on the fringes of society, but rarely did anyone question their status as mothers.

The new psychological explanation of white single pregnancy had a number of dramatic and swiftly applied implications. First of all, the psychological explanation was an important ingredient in the postwar cultural consensus that broke the relationship between biology and motherhood. After the war, public policy makers and implementers and large segments of the public at large came to believe that for whites, motherhood was not determined by biology, by giving birth. Rather, it was determined by marriage. A white girl or woman who had a baby outside of marriage was diagnosed as mentally disturbed. The fact that she had no husband to protect and love her was proof of her neurosis and her unfitness for motherhood.

Second, the psychological explanation of white single pregnancy was crucial to defining white illegitimate babies as valuable and adoptable. The women who had given birth to them, experts now argued, were not marked by fixed, inherent traits of biological inferiority. They were seen, rather, as nongenetically, temporarily, and treatably neurotic. Consequently, unlike bastard babies born of "tainted" mothers in the early decades of the twentieth century, illegitimate white babies born after the war were defined as free of maternal taint. These two innovations supported, naturally, the third innovation: that white unwed mothers must give their newly valuable illegitimate babies up for adoption.

Beginning in the late 1940s, community and government authorities, together with maternity-home personnel, developed a raft of strategies, some quite coercive, to press white unwed mothers to relinquish their babies to "deserving" couples. The strategies were astoundingly successful. Most maternity homes reported relinquishment rates of 90–95 percent by the mid-1950s.

Thousands of white girls and women surrendered their newborn babies between 1945 and 1973 under these new rules. In 1976, a few women who had surrendered their babies some years earlier found each other in the Boston area and rather quickly, in the style of that era, formed a political and mutual support organization that they called Concerned United Birthparents (CUB). CUB grew rapidly in the late 1970s and early 1980s, drawing in new members from around the country.

CUB members generally identified themselves as women who had been coerced into surrendering their babies. Members recognized right away that they had developed remarkably similar language and perspectives to describe the violation they had suffered. CUB's founding members drew inspiration from other liberation movements that were active and visible in the mid-1970s, including adoptee identity groups, civil rights groups, and women's groups. The activism of many CUB members was also inspired by the growing mass of single mothers in the United States in the 1970s and their public claims for maternal legitimacy.

By the time I encountered CUB in the early 1990s, its members were typically middle-aged and probably demographically similar in many ways to their national, racial cohort: many were married, many divorced, a few were widows, some had never married. Most were heterosexual. Most had subsequent children they'd been able to keep. Many of these women had been employed for a number of years. Quite a few had impressive professional careers, as lawyers, writers, publishers, college professors, administrators of various types, nurses, journalists, and political activists. All of these women remembered a time in the 1950s or 1960s or early 1970s when they were horrifyingly powerless.

The collection of birthmothers' voices here sketch out the anatomy of choicelessness. The birthmothers make clear what happened in our recent past when family, teachers, employers, and other community authorities joined together to deny choice, rights, and motherhood to a sizable cohort of American girls.

PREGNANT AND POWERLESS
IN THE POSTWAR DECADES

Ann Hege Hughes, a publisher in Baltimore, today the mother of several accomplished, grown daughters, remembers her mother's response to news of Ann's teenage pregnancy in 1966. "You shit!" her mother screamed. "You ungrateful shit! How dare you do this to us, after all we've sacrificed for you! How could you? You're nothing but a whore! You've disgraced your whole family—me and your father, your grandparents, your brothers—all of us!"[4] Ann's mother believed that a pregnant, unmarried daughter was as threatening to the family's status as an embezzling father or a shoplifting mother—and much more threatening than having a "hood" for a son, even one whose girlfriend was rumored to have gotten herself pregnant.

Ann's mother's reaction mirrored those of parents all over the country. Pollie Robinson, who got pregnant in 1963, managed to keep the news from her parents—"pillars of the community"—for five months. But when they found out, her father, a policeman, announced he would get the boy locked up, and Pollie's mother douched her with Lysol.[5] Many parents ascribed huge responsibility to their daughters and threatened these teenage girls in ways that terrified them. Karen Kottmeier remembers, "My father, a lawyer, said that his law practice would be harmed." He asked Karen how "he could explain this terrible thing to his clients, who were all people of prominence."[6] Elizabeth Avens recalls her responsibility for the consequential, "permanent damage" caused by rumors of her pregnancy: "My mother was forced to quit her bridge club."[7] Another woman explained how her family's future was in her hands. Her parents' "reaction was so bad. I was from a right-wing military family. Getting pregnant was the last straw for my father. Either I gave up the baby for adoption or my father walked out, deserted the family and divorced my mother. My father totally supported our family financially."[8]

Eleanor Whitmore, pregnant in 1966, was confronted by her mother, who threatened to throw herself out of the window and predicted that Eleanor's father would have a heart attack. This mother's imprecations revealed another parental fear: the event was a devastating reminder of the family's precarious foothold in the middle class and their actual low origins. As Eleanor's mother put it, her pregnant daughter was no more than "a throwback from some Irish slut" on her father's side. In retrospect, Eleanor knows she "wasn't a slut," but at the time she was completely overwhelmed. "Suddenly, I became so unlovable, so wrong. The father of my baby wanted nothing to do with me. His parents hired an attorney to get rid of their own grandchild . . . and my own parents backed them up."[9]

When daughters became objects of their own parents' terror in the era of "family togetherness," they felt absolutely resourceless. Mothers and fathers worked quickly to erase these girls as social actors; what the daughters wanted for themselves was completely irrelevant. Ellen Simmons was determined to find a way to keep her baby, despite the fact that her parents pressed her hard to agree to adoption. She remembers that "when the time for my delivery drew near, my father informed me that if I did not agree to sign the papers, he would have the doctor sterilize me when he delivered the baby."[10]

Eleanor Whitmore describes how she began to fight to keep her baby immediately after telling her parents about the pregnancy, but they wouldn't hear of it. "Unfortunately," she observed, "I had no alternate plan to back up my beliefs, no money, nobody cared about me to help."

Many other adults in the community joined parents in the project of shaming and effacing these young women. When Eleanor's mother asked the family doctor if he would see Eleanor for prenatal care, he "said no; he did not want an unwed pregnant girl in his office." The doctor who *would* see Eleanor at the time was a psychiatrist who diagnosed her as schizophrenic, gave her pills for her disease, and wanted to administer shock therapy. Eleanor remembers, "He had a loud window fan that drowned out my voice when I spoke to him. He said my brother was a zombie . . . and that things like that run in families, so I'd be lucky to be rid of my baby. He hated when I cried and begged for my baby. He ordered me to talk about something else."[11]

Cindy Bhimani, who got pregnant as a high school student in 1970, reports that she "wasn't allowed to attend public school and wasn't told why."[12] Janice Fruland was twenty-three and an elementary school teacher, "alone in a new city" in 1966. "The principal was kind," she recalls, "but said, 'Go get your purse, this is your last day—you can get your personal belongings when school is out.' "[13]

The sexual partners of these young women recognized the total vulnerability of girls tossed out of the family circle, and not infrequently used that vulnerability to escape their own responsibility for sexual adventure, for the pregnancy, and for parenthood. Barbara Anderson-Keri explained one trick that boys in her community used. "If a certain male wanted to get out of being named the true father, he would get about five buddies to SWEAR they had sex with the girl . . . Branded promiscuous, the female had little recourse against the fellow, and she already experienced shame galore for birthing a child out of marriage—that behavior alone made her a pariah, even if she were raped."[14]

To many of the daughters, the most horrible aspect of the ordeal was the way mothers and fathers and everyone else denied that the girls were, themselves, mothers. Nine years after her 1968 unwed pregnancy, Mary Anne Cohen described how she was treated, "as a collection of statistics and sociological clichés, not a unique human being with dignity, with valid feelings and needs." She went on, "Because I was not a Mrs. somebody . . . I was seen, not as a mother, but as the producer of a valuable product, a white, healthy infant of college-educated parents . . . I was the means to an end." When Mary Anne insisted on seeing her baby in the hospital, "one doctor threatened to have me transferred [from the psychiatric ward where hospital personnel had placed her] to the state mental hospital if I made any trouble."[15]

Kathleen Leahy Koch, who was date-raped in 1969 ("It was years before I had a name to articulate what had happened to me"), will never forget that she was treated not like a mother-to-be but like a criminal. "I was just someone who had to have a baby for some worthy family," she wrote. "I was completely dehumanized."[16]

Most often in the United States, relinquishment is presented as the act of biological mothers who have altruistic reasons for making the choice to give up their babies (they know they are too young or too poor or too alone, for example, to be good mothers of their precious babies), or of bad women who have heartless, selfish reasons (they don't want to be tied down or they don't/can't feel any love for the infant). It has been very rare in this country to think about relinquishment as a coerced act, forced on a mother who wanted to keep her child. Many of the pregnant girls and young women in the postwar decades in fact responded deeply and positively to the idea of being a mother. These girls were horrified when adults in charge of their fate denied them that status.

Karen Kottmeier uses strong language to describe the "terrorism" she experienced in 1967 and 1968 when she was pregnant and unmarried. "The grief was so intense that I remember thinking that I would die. In a way, I did die. I was told I was not a mother when I was pregnant, but that I was . . . a vehicle so that a deserving [infertile] couple . . . could have a baby."[17]

Given the latitude and the relative power that many young women today have to make sexual and reproductive decisions for themselves, it can be hard to imagine how completely young women in the past were under the power of parents and other adult authorities. Feminist journalist Jane O'Reilly, herself a birthmother in the late 1950s, has described the problem of imagining this past: "In 1958, an out-of-wedlock pregnancy was literally disgraceful. It was also almost the only imaginable disgrace (so limited was the range of good or bad behavior for a middle class girl). Ironically, my generation's revolution was so successful in expanding these limits that now my [relinquished and found] child cannot begin to understand what it was like."[18]

For the women whose motherhood was denied, the anguish is unforgettable. The language these women use to express their anguish is powerful. In many cases it seems to suggest that what surrenderers suffered was a near-fatal blow—a blow that struck at their *biologically grounded right* to be mothers of the children they bore and were forced to "give away." Today many people are uncomfortable with or simply reject the idea that motherhood is essentially a biological phenomenon or status. Yet the stories here press us to consider the implications of this: women who become mothers in other-than-biological ways very often do so by depending on *other mothers* to provide them with children. As I discussed in Chapter 1, "other mothers" are often women whose desperate circumstances degrade the meaning of biological motherhood. We have seen that economic and cultural degradation can cancel a woman's ability to assert the biological claim to motherhood. This feature of adoption is typically overlooked. The language and the experiences of unwed mothers in the postwar decades, especially the ones who became politically active in the 1970s, draw attention to these matters. These women tell stories that force us to gauge the relevance of biology when biology is denied.

Thirty-six years after having experienced the anguish of surrender, Sue Tavela writes, "I never even read the relinquishment form. I was too crushed and just signed it . . . I was already a zombie just going through the motions of being alive . . . I felt dead inside."[19] Pollie Robinson, who had considered killing herself while a teenage "slave" at a Florence Crittenden Home for unwed mothers, referred to herself as a "zombie puppet" during and after the relinquishment.[20] Kay Ball, raped and pregnant in 1971, did attempt suicide. As she put it, "I was so ashamed and beaten down emotionally and mentally that I just wanted to end it all."[21]

All of these young women felt strangled by a rope pulled from both ends. Pulling from one end, as "Julie" explained, were the adult authorities who demanded docility. At the maternity home, "Everyone was 'giving up' her baby. 'If you love your baby, you will give him up.' None of the fifty girls at that St. Agnes rebelled. We all felt powerless. We were so obedient."[22] The other end of the rope was yanked by "the guilt [these girls] felt for not fighting harder to keep their children,"[23]—or for not being able to figure out a way to manage alone in a hostile environment.

Some unwed mothers in these decades did recognize, through the fog of despair and helplessness, that when adults denied them motherhood and their babies, it was about power. Carole Anderson, today a prominent lawyer in Iowa, remembers, "I knew before I surrendered that I had that legal right [to be my son's mother], and I also knew that it did not matter what my legal rights supposedly were because I had no practical power to enforce them. I tried to explain my rights to the social agency and my parents, but I was roundly informed that I had no moral right and reminded that I had no economic means to support myself with my child."[24]

Carole Anderson was one of many who attempted to "explain" and to resist the fate that others mapped out for her. Scores of women present the process of relinquishment as a desperate, cliff-hanging narrative. Another woman described how she resisted with such force that hospital personnel tranquilized her. Then, she wrote, "The nurse literally picked up my hand and signed my name."[25] Barbara Anderson-Keri fought like hell to keep her baby. She did everything she could think of to find a job, to raise money during the thirty days that her baby was in foster case, before he was formally adopted. But she couldn't pull it off. "I lost the battle," she wrote. "The agency, society, those with money had won. But I tried."[26]

Eleanor Whitmore believed then and now that if she'd fought any harder to keep her baby, she "could have ended up incarcerated," and Leslie Noxon reveals how hard she fought when she remembers that "the baby was literally torn from me."[27] Alison Ward, eighteen in 1968, did struggle, all the while feeling "like someone in a cattle shute with no way out."[28] "Gwen" described how she felt after signing the relinquishment papers: "They had won. I really surrendered in every sense of the word. I ceased to struggle. I almost ceased to exist."[29]

Still, many of these women castigate themselves harshly for not resisting with even more force than they did. I've heard dozens of women begin sentences, "If only I'd . . ." Even many who are completely aware that they were caught by a broad and powerful cultural consensus persist in taking personal blame for not fighting harder to be the mothers of their children. "Linda," who had her baby in 1965, reflected twelve years later that the counseling she received was "forced" on her. She wrote, "I hated it. I wish I had told them to go to hell."

Many of these women feel particularly embittered because they were denied information about resources that could have saved them and their motherhood, or allowed them to make their own decisions about being mothers. As Gail Hanssen put it, "Imagine the frustration when you realize the alternatives and resources which were available but hidden from you."[30] Carole Anderson writes of her ignorance about welfare: "I knew there was something for poor people, but never having classified myself as a poor person, it never occurred to me that whatever it was, it would be available to me. When I [worked at the Illinois Department of Public Aid, and I] figured out eligibility requirements as a worker, I'm going, oh my god, this was available to me. Nobody told me about it. This was a source of real anger."[31] Ironically, it was *ignorance* about welfare benefits that rendered a number of these women powerless, defenseless, and dependent in the 1960s.

Abortion was out of the question for many of these girls, as well, even though certainly hundreds of thousands of girls and women were finding ways to terminate their pregnancies each year before national legalization in 1973.[32] According to the Centers for Disease Control, in 1971 480,259 legal abortions were performed in twenty-four states and the District of Columbia. New Jersey, one of the other twenty-six states, reported no legal abortions that year, but did report that 21,207 residents of that state got abortions elsewhere.[33] Many of the unwed mothers who speak in these pages, and many who formed CUB in 1976, were Catholics and did not consider abortion, legal or criminal, an option. Others came from families that forbade their daughters to break the law. Many of these girls wanted the babies they carried, and others simply knew nothing about abortion at all.

Many transformed their violent resistance at the moment of surrender into a secret resistance that, at the time, they shared with no one, but that they hoped would sustain them. In 1970, Becky, for example, "lost the battle" that had pitted her parents, the birthfather, and his parents against her desire to keep her child. "From the moment I signed the papers," she writes, "it was etched in my heart that I would always be the mother of my daughter and would search for her."[34] Pollie Robinson resisted her effacement in 1963 by secretly exercising a parent's first prerogative: she named her daughter "Jacqueline Hope, after Jacqueline Kennedy because of her courage and Hope, in hopes that I'd see her again."[35] Randa Phillips reports doing what most of these women could only dream of: "I read the adoption social worker's records [of her child's placement] upside down when I was meeting with her for 'counseling' aka brainwashing."[36]

Many girls who resisted overtly, many who were outwardly obedient, and many who resisted secretly were enraged by the way that social workers and others cravenly and unselfconsciously assessed their babies as valuable commodities. Lee Campbell, the first president of CUB, was aghast when she got hold of a Florence Crittenden interoffice communication about her case that referred to her resistance to giving up her baby and expressed relief that she had finally signed. The memo went on,

"The baby is lovely and should be excellent material for adoption."[37] Another woman described what she thought when a worker from the adoption agency came to the maternity home "to look over the product, the fresh inventory." This mother sized up the worker as on a mission "to make sure [the baby] wasn't Afro-American."[38] "Angie" believed then and still thirty years later that to the adults in the adoption arena, "I was the naive whore that was providing them with that precious commodity, my beautiful son."[39]

Barbara Anderson-Keri describes how she was fired from her job in Boston in 1959 when the management found out she was pregnant. But then they offered Barbara a deal—if she would sell the baby for a few thousand dollars. Barbara refused, but she writes that until the day she left the firm, "I got numerous calls at the pay phone from Scarsdale and other rich enclaves. As an unwed pregnant female, especially since I'd attended college and could be considered reasonably intelligent, I was fair game for everyone wanting babies . . . My kid was 'up for grabs' by the various vultures. I got offered thousands to sell him on the Black Market . . . But no one would help me in any way to raise him! What a crock."[40]

Almost as enraging as the commodification of their babies, according to many unwed mothers, was the social workers' standard line, calculated to soothe troubled, relinquishing mothers: "The girls forget they even had babies."[41] One woman described this prediction as more than wrong; it was "maddening," and she coupled it with the thoughtless advice she received from "everyone" in those days: "Oh, just go on with your life. You can have other children."[42]

Far from "forgetting," almost all of the unwed mothers whose voices are offered there felt that coerced surrenders filled their lives with "sorrow and anguish." As "Kathy," now living alone in Utah, put it, "The whole experience of relinquishing my son has been emotionally and psychologically debilitating. Relinquishment [twenty years ago] broke my spirit, murdered my soul, and disabled me. It made me dysfunctional."[43] "Elizabeth," who became an unwed mother in 1963, had been a "star pupil in a rural New England village high school, an honor student at college, and a graduate student in biology at an Ivy League institution." In the years after she lost her baby to adoption, she was "swamped by depression and suicidal thoughts."[44] A woman whose child was taken thirty years ago reports that because of the loss, "My whole ability to love or trust people, to have people get close to me, has been forever affected." She adds, "No one told me about the lifelong trauma I would have from this."[45]

Eleanor Whitmore, like many of the other women, describes how the experience of having her first-born child removed from her arms forever deeply affected her ability to relax into straightforward maternity with her subsequent children: "Something like a normal visit to a pediatrician was difficult for me because I knew the power people like that had if they chose to use it . . . I am a kind, decent, moral, hard-working woman, yet I was always thinking up escape plans in my head in case the day came when the authorities decided to take my children."[46]

The ways that these women describe the long-term impact of surrender can be read as uniformly melodramatic, solipsistic, Oprahatic. Some readers might imagine they detect a "party line." But the more than one hundred women who've supplied these descriptions come from California, South Carolina, Maine, New Mexico, and many places in between. Few of them know each other. They are in their late thirties, their early sixties, and most ages in between. Many are CUB members, but a number are unaffiliated, and individuals from both groups describe similar, traumatic surrender experiences and eerily similar and devastating long-term consequences. Carole Whitehead, who now lives on Long Island, thirty-five years after surrendering her baby observes, "Once you have had your self-esteem destroyed as many of us have had by surrendering our babies, it is an everyday struggle to feel that you are okay as a person or as a woman."[47]

Lynn Kopatich captures the long-term impact of her loss in particularly affecting language: "I left my heart and soul, as well as my baby, in that drab little institution. I left my youth, my innocence . . . my trust, my laughter, and my love . . . Pieces of that girl who entered the Home in August, 1962 are still missing today . . . I have not been and never will be whole again."[48] "Angie's" loss captures the literal—and metaphorical—experience that many of the women identify with very deeply: "I was a singing teacher, but I lost my voice after the relinquishment. Losing my voice was the result of almost dying of a broken heart."[49]

Most of these former unwed mothers sank very low before they began to craft egress. One woman saw no opportunities for sixteen years, but then she heard about CUB. The letter she wrote to the fledgling organization reads in part, "I would love to know that my child is alive and in a good home. I suffered a nervous breakdown after my baby was born. At the time the question of adoption came up, I had no money, no husband, no home of my own. My life has been a gradual deterioration of a smart, intelligent, fun-loving, happy girl into a nervous, depressed, sad woman. Please help me find my child."[50]

In general, these women say that moving toward mental health and personal strength involved the combination of two factors: coming to believe they had the right to search for their lost children and finding Concerned United Birthparents.

GATHERING STRENGTH

In the middle 1970s, some former unwed mothers—most of whom were by that time married and the mothers of children they were able to keep—began to reconstruct themselves. As Pat Taylor, who lived in a Connecticut "bedroom community" at the time, put it, "I started to re-create myself, molecule by molecule. I didn't have much to work with. I had to figure EVERYTHING out, in every arena."[51] A number of these women, like Pat, had separated or gotten divorced in the mid to late 1970s and recognized then and in retrospect that the strength they needed to manage their households and families as a lone adult helped them rebuild personal strength.

Pat Taylor describes how when she divorced, her "whole life shattered—the life that I had built on the ashes of that disaster [the relinquishment]—the life that was supposed to rescue me from my tragedy." Soon after her life "shattered," Pat, who was in graduate school at the time, realized that "the mother who was told she would not be able to complete her education [as a pregnant teenager, then mother in the 1960s] with one child, was now pursuing an advanced degree . . . [and] an internship, and she was raising four children alone." This recognition led to Pat's "summer of autonomy" in 1979, when she located a private detective in New York who specialized in searches—and she found CUB.[52]

At about the same time, in a suburb of San Francisco, Carol Schaefer also separated from the husband who had rescued her from the disaster of surrender. "Finally," she writes about this period, "I had to deal with re-pair people, insurance companies, the world, without a phantom male presence to keep them all at bay. I had to become strong enough to deal with problems entirely on my own." At this point, Carol unearthed a newspaper clipping she'd hidden among her things years before, a small story about an organization of adoptees who were searching for their birthparents. With her new strength, Carol felt she could make contact with others in the adoption arena.[53]

Gail Hanssen, in a Boston suburb in the late 1970s, was one of a few birthmothers at this time who began to gather strength with the help of a counselor, in her case, a pastor. This man suggested that Gail might consider that she could stop apologizing for her sexual transgression, her pregnancy, especially the loss of her child. She might learn to burn the debt note, he said, because she'd paid her debt. In 1978, Gail described how she interpreted the pastor's lesson in her own way. "I realized that I had been apologizing for a decision which, in all truth, I had been forced into . . . Since that time, I have found the strength to speak out and the courage to right the wrongs I felt had been done."[54]

Another woman in the Boston area reflected on the time when for-mer unwed mothers began to analyze what had happened to them in po-litical terms, and to find each other. Janice Chalifaux said, "You know, by that time, we grew up. A lot of us got education and power. None of us are dummies. We weren't at the time we lost our children either. But we were made to feel as if we were."[55]

It is true: many of these women did grow up in the 1970s, and what a time for them to have done it. Before considering the broader context that supported efforts of former unwed mothers to organize in strength at that time, I will look at the impact of one group, ALMA, the Adoptees' Liberty Movement Association, founded in 1971 by Florence Fisher, au-thor of the hugely influential book, *The Search for Anna Fisher*.

In many ways, the idea of adoptees searching for their biological roots and claiming rights to information about themselves was, itself, shaped by liberation movements emerging in the 1960s. In the 1970s, through ALMA and other organizations, adoptees claimed the right to own the truth about their origins. Among the pioneers of "identity politics," adoptees fused liberation, the search for selfhood, and special group iden-tity to define and assert a political cause.

Betty Jean Lifton, an adoptee and another extremely influential writer and figure in the adoptee identity arena, described how adoptees were isolated and neutralized before the liberating upheaval took hold. "Until recently in this country—until the ferment of the 1960s spawned the various liberation movements—the Adoptee was in the closet. If he was adopted, he didn't tell others. If she wanted to know about her past, she didn't ask questions. If they felt rootless and alienated, they endured it . . . They were the silent majority."[56]

Another adoptee, Susan Darke, who is also a birthmother, explained why she and others felt they could "come out of the closet" in 1970 and demand answers about their origins. "After all," she said, "with the sexual revolution and ordinary talk about birth control, abortion, adoptees felt they could speak out. With abortion rights and the women's movement backing us up, we could ask questions."[57]

Thousands of adoptees did begin to speak out in this period. And they spoke as rebelliously as other civil rights claimants, drawing on broad, liberatory concerns to justify their cause. They explicitly tied their cause—their right to search for their biological parents—to the civil rights movement. By the mid-1970s, "adoptee liberation" was referred to as a *civil right*[58] and was identified in the *New York Times* as "another in the series of liberation efforts that started with the black struggle in the South."[59] One adoptee spoke for a growing cohort when he crafted an explicit analogy between adoption and slavery: "As an adoptee, I am expected to respect a contract made over my body when I was too young to give my consent. Am I to respect this contract while my past is buried? So long as this inhuman practice continues, adoption can only be regarded as slavery. We damn sure have been bought and sold on the open market."

Another adoptee in this era expressed himself, and the feelings of many others, in the prevailing terms of anti-authoritarian youth culture, while claiming adultlike self-ownership. He wrote: "In a way, I am very angry toward the law. The law still refers to me as a child when they refer to 'in the best interests of the child.' I resent that because in my opinion, I am twenty-one years old and I feel I am quite old enough, mature and responsible enough to be making my own decisions. I don't feel as if any decision concerning my adult life should be left up to a judge or to anyone else." This writer added, drawing on a vibrant charge of that period, that being adopted prevented him from knowing "the name I was born with" and who his biological parents were; it "made me feel like a second-class citizen."[60]

When Florence Fisher politicized the experience of the "identity crisis" and the project of looking "for answers" about herself—she called herself "a militant" in 1973—her claims and her legislative and public relations programs resonated with so many adoptees because of how her activism fit the political temper of the times.[61] But they also resonated because, in the new era of working mothers, the subject of mother-child separations was of great interest to many child development investigators. Adoptees had access to a postwar psychological literature in the 1970s to justify their claims for information and reconnection. In addition to Freud, other psychiatrists and psychologists such as D. W. Winnicott, René Spitz, Melanie Klein, Anna Freud, and John Bowlby had argued strenuously that "separation" was dangerous.[62] When these experts cited the dangers—Spitz had referred to the "human wrecks" that resulted from "the absence of . . . emotional interchange with the mother"[63] —they were not usually describing the separation of adoption. Many used examples of wartime mother-child separations to study the subject. Nevertheless, these experts were cited in support of adoptees', and later birthmothers', claims.

At the same time, the subject of adoptees searching for their origins was picked up by the mass media. Mainstream newspapers and magazines started publishing articles that focused on such questions as whether unwed mothers should place their children for adoption or not, whether adoption records should remain sealed or be opened, whether an adoptee had the right to search, and whether searching was a sign of mental health or maladjustment.[64] Academic psychologists conducted and published studies focusing on these questions, as well, and their results were widely cited in the media. A typical article, published in 1974, announced, "Now there's new evidence to show that it may actually be good for adoptees to know who their parents are." A social scientist quoted in the piece pointed out how times had changed: "We always used to say, if it's a good adoption, your child won't want to seek his birthparents . . . But we've found it's a natural genealogical curiosity."[65] Children's books, too, began to suggest at this time that "searching" was a natural and socially acceptable thing for adoptees to want to do and that even a young adoptee might want to find out about her origins.[66]

Searching for one's origins meshed well with the emergent fascination with "self"—and even with sharing one's search for self with the public. *Psychology Today* published an essay in 1975 called "I Take After Somebody; I Have Real Relatives; I Possess a Real Name," in which the author, an academic sociologist and an adoptee, chronicled her own search. The author explained that she began searching in 1973 after having decided that her urge to locate her biological mother was "natural," not the result of "morbid curiosity."[67] Other mainstream media followed suit, quoting adoptees' heart-wrenching expressions of their need to find themselves by finding their lost parents.[68]

The sensationalized story of "Baby Lenore" in 1970–71 reflected both the new uncertainty about adoption as a completely efficient solution to unwed pregnancy, and the emergence of the possibility that ordinary Americans might be able to accept the rights of unmarried women to be mothers even without husbands. In this case, Olga Scarpetta, a thirty-one-year-old unmarried Colombian woman with a master's degree in psychology, had come to New York to have her child and to put the baby up for adoption. Four days after the child was born on May 10, 1970, she was placed with a New York adoption agency. On June 18, the agency found a "suitable couple," the DeMartinos of Brooklyn. Five days later, Olga Scarpetta changed her mind and decided to keep her baby. Despite the fact that Scarpetta had acted to reclaim her mother's rights within the allowable period—six months—both the adoption agency and the DeMartinos opposed her claim. The case dragged on in the courts of several states for months and received "worldwide attention."[69] The public discussion it stimulated provided a high-profile forum for both advocates for and opponents of adoption. The DeMartinos' lawyer argued in press conferences that the case revealed the "second-class citizen rights" of adoptive parents.[70] Sixty "Brooklyn housewives" circulated petitions on the DeMartinos' behalf ("No family should be torn apart").[71] And those interested in holding the line on illegitimacy and unwed mothers built their soapboxes from planks of the DeMartino case. As one letter writer to the *New York Times* put it, "Mothers who surrender their children for adoption are to be congratulated for using their better judgment in placing the welfare of the child before their own selfish ego."[72]

Florence Fisher spoke for many adoptees poised to come out of the closet in the early 1970s (and for birthmothers still deeply closeted but watching the proceedings closely) when she described her obsession with this case: "So profoundly was I affected by the Baby Lenore case that . . . I bought every newspaper on the stands and listened to all the news broadcasts . . . The case haunted me." When the New York State Senate passed a bill (with forty-four out of fifty-one senators voting in favor) providing that thirty days, instead of six months, after surrender the adoptive parents would be presumed the more fit parents, Fisher went to Albany to lobby against the bill. She also placed ads in several New York newspapers, appealing to other adoptees to join her. The response was overwhelming: "I was soon inundated by mail from all parts of the country . . . literally thousands of letters [supporting Scarpetta's rights and Baby Lenore's needs to be with her biological mother] poured in." This case brought adoptees out of the closet in flocks and increased public interest in adoptees' identity claims. Ultimately, a New York court ordered the DeMartinos to surrender Lenore to Olga Scarpetta. The couple fled to Florida with the baby, and in June 1971 a court in that state awarded Lenore to the adopting couple. During the case, Florence Fisher received invitations to appear on TV and radio panels and to give talks before conferences of social workers, departments of public welfare, and religious organizations providing children's and family services. Newspaper reporters sought her out for interviews.[73] Soon after, she founded the Adoptees' Liberty Movement Association.

ALMA had a constituency eagerly waiting for it, indeed. The organization grew quickly in the early 1970s. Before it reached its first decade of life, it had chartered fifty chapters nationwide and drawn in 50,000 dues-paying members. By 1982, it maintained a national registry of 340,000 searching adults.[74] Organizations with allied missions, such as Truth Seekers, an Illinois group founded in 1973, were cropping up around the country. ALMA's mission—to justify and facilitate adoptees' searches and to pursue judicial and legislative remedies for adoptees, such as unsealing adoption records—appears to have matched the interests of a great many adoptees in the mid-to-late seventies. When the Children's Home Society in Los Angeles conducted a survey, 86.4 percent of the 1,891 respondents reported that they would feel "other-than-negative" if their birthparent sought a reunion.[75]

ALMA's mission also matched the interests of the white women who had surrendered their babies. In fact, ALMA's mission, together with the high-profile public statements it occasioned, catalyzed them. Susan Darke, one of the founding members of CUB, remembers how she (and others) felt in the early 1970s, when she began to hear adoptees talk about their need and their right to search for their mothers. "As adoptees started to talk," she recalled, "we thought, oh my goodness, my child may need me . . . my child may have questions. We could be silent as long as we didn't realize that our children may need us. Once adoptees started to speak out . . . birthmothers spoke out, too." Susan added, with fervor: "You can hold a woman down pretty easily, but once you think your child is in trouble, at risk, needs you—THAT'S what made us rise up."[76]

Lee Campbell, like many in her cohort, encountered ALMA through a newspaper article soon after the organization was formed. Reading the clipping from the *Boston Globe* convinced Lee that she had to—and could—"do something." First she phoned the ALMA office in New York, asking for information about the organization. Then she spent days trying "to squirrel the courage to go to the Brewster's Ladies' Library" to find a copy of Florence Fisher's book, *The Search for Anna Fisher*. Lee described what happened as she gathered information from ALMA, read Fisher's book, and saw additional articles about adoptees, searches, and reunions: "[M]y secret life grew."

By early 1975, Lee was attending ALMA meetings and accepting adoptees there as her guides and gurus. After a few meetings, Lee began writing "outreach notes" to the "Confidential Chat" section of the *Globe* in an effort to make contact with other women who, as unmarried mothers, had lost their babies to adoption. She signed her letters "Biological Mom."[77] Lee Campbell was on her way out of the closet; she was asking shamed women to come out from under their shame and write about the violation they'd suffered. She was becoming an activist.

Sandy Musser was being transformed by adoptee rights meetings at about the same time. She has described her response in terms that make it clear these events functioned as "consciousness-raising" groups, alternate "women's groups" for a population that included many who had probably not heard of the Redstockings or the Chicago Women's Liberation Union, who were probably not reading Shulamith Firestone or Kate

Millett in the mid-1970s—and yet were desperate for liberation and ready to grab it. Sandy described the first meeting she went to this way:

> As they went around the room introducing themselves, one woman said, "My name is Barbara and I am a birthmother." A BIRTHMOTHER! Another birthmother like me! She also wanted to know her daughter. How fantastic! . . . Why hadn't I realized that there must be thousands of others like myself feeling this pain of separation from flesh and blood? Why did I think I was so unique? Possibly because I was never able to share this dark secret . . . before . . . fear of condemnation . . . fear of rejection . . . Total freedom was becoming mine.[78]

FREEDOM CONTEXT

Neither Lee Campbell nor Sandy Musser had been activists before they found the adoptees' movement and became founders of the birthmothers' movement. But many other women who joined CUB as soon as they heard about its existence, sometime between 1976 and the early 1980s, *had* been activists, had spent years following the surrender involved in social justice work of various kinds. Most of these women kept the story of their lost babies secret during these years. Most did not yet overtly associate what had happened to them as unmarried pregnant girls with social justice issues and the claims of other oppressed and exploited groups. But their involvement in "causes" was transformative.

Janet Fenton, a longtime president of CUB, looks back on her pre-CUB, post-relinquishment life this way:

> I have to say the really important thing for me was getting involved in organized labor. I didn't stay in school, didn't get a degree, but you didn't need it to be a leader in those areas. Working in organized labor fed my self-esteem, which really needed feeding [after giving up my baby]. It was a good time to be involved, women on negotiating teams, in bargaining units. And no matter which corner you went around, there was a new group, new battles. Causes. The Great Society—getting those programs going

in Des Moines. I started out with the Communication Workers. I worked the night shift and found out that if you were a steward, you could get time off from that supervisor! I was on the City Central Body before I was old enough to buy a drink![79]

Carole Anderson worked in the 1970s with a group of "strong-minded women" in a welfare office. These women, she says, cared about the same things she did: "children's issues, policy issues . . . we were looking at how women who had no power ended up on public aid." Carole described her approach to the bureaucracy:

> Here are the rules. So, how can we accomplish our goals within the rules, even though they aren't part of the rules? We did things like put together our own referral systems since the department had no plans for referring clients for other services. We stopped going on visits as if we were police inspectors. Instead, we used the visits to let people know where and how they could get services. There was lots of feminism in our group of six. Among us, one is now a university professor, one started her own business, I'm a lawyer. When I look back at this group of women, god, it was a talented bunch.[80]

Barbara Anderson-Keri "wandered on the periphery of emerging radical groups in Ann Arbor in the late 1950s," but learned lessons about "the dangers of isolation for those fighting a battle," from following the civil rights movement in the newspapers and working as a teacher amid racism in the Detroit public school system.[81] Eleanor Whitmore describes herself as having been "a sixties kid" before and after she surrendered, "supporting the civil rights movement, the anti-war movement, youth culture and the counterculture" while at college in the mid-1960s. When she was forced to give up her baby, she writes, "I knew beyond a doubt that they [the adoption authorities] were the ones out of step, not me."[82]

Like many of these " '60s girls" who got caught and punished, Leslie Noxon's pre-CUB activist sensibility took form before second wave feminism was a widespread, vibrant force on campuses. Leslie writes, "I rebelled against everything . . . the Church, the Republicans, the White

House, and the horrible Pentagon, the war in Viet Nam, the poverty in the Third World countries whose evil regimes were supported by U.S. tax dollars. I became an environmental rebel, asking startled women in the grocery store to boycott Dow. I was there at marches on the Pentagon and the U.N. building and fell in love with a Freedom Rider." Ruefully, she adds in retrospect, "My new hero was still male."[83]

Judy Darst spent several years after her 1966 surrender "trying to deaden the pain with drugs." By the time she found a "new outlet for [her] rage"—political activism—feminist analysis was available, and Judy used it. She describes her commitments at the time as "the anti-war movement, the civil rights movement, and the women's movement, all of which helped me develop my own set of values. I wanted to create a world that didn't insist on separating babies from their unwed mothers. I finally had new words—sexism, discrimination—to explain the terrible injustice that had been done to thousands of birthmothers during the 1940s, 1950s, and 1960s . . . I wanted to be a revolutionary and smash it all to hell." Today, Judy writes that her fervor and idealism were "in part an antidote" to the "overwhelming pain" she experienced after being pressed so hard to give up her child. Judy also writes that even then, seven or eight years before the founding of CUB, she "knew it was only a matter of time before birthmothers organized. After all, everyone else was demanding their rights, why not us? We certainly had every right to."[84]

Mary Redenius married in 1962 and immediately began having children she could keep. Today she is very certain that the trauma of relinquishment made her into a feminist-activist. For Mary, pre-CUB "causes" involved pushing Washington, D.C., area obstetricians and pediatricians to listen to mothers and learn from them. She describes her "revolutionary" role in pressing hospitals to adopt "rooming-in" policies and policies that permitted unmedicated labor and husbands in the delivery room. Rooming-in was so important to Mary because, as she puts it, after what she had gone through losing her first baby to adoption, "I just couldn't tolerate a moment of separation from this [subsequent] baby." Mary describes her work in this arena and with La Leche League as imbued with the conviction that she and other mothers "could be women in the world without having to measure their worth by the patriarchal standards." More particularly, Mary describes the consequences of her feminist activism in the 1970s: "We took the power away from our obstetricians and pediatricians, almost 100 percent of whom were men—and sometimes they respected us a lot and if they didn't—snap!—we just found another doctor who did."[85]

A number of birthmothers cite Ms. magazine as crucially responsible for their feminist education in the mid-1970s, after their surrenders and before they found the "special sisterhood" of CUB. Pat Taylor was embarrassed to admit in the late 1990s that back in the mid-1970s, her only window out of the "patriarchal world" she inhabited after relinquishing her child was Ms., "a pretty wonderful connection."[86] Peggy Matthews-Nilsen identified Ms. as the vehicle for convincing her "that the patriarchal system had been wrong about the simplicity of adoption and the rightness of separating me from my son." Yet Matthews-Nilsen and others report that they had to make these connections for themselves because Ms. was strangely unresponsive to the special vulnerability of birthmothers. "I remember," she writes, "an increasing awareness that my experience as a birthmother had been oppressive and coercive . . . but this was the only area of my life that didn't seem to be reflected in Ms. magazine or in other feminist writings."[87]

Leslie Noxon was one birthmother who, despite her political activism, describes herself as having "been asleep for years" after the surrender of her baby. But the feminist movement, in the form of a 1973 consciousness-raising group, she says, woke her up. "It was my friend, Joanie," she writes, "who first noticed that the driving issues for nearly each of the twenty women [in our group] were either abortions or loss of babies given up for adoption. That is when I began to fully feel my feminist persona rise up and when I first recognized the awful control of my sexuality by men around me."[88]

Janet Fenton sums up the impact of these years of social activism for birthmothers (and, of course, for many others) when she describes what this work did for her just before she found CUB: "I had a need to find a place where I could change things. It didn't start out having anything to do with being a birthparent, or with those issues, but it really helped me develop—the feminist movement and these other activist movements helped me develop as a person and eventually move toward CUB."[89]

Many of the women who got involved with Concerned United Birthparents after 1976 had not been activists before. As Carole Anderson put it, "Many birthmothers were so traumatized by what had happened that they simply had not had the nerve or inclination to be participants in community life."[90] Merrill Clarke Hunn confirms Anderson's observation. After her own 1963 surrender, she writes, "I didn't respond to the movements in the 1960s and 70s. I was too busy keeping my head down. Hell, I wasn't feeling *anything* . . . how could I possibly have been passionate enough to put myself out in the world in a way which would draw attention! . . . It was all I could do to function and stay afloat."[91] Ann Hege Hughes agrees and stresses how important it was for her to maintain her *invisibility* in those dramatically activist years. "I guess you could say I had a feminist soul but that the spunk to get out there and BE a feminist had been beaten out of me by my unwed pregnancy. After that shaming trauma, I would go out of my way to appear conventional, no matter how repulsive that was to me personally (and it was)."

One woman despaired at the time that birthmothers would ever become activists, much less speak out in their own behalf; they were so busy, as Merrill Clarke Hunn put it, keeping their heads down. This woman sent an unsigned letter to Betty Jean Lifton about her plight and apologized for being so "mysterious" about personal details. She explained her fear of discovery by referring to how much former unwed mothers still had to lose if their identity became known in the mid-1970s, even years after relinquishment. And, she added hopelessly in the era of liberation, "There can be no 'natural-mothers-who-gave-their-babies-up-for-adoption' liberation groups." This woman was obviously fully aware of the political context in which she was living, but defined her kind as outside of, too shamed for, the liberationist project.[92]

THE SPECTER OF THE SINGLE MOTHER —AND "CHOICE"

In fact, not surprisingly, the pre-CUB activists and nonactivists alike were sharply aware of the liberationist political context. Most of them were also acutely sensitive to the fact that aspects of their own recent experiences had become archaic very quickly. Carole Anderson says of that time, "We all watched a lot of situations where it didn't happen to other people, and that wasn't long after our surrenders. If I'd just been born five years later . . ."[93] Bonnie Bis, a former president of CUB, reflects on the incredible status change that many teenage daughters underwent between the late 1950s and 1970. "In the earlier period you didn't tell your father, 'no.' Children simply didn't do that. You might argue a little with them, that's all. Personally, I couldn't imagine standing up to my parents on anything. In 1970, you ran away."[94]

By the early 1970s, daughters in many states did not have to run away to trump parents' authority when certain sexual matters were the issue. Delores Teller could not, as a teenager with disapproving parents, get birth control materials in 1968, even though she reports badly wanting to control her fertility. But by 1972, nineteen states allowed girls younger than eighteen to consent to their own contraceptive care. Thirty-nine states accorded this right to girls eighteen, and over, even if they weren't legally emancipated. And abortion was legalized nationally, of course, in 1973.[95]

In a closely related and equally rapid shift, Americans changed their minds about premarital sex. A 1969 Gallup poll found that 68 percent of Americans believed unmarried sex was wrong. But four years later, another Gallup poll found that only 48 percent took this view. In this second poll, 43 percent of the respondents believed that neither for the male nor the female was premarital sex "wrong."[96]

Growing public tolerance of premarital sex and public enthusiasm for the so-called sexual revolution in the 1970s had a big impact on the lives of many birthmothers, especially because these developments contributed to their ability to "come out of the closet." Susan Darke notes that just a few years earlier,

> We birthmothers weren't supposed to tell potential husbands [about our unwed pregnancies and relinquishments] . . . We even faked virginity, for God's sake. But then the sexual revolution comes along, and right away men didn't expect to marry virgins anymore. So you could tell your husband. And if you could tell him, you could tell the world, practically! You weren't going into marriage as a little virgin. Now husbands knew there had been a relationship, a baby: sex. That's what it came down to. Suddenly women had the freedom to say this, at home, with their husbands . . . anywhere.[97]

Pat Taylor says that in the early 1970s, "the feminist movement was happening, but not in Brookfield, Connecticut," where she lived. She believed her upper-middle-class women friends there "would have died rather than go to a feminist meeting." But then in the late 1970s, Pat acknowledged to herself that "the emperor had no clothes," and divorced her husband. She was the first, but soon she wasn't alone: the divorces "proceeded like dominoes." Of the thirteen couples Pat and her husband socialized with, only one couple stayed married.[98] Janice Chalifaux saw the same thing in her town, and explicitly connects the quick-spreading divorce phenomenon of the 1970s with her movement toward CUB. "So many families were breaking up then," she says. "In my middle-class neighborhood, Catholic and all that, suddenly whole neighborhoods were getting divorced. Kids were running away from home, girls were getting pregnant. Suddenly, there were all these kids with single [divorced] mothers." Janice was looking, straight on, at the family form she'd been told only a few years earlier was an impossibility.[99]

One reason many authorities cited for denying Janice's cohorts their babies and their motherhood was that these unwed mothers had no way to support their babies. After all, mothers needed to stay home with their children, many postwar experts still claimed. Here was another rapid social and cultural change in the mid-1970s for birthmothers to digest: nearly 40 percent of *married* mothers of young children were working for pay in 1976 and a higher percentage of single mothers.[100] Only a few years earlier, birthmothers had lost their babies in part because their parents, teachers, and clergymen could reject, as an oxymoronic construct, "working mother."

All of these rapidly consequential phenomena—the decline of parental authority, teenagers' access to birth control and abortion, growing social tolerance of premarital sex, escalating divorce rates and rates of employed mothers—had special salience for young women who had so recently been sharply pressed to relinquish their babies. By the mid-1970s, all around them were girls and women near their own ages having sex and getting pregnant without suffering this punishment. There were mothers getting divorced, going to work, and maintaining their families as single mothers.

Moreover, at the same time, this cohort recently defined as not-mothers of their babies witnessed other women, in situations not so different from their own only several years earlier, making powerful and public claims for their right to be mothers, even when these women were in compromised and straitened circumstances. Members of the National Welfare Rights Organization, for example, were loudly linking their right to government benefits to their right to be mothers.[101] Lesbian mothers' rights groups, and other single mothers' rights groups of various types, were speaking out and garnering respectful treatment in some mainstream venues.[102]

The Sisterhood of Black Single Mothers, a Ford Foundation–funded organization in Brooklyn with 256 members in the late 1970s (the group was founded in 1974), paired older women with younger single mothers. The older women aimed to pass on positive lessons, including this one: "Before you can raise a child, you must feel good about yourself." The younger women were being exhorted to claim their motherhood status wholeheartedly and do a good job. In this transformative period, perhaps the most radical and rapidly consequential claim of a previously marginalized group was the claim of unmarried women to be mothers. The "primary goal" of the Sisterhood of Black Single Mothers was to change the public image of their members. As one single mother from Bedford Stuyvesant explained, "Look at the labels put on single mothers: 'unwed mother,' 'illegitimate child,' 'broken home.'" Then she said, "Society puts those [labels] on you and then asks you to function in a positive way."[103] In the 1970s, this was a bold, fresh observation, and untainted single motherhood was an innovative claim. Ultimately, of course, the sisterhood did not achieve its goal of detaching negative epithets from unmarried mothers, particularly young, Black ones, though this group joined many other such pioneering "sisterhoods" cropping up in the late 1970s and early 1980s to argue that single motherhood should be a normalized status and single mothers deserved respect.[104]

It was no coincidence that the more autonomous-sounding term "single mother" replaced the pitiful and old-fashioned sobriquet "unwed mother" in the early 1970s, or that single mothers were forming organizations, speaking out, and getting attention then. After all, the National Center for Health Statistics reported that 1976 was the first year that more Black babies were born to single women than to married ones, 50.3 percent. A much smaller percentage of white babies were born to single women, but this rate was rising very rapidly. Between 1969 and 1976, the white rate was rising on average about 15 percent a year (5.5 percent to 14.8 percent, a 169 percent increase).[105]

With so many single mothers in the United States, these girls and women could no longer be hidden; in fact, many refused to hide. An early advice book on single parenthood, published in 1973, stressed the new latitude this population could claim, in racially neutral terms: "Almost any [single, pregnant woman's] decision is now acceptable within the culture. Abortion is sanctioned, the pregnancy itself is at least tolerated by most of society, and a kind of counter-culture prevails that makes many girls feel . . . totally capable and unapologetic about raising children outside of marriage."[106]

The new "acceptable" status of single motherhood was quickly and dramatically revealed in one arena: the precipitous decline in the number of white infants available for adoption. Study after study in the early 1970s reported steep declines. One study published in 1975 indicated that among forty-nine prominent adoption agencies, the number of children accepted for placement dropped 45 percent between 1971 and 1974.[107] Lynn McTaggert, a journalist who conducted an undercover investigation of the booming "black market" in white infants at this time of scarcity, found that "by the mid-1970s, New York adoption agencies were averaging five white infant adoptions per year, compared to an annual average of fifty the year before Roe v. Wade." McTaggert argued that agencies were hurting for babies not so much because of legal abortion as because single mothers were keeping their children.[108] One report noted that the peak year of adoptions in the United States, 1970, when 175,000 placements were arranged, was followed by steadily declining numbers, so that by 1977, there were only 104,000 placements, a 41 percent decrease.[109] This downturn occurred during the period when ever-larger numbers of single women were giving birth. The National Center for Health Statistics reported that in 1975, 447,000 babies were born to unwed mothers, almost twice the 1965 number.[110] The combination of legal abortion and the rise of single motherhood changed the adoption scene for the remainder of the century.

Despite the fact that thousands of white couples, most adoption agency personnel, and black market operatives were clamoring for babies in the 1970s, mainstream experts began to stand up in some unusual and unprecedented places and speak out in support of the single mother's *right* to keep her child. In 1975, Joseph Reid of the Child Welfare League of America (an organization that had supported the adoption mandate for many years), for example, pressed a U.S. Senate committee investigating adoption practices to consider this: "To measure success only by a high count of decisions *for* adoption is tantamount to disregard of parents' rights and needs. It is tantamount to saying the parents' well-being is subordinated to the objective of securing a child for someone else."[111] For the first time, some experts began to recognize that the *choice* of a middle-class couple to adopt a baby had to be counterweighted by the birthmother's *right* to be the mother of her child.

Two years later, the U.S. House of Representatives held similar hearings as trafficking in white babies proceeded out of control. At these hearings, *Chicago Sun-Times* reporter Pamela Zekman and other investigators pressed politicians to stop effacing the worst victims of this traffic: resourceless birthmothers manipulated by desperate circumstances to surrender their babies. Zekman testified: "The experience can do years of damage to these girls, and we interviewed many who suffered feelings of tremendous confusion and guilt after they gave up their babies. Many were in desperate need of counseling after giving up their babies, but such services are not part of the baby business."[112]

More than sympathy and concern for normalization were expressed for single mothers in these years. The U.S. Supreme Court decision *Ordway v. Hargraves* (1971) made it illegal for schools to expel unwed pregnant girls, and with Title IX legislation in 1975, Congress acted to deny federal funds to schools that didn't comply with *Ordway*. Hundreds of programs sprang up around the country in the early 1970s to accommodate the educational needs of girls who only a few years before would have been summarily tossed out of school.[113]

Even adoption agencies began to alter their practices in the 1970s in ways that recognized the passing of the adoption mandate for white unwed mothers. Spence-Chapin, the premier New York City agency, created new programs dedicated to "helping the unmarried mother if she wants to keep her child."[114] The National Conference of Catholic Charities, formerly a leading facilitator of white adoption in the United States, did not fault the maternity home and school-based programs *supporting* unwed motherhood that were catalogued in a 1974 Catholic Charities report. These included a "Keepers Club" for girls refusing to surrender; a program giving academic credit in child care to unwed mothers who worked in a school's day care facility tending their own children; and programs providing "a homelike residential setting in which young mothers who are keeping their babies can develop into self-sufficient, effective parents and homemakers."[115]

Most dramatic and accessible to the cohort who had recently surrendered were the numerous "testimonial" essays that appeared in mass media venues in the mid-1970s. In a *Redbook* article, "To Be an Unmarried Mother: The Most Important Decision I Ever Made," for example, "Martha" (a pseudonym; the author notes, "Public exposure is simply too dangerous for me") acknowledges herself as a delighted pioneer because she kept her child and became a single mother. "A generation ago I never would have been able to do with my life what I am doing now . . . I am . . . an unwed mother whose family background, education, and career are of the so-called 'professional class.' There are going to be more and more of us, I feel." Despite the "danger," the difficulties of single parenthood, "the tight money and fatigue," Martha offers herself as a role model, "so very happy that I did what I did."[116]

In 1975, *Mademoiselle* recognized the trend and published "So You Want to Be a Single Mother . . ."[117] Even *Seventeen* gingerly endorsed single motherhood in 1977, when it ran "I Refused to Give Up My Baby." This piece emphasized the hardships of mothering alone and young, but portrays "Sue-Ellen" as a good mother whose family hesitantly "comes around." The article casts maternity homes as "relics of a bygone day," and quotes Sue-Ellen's self-determined argument to her father and, perforce, to readers: "You don't understand: The baby is MINE. I'm going to get a job and raise my baby . . . I wanted the baby, and I wanted it for myself."[118]

Carole Klein, one of the first to write a book about single motherhood, noted in the early 1970s what simply could not have been said only a very few years earlier: "It seems reasonable to conclude after meeting many single mothers that unmarried motherhood can be rewarding to all kinds of people." Essentially complimenting women who refuse to relinquish, she characterizes this group as sharing "a tenacious determination to steer their own lives."[119] Libbi Campbell, one of the founders of CUB, spoke for many mothers who had surrendered children when she considered why, by 1976, a critical mass of former unwed mothers was ready to find each other and organize. "We all in our own way," she said, "came to the conclusion that there were some great injustices done. And we were able to speak up . . . Whether it was the sexual revolution or women's rights, or feeling empowered . . . that whole situation we'd gone through, it just began to seem so archaic, so medieval."[120]

By the mid-1970s women like Libbi Campbell were grappling with a fundamental recognition: that they were living in the new era of "choice." Perhaps more than any other group of females in the United States, these women were stunned by the rapidity and totality of the change and its implications. Just a few short years ago, as daughters, as rejected girlfriends and lovers, and as maternity home inmates, unwed mothers had been dependents and thus denied choice absolutely. Sheila Ganz, raped, pregnant, and the resident of a Pennsylvania maternity home in 1969, put it this way: "I was in a home for unwed mothers the last four months of my pregnancy. No one there ever said to me, 'Ok, Sheila, do you want to do A, B, C, D, or none of the above?' As a single mother . . . I had no choice."[121] Now that "choice" was constituted as the very essence of modern, autonomous womanhood, many surrenderers identified their total lack of choice as the facilitating condition of their violation.

Worse yet for these women, "choice" was integrated so smoothly and completely into the lifestyle perquisites of contemporary (white, middle-class) women that, after 1973, Campbell's cohort was routinely and explicitly charged with having simply made their own freewill choices to relinquish; thus, many observers argued, they should quit complaining. As Gail Wolthius wrote in 1977 to her sister birthmothers, "How many times did you hear the words, 'But you had a choice, you could have kept your child.'" Gail begged to differ: "Did you really have a choice? Adoption agencies, parents, relatives, friends all [lent] their subtle pressure. That's not a choice."[122] Marsha Riben agreed, pointing out that, as a matter of course, "The world looks upon [birthmothers] as 'bad' people for having done just what they were told to do."[123]

Birthmothers began to recognize in the mid-1970s that not only had they been denied choice as pregnant girls a few years earlier, but "choice" itself was a slippery concept, one that, as it turned out, had most relevance for women *with resources*, including some combination of money, maturity, and a marriage partner. These special conditions for choice existed during the peak years of relinquishment. And they continued to be relevant, according to many adults resisting unmarried women's right to keep their children into the middle 1970s and beyond. Despite the normalization of single motherhood in these years, *real choice* remained elusive for those who lacked this cluster of resources.

When the issue of choice was raised in connection with girls and women without resources, the assumption was all too often that such females were incapable of choice or associated with *bad choices*. Young girls who sought birth control, for example, were all too often defined as the ones "whose sex impulses cannot be controlled." Experts warned that not every young woman possessed the personal traits necessary for using "the new freedom." One commentator pointed out that "the ability to make an absolute and free choice as to the purpose and result of . . . sexual activity . . . still required intelligence."[124]

Similarly, girls who relinquished after 1973 were often presented as alienated from "good choices" because they were "being seduced with dollars to place their children." In 1975 a Florida detective investigating black market adoptions quoted a lawyer who "says to a girl, 'We're going to pay all your expenses and give you $1000 or more, to boot.'" The detective tagged this strategy as "a fairly good inducement, especially staying down here where the climate is good."[125] The "mothers" in question here were "girls who are paid to stay pregnant and . . . girls who are paid to get pregnant," that is, young women willing to make the bad choice to debase their bodies and degrade motherhood for money and a Florida "vacation."[126]

As more unmarried girls and women refused to relinquish, mainstream media acknowledged the trend, but often withheld approval by implying its bad-choice basis. As *Time* magazine argued in 1971, "keeping" may be good for single mothers, but experts doubt that it's good for their babies. Reviving decrepit research from the 1950s, the article stressed that "psychological studies suggest that among unwed mothers, it is the most unstable who keep their babies."[127] In the same season, *Newsweek* identified the keeper as typically a mother likely to "take her baby home and care for it as long [and only as long] as it's still a toy." Alternately, and without citing evidence, the article claimed that in San Francisco, "sometimes a bellwether for youth trends, mothers twelve to fifteen years old are starting to bring their babies in for adoption once they find out they can't live within welfare allowances."[128]

Unwed mothers who had lost their babies to adoption in the 1950s and 1960s were simultaneously grappling in the 1970s with the long-term consequences of their own losses, with seeing other young women able to choose motherhood, and with the ways that "choice" could still hurt their kind. By this time, though, a woman pressed very hard to surrender her baby in the past could speak out, even if anonymously, as "Dead Violet" did in the mid-1970s, when she wrote to Ann Landers: "If you tell one more young girl to give up her baby born out of wedlock, I'll go through the roof." She explained what a terrible experience it is for a girl to give up a baby, "all [that she] has left in the world." In this woman's case, she gave up her son fourteen years before because of the social worker's pressure. As a result, her life was utterly "empty." She told Ann Landers, and thus a good part of America, that because of this horrible, life-changing episode in which she'd had virtually no choice, "I cried myself to sleep every night since then." Many birthmothers in the process of evaluating the cultural context, wondering whether to feel empowered or disempowered by the strong, though contradictory, currents shaping the 1970s, surely gulped hard when they read Ann Landers's response. The advice columnist implicitly suggested that unwed mothers, especially those who mourned their loss, were undeserving of choices: "A woman who has cried herself to sleep every night for fourteen years," wrote Landers, "would probably have raised a child with a million problems."[129]

Others agreed with Ann Landers that girls who had relinquished had forfeited choice. On the other hand, Landers and others sized up *some* in the adoption arena as legitimate choice makers whose options should be protected or promoted. Adoptive parents, in particular, were often identified as beneficent and able choice makers. Their choice could transform an "unwanted" baby into one who was "loved and cherished." Equally important, adoptive parents had a fundamental association with a marketplace activity, wherein they could spend their resources freely. One commentator in 1977 typically defined the "adoption market" as a place where "the adopting couple [can] receive the most precious gift in the world in return for a price they are willing to pay."[130]

Policy makers and service providers, too, were easily defined as choice makers in this realm. Both groups were empowered to transfer babies around (or to propose such transfers) in efforts to solve vexing social problems such as homelessness and poverty. In 1977, a group of policy makers proposed creating a "national data bank" of homeless children as the basis for a registry of adoptable youth.[131] Early in Ronald Reagan's presidency, many adoption workers expressed their sense of purpose by referring to the fact that "adoption is one of the main ways of breaking the poverty cycle by moving a poor child to the middle-income level."[132]

Many women who had lost their out-of-wedlock babies in the 1950s, 1960s, and early 1970s assessed the post-*Roe* promise of choice—as well as the limits of choice—for the relatively resourceless, and began to come alert to a context in which they had something to say and, perhaps, something to gain.

4

CLAIMING RIGHTS IN THE ERA OF CHOICE

PART II: CONCERNED UNITED BIRTHPARENTS

———

GETTING ORGANIZED

Many women scattered around the country were thinking about "coming out of the closet" in the early to middle 1970s, as former unwed mothers who had lost their children to adoption. But one married young woman raising two little boys in the Boston area took the first concrete steps to build connections among them. Lee Campbell described how important the "Confidential Chat" section of the *Boston Globe* continued to be to her efforts. After the section editors facilitated connections between Lee and women who responded to her notices about unwed mothers and child loss, she "published a letter in the paper asking 'biological' mothers who were interested in exploring issues to get in touch." In short order, a group of these correspondents began to form around Lee in early 1976. The women went to ALMA meetings together, and under Lee's direction and with the help of Betty Jean Lifton—who had published a memoir called *Twice Born* about adoption and search—they began to develop a series of "clinics" especially for themselves. The group wanted "help to cope with our peculiar loss, to integrate our past with our present, and to prepare us for a future when we might be reunited with our children."

After only a few months, Lee and others realized that in some fundamental ways their issues were different from those of the ALMA adoptees, and they "needed an ALMA-type organization just for us." Their early efforts to form common purpose were sometimes tension-filled. After all, what these women shared most explicitly was a sense of degradation, shame, loss, and long-term isolation. Lee Campbell's description of her first meeting with Joanne MacDonald, a woman she would work closely with for years, illustrates part of what it took for this initial band to cohere. First, Lee heard from Joanne through the "Confidential Chat" column and realized that her correspondent lived in Orleans, Massachusetts, "just north of me." This proximity worried Lee. "It seemed too close for comfort. What if she couldn't keep a secret? And though I'd met many birthparents at Flo Crit [the maternity home] and a few more at ALMA meetings, I worried she would be an 'unacceptable' birthmother, a trashy one." Lee describes her preoccupations when she first met Joanne this way: "I dressed extra-conservatively so she wouldn't think me trashy. But when she opened her back door to me, all bets were off. While I wouldn't have classified her trashy, she definitely wasn't middle class . . . and she was proud of it."

Breaking through class, status, and sex/gender stereotypes, Lee and her new colleagues got to work quickly, with Betty Jean Lifton as mentor, to develop "terms to identify us, descriptors to define us, and analogies to explain us." Members of the newly forming group were thrilled by these tasks. According to Lee, "It was as though we had waited our collective lives for this opportunity. When we brainstormed, the air crackled with electricity."[1]

Following the conventions of new identity/political action groups in the 1970s, this group determined that the language it chose for itself was crucial, both personally and politically. (One woman, struggling by herself in the Midwest in this era, also recognized the importance of language: "Some folks were buying that we weren't mothers; I knew perfectly well that I was a mother. Our society [said] you were an unwed mother until you signed those papers and then you weren't a mother at all. Some of us were saying, okay, I'll try not to be a mother at all. Others were saying, are you nuts? Of course I'm a mother. But still there was no recognition. We had to find some way of saying what this was: okay, we surrendered . . . but we ARE mothers.")[2]

According to Lee, in the summer of 1976 "we agreed on 'birthparent' and 'birthparenthood.' We didn't want to upset adoptive parents with 'natural.' And 'biological' now made us gag. 'Biological,' we felt, was descriptive of a mechanical incubator or unfeeling baby machine. 'Birth' was key. With 'birthparents' as one word . . . we were like other one-word progenitors, like grandparents." As for the adoption experience, the women decided to call that a "surrender" rather than to use a term such as "given up" or "placed." "To us," Lee wrote, "surrender fit the experience. We had been involved in a social war to which we had surrendered without options and without compensation for our loss."

Newly named, Concerned United Birthparents began to craft its mission and set its agenda. The Boston group immediately identified several areas it would concentrate on: legislation and policy initiatives to enable birthmothers to exchange nonidentifying information with adoptive parents; community education; and mutual support. At the beginning, CUB did not *officially* discuss or assist with search matters, although many members, perhaps most, were searching for their children in secret. Lee explained the dynamics and determination that allowed the founding group to tackle its ambitious program: "Susan kept us accountable to adoptees. Mary Anne served as our resident critic. She encouraged us to be more radical, as did Kathy and Joanne. This tested Susan, Gail and me, who were more conservative. At any point these differences could have had us lunging for each others' throats. CUB could have been over before it began. But the work was too critical to 'give up.' To us, CUB became a symbol for not giving in, again, to the system."[3]

Almost immediately, CUB found that it was remarkably easy for the group to get media attention. As Carole Anderson put it later, "We were a novelty, something totally new and slightly titillating." Whatever the media's interests were, the coverage was extremely useful to the new organization. Anderson noted, "Mothers were so hungry [then] to share their experiences with others that a letter to the editor in a Peoria newspaper could result in a new member from Poughkeepsie, as relatives and friends sent clippings to suffering moms."[4]

Lee Campbell, who was personally involved in most of the early media efforts, catalogued CUB's success:

> In addition to small town . . . newspaper coverage, word of our work was also featured in national publications from *Business Week*, *The Christian Science Monitor*, *Parade*, *Family Weekly*, *Newsweek*, *Good Housekeeping*, *Woman's Day*, *Family Circle*, *Woman's World*, and *McCall's*, to *Dear Abby*. Radio was another popular medium, especially after we protested the adoption-marketing angle of the original Cabbage Patch Kids craze. In addition to local television coverage across the country, [The Phil] Donohue [Show] hosted us four times.

Years later, Lee described her fear about going public on TV as a birthmother. She feared her husband "would have a stroke." She worried about the impact on her two little boys at home whom she had not yet told about her first son, lost to adoption. "I can't risk they will somehow get wind of it . . . I also thought: My Boss? Dave's boss? My friend Marie?" In the end, Lee made up her mind to go on *The Phil Donohue Show* and other TV programs, but, she decided, "I would be photographed in silhouette."[5] According to Carole Anderson, Lee's first appearance on *Donohue*, in shadows, "brought the biggest barrage of inquiries CUB ever had . . . Letters came by the thousands. Some had pictures in them, copies of documents, amazing things."[6] Following Donohue's interest, media coverage of CUB "continued strong" in the early 1980s. When *Parade*, the national Sunday newspaper supplement, ran a story entitled, "Shadow of Motherhood," CUB heard from 500 birthparents. Articles followed in the *New York Times* and the *Wall Street Journal*.[7]

Such extravagant media attention helped CUB members feel much more confident about making their claims for birthmothers' rights among each other and now in public. Also adding to their confidence was the fact that, at this time, "people were rebelling . . . everyone had causes. All of a sudden, causes were okay."[8] The formerly shamed girls who joined CUB immediately began to connect their cause with justice movements in general. In a 1977 CUB newsletter, Lee Campbell emphatically invited readers to identify with all marginalized people: "EVERY BIRTHMOTHER—INDEED EVERY MINORITY—MUST

HOLD A SEMBLANCE OF THESE FEELINGS IN THEIR CON-
SCIOUSNESS . . . IT'S A HUMAN FEELING—SOMETHING TO
DO WITH 'GETTING EVEN,' REVENGE AT PEOPLE WHO HAVE
NOT ALLOWED YOU [TO BE] THEIR EQUAL . . . I WANT TO IS-
SUE A PIERCING SCREAM OF DEPRIVATION."[9]

Many birthmothers were thinking in these terms, explaining their
cause in terms of other, larger, more publicly acknowledged causes. One
woman who had lost her child in the 1960s wrote in the mid-1970s that
she had been crying herself to sleep for twelve years "over what happened." The worst part, she wrote, was the nightmare that stained her
sleep nightly, of "concentration camps with parents separated from children, slavery with parents separated from children, and Viet Nam with
the children being blown out of their mothers' abdomen by bullets."[10]

In the mid-1970s, these images were both vibrant and accessible for
many Americans, as movies, TV shows, and the nightly news dramatized
"history from the bottom up" and its legacies. Birthmothers easily identified with marginalized, victimized groups whose stories were being produced and consumed at least in part in the spirit of atonement. They also
identified with members of newly defined or newly activist victim groups,
such as battered women, abused children, and rape victims.[11] Some associated the awakening of their political consciousness as birthmothers
with observing the new political activism of other marginalized groups.
Sheila Ganz remembered witnessing a Hopi ritual in which the elders
were deciding what actions to take against a government that had broken every treaty it had ever signed. Watching that ritual awakened
Sheila's political consciousness as a rights-claiming birthmother forever,
she writes.[12]

In 1978 Lee Campbell, well known by then in adoption circles because of the media attention accorded CUB, was appointed to the
federal-level Model Adoption Legislation and Procedures Advisory
Panel. She described her frustration with the panel members' insensitivities in terms she knew would resonate with her sister birthmothers. After only a few meetings, Lee had felt put down by the group; she believed
they thought she was too uppity for an unwed mother and wanted to put
her back in her place. To do this, she believes, panel members rejected
the term "birthparent." Lee was "stricken" by the members' disregard for
her preference: "It was as though I were an African-American, sur-

rounded by dominant powers who were callously insensitive to what I preferred to be called." When the panel rejected Lee's compromise suggestion, "natural parents," and voted to use the term "biological parents," Lee's identification with the oppressed deepened: "Now I was not only an African-American surrounded by insensitivities, I was also an African-American surrounded by those who called me the N-word."[13]

Among the first acts of CUB was to produce its own media outlet, the CUB Communicator, a newsletter first issued in the summer of 1976. In the pages of the Communicator, birthmothers used the language they preferred, routinely described their surrender experiences in thoroughly political terms, and explored the meanings of being activists. There, and at early CUB meetings, members were determined to recapture their dignity and reconstruct themselves as "whole, complete persons."[14] One way to do this, they figured, was to provide services to the many birthmothers who felt disillusioned and left in the lurch by the social agencies that had managed their adoptions. Libbi Campbell, one of the early Boston members, spoke for many when she asked, "Where were these agencies after they took our children? They never asked if you wanted to talk about what happened . . . if you wanted counseling." So Libbi explained, through the Communicator and the meetings, "we decided we had to do it ourselves."[15] According to many accounts, CUB was successful in these efforts. Pauline Evans in the Midwest described her first meeting as "unforgettable," and Laura Lewis in the Washington, D.C., area remembered feeling "reassured" the first time she attended a meeting because the women there were "mature," and, most important, they "were thinking for themselves."[16]

Most CUB members at this time were thinking about establishing their right to search for their lost children and supporting each other in claiming this right. Before CUB, some birthmothers had made tentative, lonely efforts to locate children, but working without support—and without the certainty that their efforts were legitimate—was hard. Carol Schaefer described what it felt like to move in this terrain alone. "I was a pregnant, powerless teenager again, looking for help, expecting only reproaches. I was going to be exiled from my life and hidden away again."[17] Becoming part of CUB gave many women the ammunition and support to trump these reproaches, imagined and real. Pauline Evans explained, "For the first time in my life [at a CUB meeting] I actually . . . met other birthmothers who had been able to find their long-lost children. And for the first time in my life I was being told that I could look for my son too. And I was even encouraged to do so! And for these reasons, I felt some degree of empowerment!"[18] Pat Taylor remembered her first meeting, on a night she drove secretly "half-way across the state of Connecticut to the small town where the CUB coordinator lived." The event "was the beginning of empowerment" for Pat because of what she began to feel about her lost daughter that night: "I began to feel as though I might even have a right to love her."[19]

Lee Campbell captured the flavor of early meetings and the importance of the search issue this way: "At every meeting we greeted new members and shared educational, legislative, and personal stories. Crying was not uncommon for those who didn't know [the whereabouts of their lost children]. Frustration was not uncommon for those who did. We who had found [our children] were living in limbo, which was better than the hell of not knowing . . . We leaned on each other."[20]

HAVING A BASE, DEVELOPING AN ACTIVIST PROGRAM

When the women who formed CUB found each other, they did not have to thrash through ideological differences to craft the group's doctrine. Early members agreed that their mission would embrace activities to "humanize adoption."[21] They specifically determined to "raise the consciousness of as many people as possible to the long-ignored feelings and concerns of the birthparent."[22] CUB members agreed to work on projects protecting the rights of vulnerable pregnant teens, educating the public about the impact of coerced adoption, and supporting each other. The initial group immediately started drafting legislation and writing grant proposals in support of some of these goals after its first meeting in July 1976 at the Paulist Center in Boston.

Early CUB members thought of themselves as "pioneers": "Everybody was full of energy, everything was new, nobody had done any of these things before. We were discovering whether any of these things worked. There weren't any books on this subject out there. It was an exciting time."[23]

A lot of early energy was focused on "how to come out of the closet," when and whether to search.[24] At the same time, though, Lee Campbell and others jumped into the legislative and political arenas. First CUB wrote a bill submitted to the Massachusetts state legislature that would have provided for "release of protection" for birthmothers, enabling adoption agencies to forward nonidentifying information about birthmothers to adoptive parents. Later the group drafted legislation that would have enabled "open records" in Massachusetts, and they participated in efforts to convince legislators that health registries were important for adoptees otherwise cut off from their medical heritage.[25] CUB was vigilant in tracking (and often testifying regarding) adoption-related legislation pending in California, Minnesota, Pennsylvania, New Jersey, and elsewhere, always attempting to protect the interests of vulnerable mothers.

Most of these efforts were not successful. Some stimulated organized opposition from adoptive parents, fearful that birthmothers were laying the groundwork for snatching their babies back, a fear Lee Campbell called "absurd."[26] Despite these setbacks, Campbell remembers the group's optimism: "We had high hopes the need for CUB would be short-lived. With ongoing publicity, we were convinced society would begin to understand the need for openness to replace secrecy, and for love to replace fear of the unknown. To us, each new article or television show or radio broadcast could be 'it,' the candle whose flame illuminated lasting change. We were idealistic."[27]

Even in these first idealistic years, CUB did have a national impact, in its contribution to the project of establishing the American Adoption Congress in 1979, in placing its first president, Lee Campbell, on a federal-level adoption policy panel, and in having Lee and then Carole Anderson, who edited the CUB Communicator for years and was also a CUB president, appear on The Phil Donohue Show.

Other CUB programs aimed to provide practical assistance to mothers and their babies. Charlene Justice, an early member, ran the CUB Sister Program, an effort to help resourceless girls and women keep their babies. Members invited mothers and their newborns to live with them long enough to get started together. In the late 1970s, the group secured federal funding for a BET on Youth program to help teenage mothers keep their babies. Carole Anderson described how "young moms worked [through this program] at CUB's office and learned office skills in a setting to which they could bring their babies to work." Carole reported visiting the CUB office, where she was impressed to see "cribs, playpens, babies, and happy young moms with their babies."[28]

By spring 1978, less than two years after its founding, CUB was bursting at the seams. Articles in the *Communicator* regularly reported CUB's successes. A typical piece, entitled "CUB Sisters: It Works," described the most cherished kind of success:

> A seventeen year old teen found herself being pressured by her California agency to surrender within a week of the child's birth. The teen called CUB and revealed a horror story of counseling, including outdated films depicting the majority of teen moms electing adoption . . . and all the ills of single parenthood . . . Although the girl was across the country, we were able to put her in touch with a local birthmother who will see to it that the decision is made without pressure or biases.[29]

Carole Anderson explained years later why these kinds of efforts were so important to CUB members: "You just couldn't think about what happened to you and the injustice of that . . . the negation of you as a person . . . and the continuing punishment . . . without wanting to stop it from happening to others in the future."[30]

In 1979 CUB counted sixteen branches "with requests for new ones all over the country."[31] In 1982 there were forty branches and the group reported having served 35,000 individuals between 1976 and 1981.[32] In this context of expansion and growing acceptance, many CUB members had grown brave enough to seek and accept speaking engagements; they were particularly interested in speaking to groups of prospective adoptive parents, to urge these couples to consider the meaning of adoption for birthmothers, to remind them that birthmothers were part of the picture, too. These were difficult assignments. Susan Darke remembers taking a train from Boston to Springfield to address such a group but found herself waiting and waiting on the station platform for the social worker who was to meet her. Finally, Susan approached a woman who had been pacing the platform and asked, "Are you waiting for me, Susan Darke?" The social worker started, flushed, and took Susan's hand, apologizing, "I'm sorry, you just didn't look like a birthmother."[33]

Libbi Campbell tried to steel herself against such stereotyping. "One of the first times we were asked to speak publicly, in Worcester . . . I remember, my lip was trembling. The one thing I wanted to say and get across was that Grace [another birthmother] was a nurse, not a slut, a nurse . . . and that I was a college student . . . Whatever projections people had, they had to know this right off the bat, that we weren't scum, lowlife, sluts."[34]

Some early CUB members claimed dignity and rights for birthmothers with eloquence at the end of the 1970s. Gail Hanssen, a birthmother who later earned a Ph.D. in psychology, wrote an "Adoption Bill of Rights" in 1979 that was endorsed by the fledgling American Adoption Congress that spring. What is most striking about this document is how, by claiming citizenship rights for "parties to adoption," it establishes that many experienced the loss of these rights in the adoption transaction. It also establishes, in the tradition of bills of rights, the determination of this group to assert and attain its due and its protection. After defining adoption as neither "punishment" nor "reward," this bill of rights asserts that birthmothers, adoptees, and adoptive parents are "free citizens," guaranteed the same basic freedoms as other citizens. It invokes the Thirteenth and Fourteenth Amendments and calls for "the emancipation of all adoption-related adults." In particular, the document seeks to establish that birthparents "shall have the same access to records kept about them as any other citizen."[35]

Through the end of the 1970s, CUB members' "idealism" and "high hopes" prevailed. Many believed that the claims asserted in the Adoption Bill of Rights were reasonable, just, and attainable. But by the early 1980s, as the Reagan era took hold, many early CUB members could see a long struggle in front of the group.

Having come to understand their adoption experiences in the 1950s and 1960s in political as well as personal terms, many of these women were sharply aware of the impact of the new administration's policies on young, unwed mothers after 1980. Following *Roe v. Wade*, "teenage pregnancy" was far less often associated with pathological maladjustment than it had been in the 1950s and '60s. The term "teenage pregnancy," according to sociologist Kristin Luker, was coined in 1975, during Senator Edward Kennedy's hearings on the doomed-to-failure National School Age Mother and Child Health Act.[36] Public policies and community strategies now aimed to blunt the consequences of young girls having sex and getting pregnant, not by sending them away to maternity homes for psychological treatment and relinquishment, but by making contraceptives and abortion just as available to this population as they were to older women in the 1970s.

With the ascendancy of Reagan conservatives after 1980, however, public funding for contraceptives and abortion was decimated, and the pregnant teenager was reconstructed, paradoxically, as a dependent daughter and an aggressive source of social pathology. She was once again denied personhood in her own right and pressed to see herself as unworthy of being her child's mother. The Adolescent Family Life Bill of 1981, also known as the Chastity Bill, and the numerous attempts in the 1980s to establish parental control over the abortion decisions of young women, were depressing indications to CUB members (and many others) that all claims for female self-determination regarding sex, pregnancy, and motherhood were now out of sync with the prevailing political score. Politicians and others in this era routinely urged adoption of illegitimate children as the stone to kill several nasty birds at once: unwed motherhood, poverty, childlessness, and the dearth of white adoptable infants. Many CUB members, having so recently defined themselves as victims of gross injustice, having so recently claimed and attained a public platform and a measure of public attention—and even a small measure of public funds to protect the current wave of unwed mothers from losing their babies—were dismayed to discover that many powerful political and cultural authorities in the United States were once again determined to define unmarried pregnant young women as public problems and their babies as potential public resources.

Equally troubling to CUB members after 1980 was the realization that while individually and as a group many birthmothers emphatically identified with the feminist movement and its goals, feminists didn't seem to identify with them.

FEMINIST RELATIONS

When early CUB members joined the organization, they identified with the women's liberation movement to varying degrees. For many, becoming affiliated with a women's group concerned with rights and justice quickly convinced them that their issue was, as Pat Taylor put it, "yet another woman's issue."[37] In the late 1970s, Pat and others came to frame their experience in terms of gender discrimination: "we, as females, were told that we did not have the resources, ingenuity, creativity or strength to be parents to our children." In general, the members who took on the responsibility for writing CUB documents for internal and external consumption, such as Carole Anderson, were already ardent feminists when they joined CUB, so they infused the organization's publications with a strong feminist perspective.

Carole Anderson wrote emphatically for the group in 1981 when she claimed, "[O]ur pain is a feminist issue." In the late 1970s and early 1980s, when Anderson, Lee Campbell, Mary Ann Cohen, and Sandy Musser defined the birthmother's experience, they connected it to all the major claims of the contemporary women's movement. From their point of view, the coerced adoptions they'd experienced were meted out as "punishments of inappropriately sexually active women." As girls rendered defenseless by society's gender imperatives, they felt strongly that they had been manipulated and lied to.

Feminist CUB leaders associated coerced adoptions specifically with the lack of reproductive freedom women suffered before *Roe v. Wade*. Carole Anderson cited the experience of one girl "who wanted an abortion but couldn't get one because abortion was illegal. Then later she was told she had to relinquish her baby because her desire for an abortion proved she would be a bad mother." Anderson, like others, also associated losing her son with sexual violation, identifying coerced surrender as the "ultimate act of rape."[38]

Sandy Musser explained how she and most CUB members viewed the practice of sealing adoption records as "an affront to the basic dignity" of women who had given birth while unmarried and lost their children. This policy, she argued, denied a group of women "the right to take charge of our own affairs" because of their gender: "[I]t perpetuates the assumption that [birthmothers] have sinned, that we should feel guilt and thus be 'protected' from exposure to the 'sin.' The closed record implies that we are incapable of emotional depth, of accepting a new situation, and coping and growing with it. The closed record limits [birthmothers] socially, imprisons us emotionally, and discriminates against us morally."[39]

Lee Campbell focused on the importance of CUB as a community of women whose identification with each other could create a collective voice and an activism to improve women's lot. As a teenager, Campbell had been elected president of the residents' council at the Florence Crittenden maternity home, where she'd spent her illegitimate pregnancy. Now, she transferred her leadership skills and her understanding of what women shared—and their potential strength—to CUB's agenda. Years later, Lee made the connection explicit:

> My relationship with CUBbers reminded me of Flo Crit. Had we CUBbers met under other circumstances, say, socially, we might not have taken ourselves to the next step . . . to revealing our deepest, rottenest, most vulnerable and caring selves. But [in CUB] it didn't much matter what our backgrounds were. Who our husbands were or what we or they did for a living. Our educational level was not an issue either. Nor our age. [We were] women joined at the hip with other women.[40]

While CUB leaders conceptualized birthmothers' experiences and CUB's mission in feminist terms, the rank-and-file members described their day-to-day involvement as shaped by practices commonly associated with the feminist movement. Barbara Shaw, for example, remembers the connection between shame, personal testimony, and liberation that she found through CUB: "I sat paralyzed at my first meeting. I think I said my name. Did I have to say I was a birthmother? What will happen to me if I utter those words? Oh no! They're getting closer. I began hyperventilating. It's my turn, a quick intake of air, a final wave of nausea. My name is Barbara Shaw. I am a Birthmother. FREEDOM."[41]

When Ann Hege Hughes found CUB, she had a counsciousness-raising experience and described it in the same terms that women used to explain the impact of their feminist consciousness-raising groups in the 1960s and 1970s: "Reading the *CUB Communicator* articles made me bolder . . . Those other birthmothers were talking about things I'd never had the nerve to voice. They were responding loudly in ways that were socially unacceptable . . . This blew my mind . . . Step by step, I expanded my thoughts . . . I started to bond with the phantom sisterhood somewhere in space."[42] Pat Taylor remembered how almost immediately after beginning to go to CUB meetings, she translated sisterhood into political activism. "Thinking about . . . young women to whom [coerced adoption] was still happening," she began to speak at public meetings and before the Connecticut state legislature. She wrote reams of letters to newspaper editors, and began to write a book about her own experience of loss in the 1960s.[43]

Mary Anne Cohen reflected the preoccupations of many birthmothers—and many second wave feminists—when she described the ingredients of her activism: altruism and revenge. As she put it, "I was and am furious at the system that took my son, and have directed my rage toward helping others 'get over' on it."[44] In general, CUB members remember that the most important effect of joining was having the feminist experience of repossessing ownership of their selves. Elizabeth Avens captured what many have alluded to: "When I came out and joined CUB, it was so powerful to me. To take my heart and soul back and call it my own . . . The judgment was finally over."[45]

Unfortunately, the feminist insights and feminist experiences that birthmothers were having at this time did not apparently resonate with many mainstream feminists, often NOW members, to whom they turned for support. After all, women affiliated with NOW and other feminist organizations in the early years of second wave feminism were deeply concerned with articulating resistance to the idea—and to public policies supporting the idea—that motherhood was *the* life-defining activity and status for women.[46] CUB women who approached these organizations with claims about their rights as mothers seemed out-of-date and non-feminist. Few feminists at the time could yet envision a future in which "reproductive rights" included both the right to sex without pregnancy and the right to be a mother.

Women who had been coerced, however, learned a lesson early about the relationship between feminism and the claim to motherhood. When Carole Anderson went to NOW meetings in Illinois in the early 1970s, she was clear that "the real issue for me was losing my son. I thought of that as a feminist issue. I couldn't think of a worse way to oppress a woman. I did connect this with reproductive rights, but nobody at the meetings did. People in this [NOW] group would look at me like I was crazy when I wanted to talk about that."[47]

During this period, Anderson went on retreat with a group of women whom she believed would have identified themselves as "radical feminists." The iconic image presiding over the retreat site was a poster of a pregnant woman on a cross, and many participants had brought abortion rights leaflets with them to the event. According to Anderson, pregnancy-as-crucifixion and abortion rights marked the beginning and the end of these feminists' concerns in the early 1970s. Insofar as this group considered motherhood at all, Anderson believed that they were "into the fact that motherhood shouldn't be limiting, and we shouldn't be forced to be mothers. It was almost a hostility at that time to the whole idea of having children. At least that's how it was in this group."[48]

In Boston, several years later, Libbi Campbell remembers that Lee Campbell spent a great deal of time trying to build an alliance between CUB and NOW and failed, specifically because NOW members "couldn't see exploitation in adoption." They refused Lee's claims that birthmothers in her era had lacked options, had experienced coercion, and had been used to profit others. Instead, NOW members insisted that adoption was a *personal choice* in the case of both the birthmother and the adopting parents. Libbi recalls that "feminists were taking the position that women should be able to get children any way they could; they didn't want to participate in anything that would curtail their options."[49] Carole Anderson met members of feminist groups at this time who stressed that adoption was not a feminist issue because women benefited most from getting adopted babies.[50]

In 1981, Anderson, Lee Campbell, and Mary Anne Cohen were so frustrated by their inability to communicate with the "feminist community" that they wrote a position paper they called "Eternal Punishment: Adoption Abuse—An Appeal to Feminists" to try to stage a breakthrough. The CUB women attempted to challenge what they encountered as the prevailing perspective, "that if a woman wasn't able to raise her child [on her own], she should have an abortion, and that failing to have an abortion when appropriate proved that she wasn't responsible enough to raise her own child." Anderson was particularly aggrieved when one "outspoken feminist," expressing her ambivalence about motherhood and her fixation on autonomy, told Carole she should "feel grateful to the adoptive mother for letting me be free and equal."

The "Appeal to Feminists" was a powerful effort to build an alliance with mainstream feminists. It concluded with a call for solidarity. "We birthmothers are openly fighting for our rights and yours and those of the young women of the future who may be threatened with our fate. Our lives are testimony to the devastating effects of the oppression of women that is our mutual foe. We are comitted to ending that oppression. Help us, and let us help you, in our common cause. We are your mothers, your daughters, your sisters, perhaps even yourselves."[51]

CUB members struggled to make their argument to feminists in these years, but never felt successful.[52] They pointed to articles in Ms. in the early 1970s, such as Babette Dalsheimer's piece, "Adoption Runs in Our Family," a justification of adoption that effaced the existence of the birthmother altogether, and to the Senate's Adolescent Family Life bill and the Family Protection Act in the early 1980s, which promoted adoption but did not provoke prominent, collective feminist objections. At the end of this period, Randa Phillips in San Francisco described how arcane the concept of birthmothers' rights still seemed to those around her, including feminists: "To nearly everyone I came out of the closet to about having a child, being a birthmother, to 99% of the people, from my mother, father, two best friends, women in NOW, lesbian and gay parenting groups in San Francisco—they all said I was wrong. I had no rights."[53]

In the early 1980s, Carole Anderson pointed out what she felt was a profound irony. The feminist movement had been at least partly responsible for the social and political changes that explained the sharp decline in American adoptions starting in the early 1970s: the accessibility of contraception, the legalization of abortion, single mothers' awareness of public assistance, subsidized day care, school programs for pregnant students, job training for single mothers, civil rights protections for employed women. Yet the feminist movement did not see the connection.[54] In this context, many politicians, policy makers, and others repathologized youthful single motherhood as an "epidemic" and began to promote "adoption not abortion" as a young woman's best choice. Feeling ignored or rebuked by mainstream feminists, marked as unfit mothers or nonmothers by politicians, CUB members figured they would have to define and claim their rights on their own.

DEFINING RIGHTS BY LIMITING CHOICE

Not surprisingly, the most consuming questions of "rights" for these women concerned their right to look for, to make contact with, and to know the children they'd lost to adoption—and the right of these children to know their lost parents. Before CUB, most birthmothers report having been obsessed with thoughts of the child, but primarily thoughts, not concrete plans. Like most who had surrendered in the late 1950s and the 1960s, the heyday of adoptions, one woman described her day-to-day relationship with the loss a decade later as a matter of mental preoccupation: "My parents put pressure on me to give the child up for adoption. I really had no choice. I was trapped. I think of her every day."[55] Even as birthmothers began to collect in CUB branches after 1976, the subjects of *actual* search and reunion were approached gingerly. Carole Anderson remembers that "in the early days . . . even mentioning the possibility of reunion was every bit as strange as promoting interspecies marriage . . . We knew of no studies, no long-established patterns, no precedents for how to contact, no role models."[56] In fact, in the early days, CUB was especially careful to dissociate itself, officially, from the search project, even though CUB leaders themselves were involved in searches and reunions and knew that many members were, too.

In any case, all CUB members were sharply aware of the horror and taint attached to the specter of the returning biological mother. CUB headquarters regularly received letters from adoptive parents warning birthmothers in general to stay away, reminding them that they had merely performed as "breeders" and so had no right to "interfere" in their children's lives. One such letter from an adoptive parent read, in part, "Keep in mind the endless joy you have given two people, feel good about yourself . . . or I'll get a restraining order if you show up." After seeing Lee Campbell on *The Phil Donohue Show*, an adoptive parent wrote, "Leave the past alone! So you're sorry—too bad." Another wrote, "You must be a selfish person and most certainly a little stupid . . . my [adopted] son . . . thinks of [you] as only an incubator. I'm glad."[57]

By the late 1970s and early 1980s, however, many birthmothers were determined to search. In 1983, Judy Klemesrud, writing in the *New York Times*, found the sources of this determination in "changing mores, the tendency of young women [today] to keep their out-of-wedlock children, and support groups." Klemesrud quoted a birthmother who agreed with CUB members that the most essential motivation for searching was enduring love for the child who had been taken away. As this young woman put it, "We can't have the years back but I can know my daughter and begin to have a relationship with her rather than continue to have a black hole in my heart."

Birthmothers finding their children in those years described the event then—and continue to describe it today—as profoundly restorative and transforming. One woman who found her daughter in the early 1980s put it this way: "It's given me peace of mind just to know she's alive and well . . . It has also allowed me to grow up in a lot of ways. Part of me was frozen at the age of eighteen."[58] Elizabeth Avens felt that finding her son "gave me back my life." "For the first time," she wrote, "I look forward to the future, I'm glad to be on this earth."[59] Merrill Clarke Hunn credits her passionate activism today to finding her child: "Once we were in re-union and our relationship began to take on its own life, I could begin to look outside myself and find a way to make my experience meaningful."[60] Similarly, after embracing her right to find her child, and doing so, Peggy Matthews-Nilsen felt she could make her loss and her life more useful; she co-led a support group, conducted workshops, and became a thera-pist.[61] Like some birthmothers who came to believe they had a right to find and know their children, Sue Tavela did not find nirvana when she found her child. She describes her reunion as "a long, long rollercoaster ride," but is emphatic that "even its worst moments have been immea-surably better than the years of not knowing what happened to my child."[62]

It is important to remember that this cohort of birthmothers had been diagnosed as mentally disturbed when they became pregnant. Many had been labeled disturbed (or horribly misguided) a second time when they fiercely resisted the adoption mandate. A significant number report sustaining a third such diagnosis when they considered looking for their children in the 1970s. By this time, though, it was harder to get the label to stick. As Lynn Kopatich says of that time, "I learned that lots of peo-ple had searched and that I wasn't crazy for not being able to forget my child."[63] In the opinion of many CUB members, gathering the strength to slough off the "crazy" label—and replace it with a rights discourse of their own devising—was the most important act of their lives.

The question is, though, how did these women define and justify their right to pursue this highly controversial activity? Some, like Carole Anderson, report that they came early to thinking in terms of rights: "I first realized that I had a moral right to raise my child . . . when I was in a sociology class in college and read about abandoned and dependent children. The text made it clear that this included the children of unwed mothers. I was horrified, then angry to see my child described as abandoned. I thought it was morally wrong to describe my surrender experience this way, and I rebelled at such a description."[64] Others, however, remained captive to the opinions of adult authorities for much longer. Ann Hege Hughes explained, "I had been heavily conditioned that it was both wrong and illegal to search for Beth," and the conditioning stuck for many years.[65]

Janet Fenton had resisted support groups and meeting any "real" birthmothers for years. She described herself in the late 1970s as afraid of so many things, especially of finding her daughter, of not finding her daughter, and of having other people say, "I told you so." Locating CUB materials in 1980 stimulated Janet's search, but even then, this union organizer felt compelled to hide in her bedroom to listen to the CUB audiotape for new members. In fact, it took Janet two years to get up the courage to mount her search. As she put it years later, "Whether or not I had the right to search: this was absolutely at the heart of the matter."[66]

Janet and others resolved this question in part by coming to believe that a successful search would benefit the child they'd lost. Drawing inspiration from the adoptees in ALMA, they believed it was critical for their children to know that their mothers loved them and wanted them. Beyond that, CUB members' definition of their search rights grew directly out of their growing sense of the "cruel injustice" they'd suffered.[67] CUB members report having waves of recognition after 1976 regarding how they had been "used" (the ultimate state of degradation for a girl of their generation). Having spent a decade or even two "experiencing [unwed motherhood and surrender] as something shameful and a secret to be lied about,"[68] many CUB women broke through personal shame and began to talk to each other about how their gender, their youth, their lack of resources (especially money, information, and parental support), sometimes their love for feckless boys, their fertility, and finally their babies, rendered them usable resources for others—in fact, constructed them as the solution to the infertility problems of others.

Over time, many CUB women developed perspectives that linked their experience of having been used in the past with the experiences of other girls and women whose reproductive capacity and their babies were targeted as the source of, or the solution to, social problems in the late 1970s and early 1980s. In the 1950s and 1960s, the problems were the ruined reputations of white, broadly middle-class girls and the infertility of white, broadly middle-class couples. In the late 1970s and into the 1980s, the solvable problems included the public expense associated with single motherhood, the threat to the integrity of the male-headed family presented by single mothers, and the dearth of adoptable white babies. In both eras, young women were cast as dependents who had made the bad choice to get pregnant outside of marriage and had to be prevented from "choosing" motherhood.

By the early 1980s, CUB was developing an orientation to reproductive politics that distinguished this group from other groups focused on reproductive matters at that time: CUB recognized some core limitations of "choice." Many CUB women defined their project as antithetical to "choice." First, they advocated the right to dismantle the apparatus that supported the continuing use of birthmothers. In particular, they wanted to abolish the structures that championed the adoption choices—even "rights"—of married couples while denying the choices and certainly the rights of birthmothers. Most offensive were the "protections" that prevented birthmothers and adopted-out children from knowing each other. Second, they dedicated themselves to safeguarding the right of fertile females not to have their reproductive capacities used in a way that could harm them. Third, they wanted to protect a child's right to remain in his or her own family. They wanted to limit the choice of any individual to acquire a child at the expense of harming another.

Repudiating the "protections" that based adoptive parents' choices (to adopt in the first place, to allow or prohibit later contact) on the denial of birthmothers' and adoptees' choices was key. Lee Campbell explained that CUB took the position that

> state-sponsored "protection" [of birthmothers' privacy] treated us like imbeciles, or as though we had done something for which we should be ashamed. We were instead quite smart, and we were determined to someday hold up our heads for giving life. WE could protect ourselves, thank you very much. We could accept or decline our child's invitation to be in our lives in the same way we could accept or decline anyone's invitation. We didn't need special protection.[69]

In 1983, when CUB took official positions on the idea of government-run reunion registries (negative), a government-run reunion intermediary program (negative), and the need for birthmothers and adoptees to have direct access to adoption records (positive), the organization explained its stance this way: "[B]irth records and court records pertaining to adoption should be treated in the same manner as non-adoption and [other] court records are . . . There is no need for state-imposed confidentiality, since all parties in adoption are as capable as non-adopted persons in dealing with interpersonal relationships."[70] In effect, birthmothers claimed that they had been forced to surrender their babies, after which government policies deepened the coercion by giving reunion-related choices to adoptive parents but not to them. CUB members became increasingly determined to make the point that in the aftermath of adoption, there are three *adult* parties (after the adoptee reached majority). When the choices of one of those parties, they argued, depended on denying or closely regulating the choices of the others, "choice" was fatally corrupted.

The second way that CUB's claims challenged "choice" focused on how class and status structured relationships among female sexuality, fertility, motherhood, and human dignity. During the late 1970s and early 1980s, policy makers and most segments of the general public used "choice" as a term laden with class content. For example, infertile, middle-class women were not publicly criticized for exercising whatever choices they could afford in order to acquire a child, including adoption and reproductive technologies. Unmarried teenagers and poor women, on the other hand, were widely accused of being bad choice makers when they became mothers. They were urged to stop reproducing or give their children away. In these ways (as well as in the public discussion regarding which abortion-seeking women could choose this option), a woman who had financial resources was accorded legitimate access to socially validated motherhood. A woman who did not was defined as lacking motherhood rights.

My reading of the public documents CUB issued in its first five years or so of existence suggests that the organization recognized that "choice" could not protect the motherhood interests of all women and that, in fact, "choice" as a governing principle led to the exploitation of some women and their children by others. My reading of CUB documents suggests that the group was developing a powerful rights-based prescription for reproductive politics in the era of choice. In these documents, CUB argued first that freedom from all reproduction-related coercion is a core condition of human dignity. Second, the group maintained, females who become pregnant must be free of social, economic, political, or other kinds of coercion. Third, women who give birth to a baby must be free of coercion. Fourth, pregnant or parturient women who have been coerced must not be forced to "live a lie," preserving the secret of that coercion and its effects. Finally, CUB documents argue strenuously that women who have been coerced to surrender children must be free today to act in their own behalf to redress the effects of coercion; they must be free to find and meet the children they gave birth to. These tenets established a theory of reproductive rights that protect all resourceless women and children from laws, policies, and practices that would grant women with resources motherhood choices denied to women without resources. These tenets protect women against laws and policies that would construct motherhood as a class or status privilege, that would allow some women to "choose" to become mothers by exploiting the resourcelessness of other women.

EFFACING MOTHERS' RIGHTS IN THE REAGAN ERA

As CUB was defining the injustices done to birthmothers and their babies in the postwar decades and to other vulnerable pregnant and parturient mothers and children more recently, the social and political context was becoming increasingly hostile or even deaf to their claims after 1980. This was so in part because in the Reagan era, mainstream feminists, NARAL, Planned Parenthood, and others focused on the need to safeguard *women's choice*, while conservatives claimed that the polity was being poisoned by the *bad reproductive choices* of many females. "Choice" defined the rhetoric on both sides, and the notion of reproductive rights faded in the public and political arenas.

There were seven powerful, interrelated political and cultural shifts in the early 1980s that contributed to muting CUB's voice and deflecting attention from the bases of their claims.

First, the shifts in the adoption arena were deeply consequential. White middle-class couples who would have been able to get babies to adopt relatively easily in the 1950s and 1960s were having a much harder time in the 1970s. By 1980 the situation was desperate. A survey of one hundred adoption agencies in the late 1970s reported that 97 percent of them had experienced a steep decrease in white infants available for placements over the course of the decade; 70 percent of the agencies noted a decrease of 50 percent or more.[71] Many agencies had waiting lists so long that they stopped accepting applications.[72] One effect was that distraught white couples—and adoption service professionals—regularly spoke out in public venues about their shared need to find adoptable babies, and also about the responsibility of unwed and other resourceless women to find good adoptive homes for their babies.

The scarcity of white babies immediately and dramatically boosted their monetary value. This development, in turn, increased the desperation of white child-seeking couples and narrowed the band of those who could acquire one of the few available babies. In the 1980s, the director of public policy of the National Committee for Adoption estimated that there were two million couples waiting for a baby to adopt in what had become, emphatically, a sellers' market.[73] Reports of adoption costs for a white baby at this time gyrated wildly, from more than $7,000 to $50,000. A consumer newsletter costed out white babies at "three thousand dollars a pound," at about the same time that Korean babies were said to be obtainable for $2,500.[74]

Not surprisingly, the scarcity and the high cost of white babies caused many people seeking adoptable infants to turn their frustration and resentment toward the mothers they held responsible for shrinking the market. Frustration was typically expressed at the time in one of three ways: by stressing that the baby's need for a good home with two middle-class parents should always come first; by stressing that unwed mothers were untrustworthy characters, probably unfit to be the mothers of their babies; or by sanctioning practices that made white unwed mothers targets for inducement.[75] One reporter found agencies recruiting unwed mothers in the early 1980s "using billboards, newspaper ads, radio and TV commercials, and even tray liners at fast-food outlets."[76]

Potential birthmothers who equivocated while under pressure to relinquish or decided to keep their babies despite the pressure were particularly vilified. A doctor who worked in the adoption arena associated such a mother with the hand of death. He explained that having to tell prospective adoptive parents that the mother had changed her mind and decided to be mother to her own child "is worse than telling someone they're going to die of cancer."[77] The editorial director of *Philadelphia Magazine*, who had published an exposé on the black market in white babies, testified before Congress to the effect that the "adoption business" had become so unsavory—so "overrun by whores and thieves"—that respectable doctors and lawyers would no longer practice within it.[78]

As white babies became ever scarcer, prospective birthmothers (as distinct from relatively independent, white, middle-class, often well-employed *single mothers*, a burgeoning cohort in the 1980s that did not, apparently, consider relinquishment) were frequently the objects of scorn, not the subjects of concern. Scorn may have been facilitated in part by the fact that these mothers were perceived as incapable of exercising choice in the style of the day. It may also have been facilitated by the abject resourcelessness of many relinquishing mothers in the late 1970s and early 1980s. Whereas many birthmothers (maybe most) in the immediate postwar decades were the daughters of broadly middle-class families, in the later period they were more apt to be like the scared young high school dropout living in a coal-mining town in the southwest corner of Pennsylvania. This was a girl vulnerable to the "offer of round-trip plane fare, spending money, medical care and clothes" in exchange for her baby.[79] One prospective adoptive mother, discouraged by how long it was taking to find an adoptable baby, expressed her own frustration and scorn in a fashion that had become all too common: "I think there are some girls who get pregnant just to make a business out of it."[80]

In a second political and cultural shift, the newly discovered vulnerability of another large group of girls and women also contributed to effacing the "rights" claims CUB asserted. As I showed in Chapter 1, by the early 1970s adoption operatives discovered third world women as sources of adoptable babies to fill the gap created by single mothers and abortion in the United States. Especially after the National Association of Black Social Workers issued a statement in 1972 against transracial adoption— "Black babies should not be used to salve the consciences of whites or to fill the gap left by the shortage of white babies"—people wanting babies turned to Korea, Mexico, Thailand, Colombia, Cambodia, and other poor countries where women could be paid as little as twenty-five dollars, or nothing, for their babies.[81] New York and other states simplified the red tape involved in making these babies available for adoption by Americans,[82] and courts and the Immigration and Naturalization Service cooperated as well. One federal immigration judge denied the claim of a thirty-one-year-old Mexican woman to the daughter she had lost to wily operatives, declaring, "It is only the welfare of the child which is of importance. Sending [the baby] back to Mexico would not necessarily be in her best interests."[83] An INS ruling in the case of a San Diego woman arrested for running a "baby-smuggling" ring in Mexico that "preyed on unmarried women" allowed couples in the United States to keep the babies if they hadn't known about "the smuggling conspiracies" when they adopted "their" infants.[84]

Reports from Colombia revealed that "some [hundreds of] babies were obtained through nurses who told mothers their offspring had been born dead and passed the infants along to . . . lawyers. Others were simply kidnapped or bought from impoverished peasant women. At times, members of the [ring] were sent out to patrol the city's red-light district to find pregnant prostitutes and persuade them to sell their babies." Prospective adoptive parents from the United States were reported to like working with Colombian authorities in these cases because the "two-to-five-day [adoption] transactions" were "attractive."[85]

With such broad official cooperation and such an unexpectedly plentiful supply of new babies, many people in the United States were eager to focus on the babies' "interests" and forget about the birthmothers' rights. By this time, Americans did, after all, have a tradition of this sort to draw on. As one woman who adopted a child from South America in this period put it nearly twenty years later, "This was 1978. Not once did I consider that these babies were being coerced away from their original moms. Since abortion was now legal, and since many single moms were keeping their babies, . . . I felt very lucky to adopt a second baby when I had friends in other parts of the country still waiting to adopt their first child."[86]

In a third major shift, in the late 1970s and early 1980s, just when CUB was attempting to arouse public empathy for birthmothers and build understanding for their rights, the pool of prospective adoptive parents began to expand in new and unexpected ways. With a replenished pool of adoptees and a newly diverse population of prospective adoptive parents, the adoption scene was more vibrant than ever; thus, CUB's claims were ever more marginalized. Two groups in particular began to act on their belief that it was discriminatory to deny them the choice of parenthood: gays and lesbians, and single persons, generally. By the early 1980s, it was possible for some female members of these groups to get pregnant via reproductive technologies. But males and many females looked to adoption to achieve parenthood.

Roberta Achtenberg, who was at the time the chief attorney of the Lesbian Rights Project in San Francisco, spoke out in terms that many gays and lesbians embraced as justifying their claim to become adoptive parents. "We have become aware that we have the freedom to become parents if we want, that it's our right. This knowledge, that we're free to if we want, has been a very liberating thing, a very life-affirming, very self-affirming thing."[87]

In a very controversial attempt "to open a dialogue in [the gay and lesbian] community between those of us who deeply desire to parent in a hostile society and those of us who have experienced the pain of a system that denies us the basic right to our heritage," adoptee- and birthmother-rights champion Celeste Newbrough complicated Achtenberg's straight-forward view of adoption by gays and lesbians when she suggested, "It is one thing to be bold in affirming one's right to parent. It's another to trample on a child's rights or a mother's rights. Just because heterosexual society has done it, and is doing it, is no reason for lesbian and gay people to follow their lead."[88]

Randa Phillips, a lesbian birthmother, also tried to persuade gays and lesbians to tread carefully in the adoption arena in a piece that she says aroused profound anger among gays and lesbians in San Francisco and did not win friends for the CUB position.[89] Phillip's effort, published in a San Francisco alternative paper aimed at gays and lesbians, reads in part:

> The movies, "The Official Story" and "Madres de la Plaza," both portray Central American mothers who have lost their children through kidnapping, never to know again where they are, if they are dead or alive. The gay community was moved by those movies. Yet the same community talks about adopting a child without re-alizing that for a natural mother to lose her child through closed adoption, to never know where she/he is, is for her a kidnapping of her child. This is true whether she is a birth/natural mother

from the United States, or from South Korea, Mexico, India, Colombia—the countries that typically export poor women's babies to the U.S. for adoption. For gays and lesbians to consent to adopting children where the natural mother never again has an opportunity to know her child, means consenting to participate in one of the systems most oppressive to women.[90]

Heterosexual single people were also making significant progress in the 1970s and 1980s in legitimizing their relationship to parenthood via adoption. The California State Department of Social Welfare paved the way for this trend in December 1965 when it revised its placement guidelines to include enabling language: "Single parent applicants may be accepted only when a two-parent family has not been found because of a child's special needs." (This revision of course put aside the paradox that the most difficult-to-raise children could command only half as much parent power as "normal" children.) The bureau defined "special needs children" as "Negro children, Mexican children, and children of all races and nationalities with severe medical problems." Early observers reported that adoption workers found the new policy "hard . . . to accept." Over time, however, many began to point to the escalating rates of divorce in the United States to justify the policy and many came to believe that one parent might meet an adopted child's need "at least as well as [one parent met] the needs of many children in broken homes." Within a fairly short period, Los Angeles adoption workers were "tremendously impressed" by the successful placements of "special needs" children with single parents.[91]

Just over a decade later, a U.S. government publication asserted, "No longer is the one-parent home considered the placement of last resort. Indeed, the single man or woman may be, for some children, the family of choice."[92] By this time, too, special interest groups, such as the Committee for Single Parent Adoption in Washington, D.C., championed the cause and "offered assistance in locating adoptable children and referrals to other single adoptive parents for mutual support."[93]

In the late 1970s, a single woman living in Colorado decided that her life was missing a child and the pleasures of parenthood. She further decided that since now single women could adopt children respectably, she would devote the year 1978 to finding a child to adopt. On January 1 of that year, she wrote in her diary (the entry would be quoted in a U.S. government publication a few years later): "My New Year's Resolution is to look seriously into adopting a child. I've already begun an investigation of agencies. Before Christmas, I phoned Friends of Children of Vietnam. The person I spoke with was most encouraging. She suggested contacting Colorado Friends of all Children and SAFE (Single Adoptive Families Everywhere). Before I could call either, Friends of Children contacted me! Good sign, I figure."[94]

Birthmothers who had recently been pressed to surrender their babies with the argument that a single woman could not be an adequate parent were shocked by the advent of single parent adoptions. As this practice became more common, one unmarried mother who had given up her baby under pressure in the late 1960s exclaimed, "Now they're giving adoptions to single parents, and with me, they were so sure, so goddamn positive, that a child had to have two parents."[95]

Increasingly in the 1980s, CUB members' claims concerning the rights of birthmothers were met and trumped by the claims of single men and women asserting the legitimacy of their choice to adopt and the righteousness of their child-saving intentions. Adopters of foreign babies and single person adopters—often overlapping groups—focused public attention on the child rescue aspect of adoption; both groups effaced the plight of birthmothers around the world who were too poor and powerless to keep their children. Both groups helped quash public policy discussions regarding strategies to bolster the resources of biological mothers and preserve biological families. Both groups offered the promise of middle-class, if nontraditional, harbors for poor babies, some of whom might otherwise have become recipients of public assistance. These developments helped support a two-tiered public perception of single mothers that has remained vibrant through the end of the century: middle-class, never-married mothers are legitimate mothers (of their own or other people's children), but poor never-married mothers are not.

The fourth cultural and political change that helped eclipse birthmothers' claims involved teenagers. Unlike the new adopters, who stimulated some public admiration, the burgeoning numbers of new teenage mothers aroused a great deal of public hostility. The emergence and public response to both categories of new parents, however, tended to undermine the innovative notion that resourceless birthmothers had rights.

Historian and public policy expert Maris Vinovskis argued in 1981 that "the American public has become increasingly upset" because of the public costs associated with large numbers of teenage girls giving birth and because of the ever-increasing number who were keeping their babies instead of putting them up for adoption. Vinovskis pointed out that the public's focus on the "financial costs" was connected to their general unhappiness with the expansion of welfare programs in this period. The public was so upset, in fact, that it quickly accepted the largely politicized terms "crisis" and "epidemic" to describe teenage childbearing when these terms were floated by politicians.[96]

The facts about teenagers having babies were rather different from the scary picture politicians and others presented, but troubling nonetheless. Briefly, the annual number of births to teenagers aged fifteen to nineteen remained fairly steady between 1960 and 1977. But a number of dramatic demographic trends emerged over that time span to change public perception of and attitudes toward these young mothers. First, the total number of teenagers fifteen to nineteen years old decreased by 58.1 percent between 1960 and 1977, so far fewer teenage girls at the end of the period were producing the same number of babies that a much larger pool had produced earlier; that is, a higher percentage of teenage girls was giving birth in the United States by 1977. And as the birth rate went down among married women, unmarried teenagers were giving birth to a higher percentage of the babies born in the United States. Second—and this was crucial—far fewer teenage girls in the later period got married once they found out that they were pregnant. For example, in both 1960–64 and 1970–74, 50 percent of babies of teenage girls were conceived out of wedlock, but in the 1960s time frame 65 percent of these were "legitimated" by marriage, while only 35 percent were in the 1970s frame. And finally, thousands of teenage girls were refusing to put their babies up for adoption in the 1970s, when the "epidemic" was diagnosed.[97]

Anthropologist Martha Ward has pointed out that by the late 1970s, teenage mothers were roundly despised because they were seen as costing the community too much money and as depriving "their betters of a valuable commodity—babies to adopt." Ward added, "Hostility toward white adolescent mothers who keep their children is barely concealed in public policy. This hostility may be linked to other issues in reproductive policy such as the growing consciousness of infertility in the middle class and new reproductive technologies."[98] In 1981 this hostility was harnessed in the proposed Adolescent Family Life Act, which strongly promoted adoption as the appropriate alternative to teenage parenthood, and in attempts to fund national adoption centers. Politicians and ordinary people who supported these policy initiatives were clearly expressing their antipathy to youthful unmarried mothers and their support of adoption. Both positions, of course, were anathema to CUB members, most of whom realized they were making their case in an ever more unfriendly climate.

Related to the public's anger about the tax burden associated with teenage motherhood was the sharpening of public hostility toward welfare mothers beginning in the late 1970s: the fifth cultural and political change that hurt CUB's crusade. Here, of course, was the central arena for defining illegitimate mothers in this period. Ronald Reagan, whose administrations were so successful in reinstating public scorn for poor, unwed mothers, began his efforts while governor of California. In the mid-1970s, Reagan proposed that the third child and subsequent illegitimate children of an unwed mother "should be statutorily removed for adoption."[99] Government policies that continued in this era to provide foster mothers with two to three times as much money as a mother living on AFDC also expressed the public's belief that women who were even temporarily without resources, even more than women without husbands, were not legitimate mothers. Throughout this period, despite the insufficiency of AFDC grants, policy makers argued publicly and frequently that welfare provided the incentive for poor (Black) women to have children, and also removed the incentive for poor (white) women to put their children up for adoption.[100]

Many of the politicians and others who decried teenage motherhood and welfare mothers in the late 1970s and early 1980s were also allying themselves at this time with the anti-abortion movement that had taken form after 1973. These forces posed yet another—a sixth—oppositional voice to the cause of those, like CUB members, who felt that girls and women should not be pushed to place their babies for adoption, and that adoption was not an appropriate or effective solution to social and political problems.

Four years after abortion was legalized, President Jimmy Carter and his secretary of health, education, and welfare, Joseph Califano, became vocal proponents of plans to persuade unwillingly pregnant girls and women to eschew abortion and choose adoption. In the summer of 1977, for example, the Carter administration proposed a plan whereby the government would "pay the maternity medical expenses of women who choose to give birth and give their babies up for adoption rather than seek abortion." Secretary Califano cited adoption as "obviously an alternative to abortion" when he and President Carter opposed federal funds for the abortions of poor women.[101] The same year, U.S. Representative Henry Hyde, the leading congressional opponent of legalized abortion, declared, "I just want to say for the record that I think maybe a poor adoption may be better than the best abortion in the world."[102]

Connie J. Downey, appointed by President Carter to head a study group charged with reporting on alternatives to abortion, felt personally compelled to disband the group in late 1977 in this climate of pro-adoption sentiment. Ms. Downey concluded after months of meetings that the only real alternatives to abortion were "suicide, motherhood, and some would add, madness."[103] For the remainder of the Carter administration, however, and throughout the subsequent Republican administrations, adoption was regularly pushed as the most responsible remedy for untimely pregnancy, and government entities made many attempts in this era to subsidize adoption.[104]

Title XX of the Social Security Act, passed in the 1970s, and the proposed Adolescent Family Life Act and the Family Protection Act in the 1980s championed subsidized adoption on the federal level, while almost 80 percent of the states underwrote adoption subsidies.[105] About half of these covered adoptions of "normal" children with no special needs. CUB's appeal to feminists in 1981 pointed out how these programs discriminated against birthmothers and all unwed mothers and advocated adoption of these women's children: "[A] single mother raising her child could not receive the tax consideration [often in the form of adoption subsidies] . . . but if she were forced to surrender her child, the married couple allowed to adopt her baby can expect a tax benefit up to $3000."[106]

A final substantial force at this time militating against CUB's effort to build empathy for the treatment of unmarried mothers was the emergence of "family values" politics. Proponents included many people who supported adoption as a solution for such social ills as teen pregnancy, welfare, and abortion. It is true that in the 1970s, many Americans perceived the term "single mother" as a signal of "the destigmatization" of unmarried mothers, a group that had formerly been divided into widows, divorced mothers, and unwed mothers—each of which carried its own degree of respectability (widow) or stigma (divorced mother, unwed mother). Now all mothers without husbands could be tagged by one neutral label. Despite this linguistic reform, many Americans were deeply upset by the huge increases in the 1970s of families headed by women, especially never-married women, and by the number of children in the United States living in families without fathers. In fact, a Yankelovich survey in the late 1970s showed that 70 percent of Americans disapproved of women having children outside of marriage, a strong indication that whatever they were called, unmarried mothers were still stigmatized.[107]

The U.S. Commerce Department reported statistics in 1980 that reflected what most Americans were seeing all around them: In 1979, 17 percent of homes in the United States were headed by mothers alone. The U.S. Census Bureau added that between 1970 and 1979 there had been a 52 percent increase in the number of households headed by women, from 5.6 million to 8.5 million.[108]

Interest groups and conservative political organizations of all sorts began to issue statements and reports documenting the negative impacts on children of mother-headed families. One such report, issued by the National Association of Elementary School Principals, was entitled "The Most Significant Minority: One Parent Children in the Schools." This document claimed that children from these families were three times more likely to be suspended and twice as likely to drop out of school as children from two-parent families. According to the report, the first group was likely to be absent from school eight days more a year than other children and more likely to be tardy. The principals' report was roundly criticized as "misleading" and "unfair" by the National Commission for Citizens in Education and others, but the study's researchers and school administrators supported many Americans' views that children deprived of a second parent could be expected to manifest negative behaviors.[109]

Perhaps the most telling gauge for CUB of the upsurge of "family values" Americans, their dislike of unmarried mothers, and their support for adoption, was the audience response to Lee Campbell's first appearance on *The Phil Donohue Show* in 1980. Campbell described her experience—from the shadows—this way: " 'So, what do you think?' he asked [the audience]. 'Lee Campbell is a woman who surrendered her son for adoption more than sixteen years ago. Does she have a right to know him? All those who say no . . .' He stepped back at the thunderous applause."[110]

While they faced deep cultural ambivalence and even hostility toward their claims, many CUB members drew strength from feminism. This was true even while many were deeply suspicious of the central tenet of mainstream feminism: choice. They recognized the marketplace essence at the heart of this concept. They recognized how the choice to adopt and the putative choice to surrender had harmed them and could harm others. They recognized how *choice* could mask resourcelessness. Even in the era of choice, CUB members defined what they'd lacked as vulnerable unmarried mothers as *rights*, and continued into the 1980s to believe that only the rights claim could protect the interests of resourceless women to be mothers of the children they bore. The rights claim was also powerful, and far superior to choice, CUB women believed, because it embedded a commitment to maintain the visibility of all other women's interests, in addition to one's own. It asserted that all pregnant and parturient women must be equally free of harm and that no child should be regarded as a "cure" for a stranger's infertility.

Through Concerned United Birthparents, many women recognized that in order to be able to make this rights claim, they would have to surrender shame, surrender dependency and obedient daughterhood, and claim independence for themselves. In the beginning many had felt as Janice Fruland had when she got pregnant out of wedlock in 1963: "I was sure God was punishing me, a 'good Catholic girl,' for having had sex."[111] By the early 1980s, a great many CUB members felt they had much more in common with Janice Chalifaux, who described what happened when she "came out" and claimed motherhood rights for herself:

I was the daughter in a Catholic family of five kids. The absolute most obedient child in the whole family. The only thing I ever did against their wishes was to get pregnant. There was no way—I couldn't stand up to that at all.

But once I went and got some education and left home, became a psych major, got some counseling, supported myself, and found CUB, I did very well. All this time, the anger that I felt was always there, bubbling under the surface, and I think I was just gearing up—not even knowing it consciously, to the day when I could go forth and find my son and tell my parents exactly how I felt about the whole thing.

When I told my parents I was going to search for my son, it was like I murdered someone. The whole family, the whole extended family, went into a horrible tizzy because it had been a secret to everyone except my few close friends before. Aunts, uncles, cousins, none of them knew. And when I came out, I did it in a very big way. Very public way. Very quickly. I started writing editorials for the *Globe*, the *Telegram*. I went on local TV, then on national TV. I came out with a blast. I exploded.

There was such a relief in it. My family was so angry, so upset. At first they shunned me, really. They were very, very angry. But then, it was as if all these little fires started in the family. People started to tell me some of their secrets, nothing horrible, but things they felt they couldn't share with anyone else in the family. So in the end, strange as it sounds, people in the family got permission from my confession to say whatever it was they needed to say . . . abuse, dysfunction, sex, whatever they weren't able to share before.

I think I started to have a lot of respect in the family, and I have a role now. It's not what it was at all. I had been a little, quiet Catholic girl who kept everybody happy, and now I was somebody different. People started coming to me. Now I'm an example, a strong role model.[112]

LOOKING BACK/LOOKING FORWARD

The women who founded Concerned United Birthparents in 1976 and the ones who have sustained it for more than twenty years have seen enormous changes in the treatment and experiences of unwed mothers. Most saw dramatic changes occur very soon after they surrendered their children. As Cindy Bhimani remembers, "Shortly after [my son was born in 1970]—like about 1973 or so, I watched other girls fight to remain in public school and fight to keep their babies—and win. You can imagine I felt shorted but there was nothing I could do."[113]

Carole Anderson and others struggled hard to celebrate the changes without feeling bitter. In 1979 Carole visited the Bethany Home West, a new residence for single mothers and their children in Rock Island, Illinois. She was delighted with the place: "I was glad to see the wonderful opportunity this program provides . . . it is truly a dream come true—yet I started crying as soon as I got back in my car and I was devastated for days. I explained to a puzzled friend . . . that it was like being a person who, years after a loved one had suffered and died of a disease, toured a hospital where people are routinely cured: I'm very happy the facility exists, but it hurts me so much that it's too late for my son and me."[114]

Some CUB members are most forcefully struck today by what has not changed. As Pat Taylor recently put it, "If someone had told me in 1978 when I was first reading all those books and first finding CUB that I would still be trying to get records opened at the end of the century, I wouldn't have believed it. Because of all our early optimism, I would have said, 'No way!' "[115]

After more than twenty years of efforts to make a case for the rights of mothers, Carole Anderson assesses the terrain today as a mixed bag.

> People are far less likely to surrender their children. People are much more likely to help their daughters and many won't even consider losing a child within their *own* family. All the reading about reunions has helped people to understand that the feelings don't go away. That's all progress. But socially and politically a lot of things are worse: the idea that illegitimacy is the source of all problems in the world. And in our day, when we were losing our children, the issue was moral in the sense that married people were considered better than we were because they were married. But today, the married part doesn't even matter. It's about money—who has enough money to be a mother, and who has enough money to adopt.

In 1997 Anderson asked herself what would happen if CUB "went away and shut up tomorrow." She rejected that alternative because, she said, "I think we have to keep the candle lit till better

days come along. If we're not there when the climate improves, the opportunity will be lost. I don't want to see a return to the dark days. But I
listen to some of the anti-mother rhetoric today and the anti-welfare
rhetoric and all that, and I can see where we could turn into the 1950s in
a heartbeat."[116]

5

CONSTRAINING CHOICE

WELFARE QUEENS AS ILLEGITIMATE CONSUMERS

——————

My name is Dian Wilkins. I am a mother of two children, and I am on Aid to Dependent Children. I attended the Congressional Subcommittee Hearings today, and
I heard the chairwoman . . . talk about all the A.D.C. mothers who had air-
conditioned houses and swimming pools. I wanted to stand up and tell them that I
certainly didn't have a swimming pool, that I was lucky to have a bathtub . . . but of
course I was not allowed to speak.   —Dian Wilkins[1]

The truth is that since the total annual welfare costs—federal, states, and local com-
bined—are $16.3 billion, and the fraud rate is 0.4%, we can calculate that welfare
fraud costs the United States $65 million annually, or $1.03 per family per year, or
2¢ a week.   —Al Sheahen, "The Real Welfare Chiselers," 1976[2]

Like the Back Alley Butcher, the Welfare Queen has had a vibrant and
reviled existence in the United States—the existence, I want to argue, of
a folk villain: not factual, but nevertheless fearsomely real to the man on
the street. Just as the Back Alley Butcher was the engine for granting
women choice, so the disgraceful Welfare Queen has justified taking it
away. It makes sense that these chimeras have been so important to the
history of chimerical "choice."

In this chapter I will look at how the Welfare Queen, like the Back
Alley Butcher, absorbs and reflects social, cultural, and political ambivalence—hostility—toward women in trouble. The nasty epithet "Welfare
Queen" did not emerge until the early 1970s. But many Americans began imagining this figure years earlier. In this chapter I use the term
"Welfare Queen" to signify widespread hostility to poor mothers receiving public assistance money—and a determination to degrade these
women by taking away their choices—from the mid-1960s onward.

In exploring the iconic Welfare Queen, I will look first at how this emblem has been constructed. Then I will consider how public frustration and anger about "the welfare mess" focused and fueled hostility toward poor mothers in the late 1960s and 1970s. When politicians leveled largely unsubstantiated claims of welfare fraud against poor mothers, polls showed that a majority of Americans accepted the idea that Welfare Queens made the immoral, even criminal choice to cheat.

As with the Back Alley Butcher, I will consider what the iconic figure obscures and why it has made sense to so many Americans for over three decades. Again, I will make space for poor mothers to describe what it was like to live in a culture that began to call their kind Welfare Queens. Finally, I want to discuss the Welfare Queen as a symbol, like the Back Alley Butcher, of a rotten spot in the consumer society.

CONSTRUCTING THE WELFARE QUEEN

In 1964 the governor of California, Ronald Reagan, told this story to a large crowd in his state:

> Not too long ago, a judge called me from Los Angeles. He told me of a young woman who had come before him for a divorce. She had six children, was pregnant with her seventh. Under his questioning, she revealed her husband was a laborer earning $250 a month. She wanted a divorce so that she could get an eighty dollar raise. She is eligible for $330 a month in the aid to dependent children program. She got the idea from two women in her neighborhood who had already done that very thing.[3]

Ronald Reagan, along with thousands of other politicians, policy makers, social commentators, and ordinary Americans, has been talking about this outrageous young woman and her too clever neighbors since about 1964. The historian wants to know, among other things, why Reagan and the others expressed resentment toward *females*, in particular, at that time. After all, families headed by poor mothers had been the recipients of federal public relief for about thirty years in 1964, and public officials rarely spoke out to chastise or excoriate such women.

Depression-era reports of public concern about undeserving poor, including perpetrators of welfare fraud, generally invoked a mass of cheaters who weren't marked as men or women, or they may have specified males. Historian Margaret Orelup found that during the 1930s, "family men" or "reliefers" were the focus of public concern. When this group was depicted in the popular media, "their manliness was undermined with descriptions of soft physiques, a 'high piping voice,' or a smirking countenance."[4]

A 1940 study of "client fraud" in Chicago reported that the public was extremely susceptible to the simple "scent" of fraud, presumably attached to reliefers of either sex. "Gargantuan" welfare expenditures in the 1930s, the author explained, "scared taxpayers" whose "hue and cry mounted to a mighty crescendo . . . The taxpayer was pictured as staggering under the weight of supporting an army of villains."[5] Even national reports of a notorious event in 1960, when the city manager of Newburgh, New York, created a plan to throw all "undeserving" welfare recipients off the rolls, invoked a nonspecific "invasion" by "chiselers" of that Hudson River city—both men and women were cast as culprits.[6] Generally, welfare resentment at midcentury seems to have been more sharply focused on Southern migrants moving north than on either males or females.[7] (Interestingly, a 1979 study found that the concentration of welfare recipients in cities was not due to continuous in-migration of the poor; rather, it was due to lower rates of out-migration among welfare recipients than among more affluent residents.)[8]

When gender did become the issue after World War II, immoral males were the ones targeted. A typical early postwar treatment of welfare "chiselers" used male-leaning epithets to describe recipients—"grafter," "leech," "racketeer," and "professional pauper"—and referred to Oklahoma, the site of the report, as "a paradise for parasites." While poor mothers weren't exactly portrayed as saints in this 1951 piece in the *Saturday Evening Post*, the author and his Tulsa informants were most contemptuous of unemployed males "who profit by our pity," of "husbands in jail for non-support," "the men who desert," the fathers who make only "casual efforts at working."

Tulsa's representative in Congress called for legislation "that has teeth to bite into the [welfare] problem." What he meant was a federal law that permitted "government crime-detection agencies to pick up these wandering hoboes and take them back to jurisdictions where they can be made to work for their child or stay in prison permanently." The local prosecutor agreed, telling the *Post's* reporter that "fathers who breed for a macabre profit, then refuse to support their children, should simply be thrown into jail for bastardy. The idea of those fathers loafing and looking at television or taking refuge out of state while the postman pads to the door with a public baby bonus . . . is senseless and intolerable."[9]

Before midcentury, it would have been quite remarkable to invoke a class of poor resourceless mothers in the United States as scammers or villains. Among women, the figure of the prostitute could be villified because her sex was linked to money, and because she was presumed to be alienated from motherhood. After World War II, the unwed mother, if she were white, was likely to be defined as not-a-mother, but that practice was largely a one-generation-long phenomenon. Her status as a producer of babies for others protected her, if not from exploitation, then from many kinds of public vilification. In the early postwar years, a poor, resourceless mother, even an African-American one, particularly one with an illegitimate child, would generally have occupied a low, marginal status in the United States. Her status as a mother may have marked her as a slattern or a slut, but probably would have protected her from classification as an aggressor, a villain, an enemy of the people. But with the expansion of welfare eligibility, this was to change.[10] In considering the emergence of the Welfare Queen, I will review here just enough about the welfare arena in the late 1960s and early 1970s to provide context for the rise of this icon.[11]

In her book *The Color of Welfare*, Jill Quadagno has done an outstanding job of showing how, in the 1960s, when antipoverty programs (including the expansion of welfare eligibility) became linked to African-Americans' pursuit of civil rights, many white Americans turned sour on these social programs that benefited the poor, especially the Black poor.[12] A 1971 study of how "the public" felt about welfare concluded: "[I]t seems fair to say that many of the objections expressed by whites to current welfare programs were in effect anti-black biases, not always so thinly disguised . . . It seems likely that negative expressions about welfare and welfare recipients are a socially acceptable channel for persons with politically conservative attitudes to express a basically negative attitude toward blacks at a time when blatant expressions of prejudice are not acceptable."[13]

In fact, many white Americans came to believe in the late 1960s and early 1970s that the chief "accomplishment" of the civil rights movement and its partner, the federal government, was the creation of this bad, scamming woman: the Welfare Queen. One expert found that the media had a lot to do with assigning Blackness and negativity to this image in the civil rights era. Newspapers and magazines usually provided pictures of white people to accompany articles about "the poor" between 1950 and 1964. When the *Saturday Evening Post* published a defense of welfare in 1952 after featuring a number of harsh criticisms, the photos illustrating "The Case for Federal Relief" showed white children nicely dressed on their way to church.[14] But "starting in 1965, the complexion of the poor turned decidedly darker. From only 27% in 1964, the proportion of African Americans in pictures of the poor increased to 49% and 53% in 1965 and 1966, and then to 72% in 1967." During this period about 30 percent of poor people were African-American.

The study of representations of the poor showed that when publications depicted poor people sympathetically, the images were usually of white people, but that "pictures of African Americans [were] disproportionately used to illustrate the most negative aspects of poverty and the least sympathetic subgroups of the poor."[15] And one of the least sympathetic subgroups was the iconic poor woman of color, a "person" many Americans associated with the figure of the prostitute: she had sex for money—the money she got from the government for having children. Since her children were so ill-gotten, this woman was imagined as thoroughly alienated from them. One commentator in the *New York Times* described such a mother in 1965 as hating her children for being alive.[16] By the mid-1960s the growing belief in the Welfare Queen was reinforced by an overlapping belief that poor Black mothers were illegitimate mothers of illegitimate children, were illegitimate caretakers, and ought to get jobs.[17] (Few Americans noticed that the typical welfare mother at this time was white or that during the great expansionary period of AFDC, 1965–70, the nonwhite illegitimacy rate was declining for women twenty and older. The teenage rates for both Blacks and whites had been rising since 1940.)[18]

The Welfare Queen was an innovative icon in the 1960s, but long-entrenched public attitudes about relief and fraud and about racial minorities as workers underlay its emergence. To begin with, in the United States, the belief that poverty and the need for outside help reflect individual failing has always chafed against the impulse to be responsibly charitable. From "warning out" laws in eighteenth-century New England villages to the widespread belief that "client fraud permeated the entire relief caseload" in the Depression of the 1930s, Americans have always specialized in distinguishing the undeserving from the deserving poor.[19] Americans have never embraced relief practices that would make the poor comfortable or guarantee them dignity, and when government, church, or private attempts to help the poor have failed, we have generally blamed the poor themselves for failing to transform a pittance into family sustenance.[20] (Indeed, one could argue that the iconic Welfare Queen has been constructed out of a certain puzzle in the minds of middle-class Americans: How can poor mothers legitimately sustain their families when public assistance leaves them so desperately short of the funds necessary for supporting the minimum standard of living?)

With accelerating frequency, poor, "dependent" mothers became targets of blame across the twentieth century, as low-waged female labor was increasingly in demand to staff the burgeoning service sector. Poverty policy experts Frances Fox Piven and Richard Cloward have described this "degradation of female relief recipients as a means of regulating labor" as a project "entirely consistent with the historic uses of welfare to enforce market discipline."[21]

The policy of granting or withholding welfare benefits as a tactic for regulating the behavior of poor people and the labor market was particularly straightforward in the 1930s when it came to the African-American poor: New Deal relief policies simply excluded Blacks by barring agriculture and domestic workers from eligibility. Political scientist and welfare expert Gwendolyn Mink has shown that from the time of slavery, Black women "were often viewed as a distinct class of womanhood to which the ideal of domesticity did not apply." New Deal welfare policies reflected this attitude by imposing on African-American women something government policies would never have imposed on white women in that era: "a presumption of employability."[22]

Between the 1930s and the 1960s, African-American women were much more likely to work for wages than white women (largely because African-American men had fewer job opportunities and were paid lower wages than white men).[23] But whether African-American women collected relief or worked for wages, social commentators assessed them as less than women. If they worked, they were unwomanly because their status as family wage earners diminished the manhood of African-American men.[24] Pressure on Black mothers to take jobs during this period and beyond also reflected, as legal scholar Dorothy Roberts has put it, "the conviction that their children were socially worthless."[25] A Black mother who didn't work was violating her natural status as a worker, pretending to fulfill a mothering role she had no feel for, and staying home to look after children whose tending would do society no good.[26]

Binding these ideas about Black womanhood and Black motherhood and work together was the idea that African-American women were unnaturally strong and powerful in relation to their men, that they presided, unnaturally, over matriarchal households. From the 1930s into the 1960s, it was quite common to encounter assessments of race relations in the United States that identified this female dominance in the African-American household as the "primary impediment to African American equality."[27]

From the mid-1960s into the 1970s, when the effects of the civil rights movement and the programs of the War on Poverty vastly expanded welfare rolls, many white Americans drew on these older attitudes about welfare, welfare chiselers, and African-American women as they responded to the changes. And the changes *were* dramatic. Between 1958 and 1977, for example, government expenditures on aid to families with dependent children rose from $800 million a year to $11 billion.[28] Put another way, in 1960 3.1 million people received this aid; by 1965 the number had risen to 4.3 million, by 1969 to 6.1 million. By 1974 10.8 million people were supported by welfare benefits.[29]

Equally dramatic, the institutions of government, perhaps most notably the U.S. Supreme Court, supported welfare expansion by creating a whole new array of rights for poor people. Many of these newly defined rights defended the dignity and the choice-making capacity of poor mothers dependent on welfare.[30] Congressional acts extended coverage to 800,000 new recipients by 1972, and welfare administrators were much more likely to certify applicants for eligibility than they had been. In Atlanta, for example, between 1960 and 1968, the acceptance rate climbed from 35 percent to 72 percent, in Philadelphia from 49 percent to 74 percent, and in New York from 56 percent to 78 percent. By 1970 the national acceptance rate was 81 percent.[31]

Exploding welfare expenditures, startling new rights accorded recipients, generous eligibility standards—and the increasing value of the AFDC check (up 67 percent from 1963 to 1971)[32]—benefited the ballooning number of poor women heading families.[33] There were many devastating causes of what came to be known as "the feminization of poverty," but one very direct cause in the 1950s and 1960s was the severe impact of deindustrialization in the United States.[34] As historian Thomas Sugrue has made so clear, cities with large industrial workforces, including African-American male workers, lost hundreds of thousands of jobs as manufacturing plants moved out of Detroit, Chicago, Buffalo, St. Louis, New York, Pittsburgh, Philadelphia, Baltimore, Trenton, and Boston. Between 1947 and 1963, Sugrue found, Detroit alone lost 134,000 manufacturing jobs. Discriminatory hiring and firing practices and selective plant closings created poor job prospects for African-American men.[35]

Deindustrialization continued across the 1960s and into the 1970s. Nationwide, young black men were "especially hard hit." A congressional report noted in this period that "their measured unemployment rate was 35.4%, five times that of the labor force as a whole."[36] A Detroit public official testified at a congressional hearing in the early 1970s that "Detroit continues to be classified as a Class C area by the Department of Labor, due to its high and persistent unemployment rate . . . Plants are moving out or closing, with workers laid off, pension benefits lost . . . [while] the cost of living has gone up six percent in the past year." The official reported that "discrimination continues against the black worker" and stressed the role these economic and social factors played in boosting public assistance payments to mothers and their children in Michigan. Payments rose 36.5 percent between January 1971 and January 1972—a time of intensifying public hostility toward welfare mothers.[37]

Elements of the public that expressed hostility toward poor mothers (especially poor African-American mothers) did not connect the plight of poor mothers to deindustrialization. They did not generally speak about how the loss of good jobs was transforming working-class families (or potential families) into the nonworking poor.[38] As legal scholar Linda McClain has pointed out, "storytelling about persons in poverty that is not attentive to such structural causes" invites conclusions about "personal responsibility and irresponsibility."[39] After the midpoint of the century, hostility toward poor women comprised old prejudices and also a new set of ideas about women, work, and reproduction. Blanche Coll, a longtime welfare policy administrator, remembered that starting in the 1960s, "Everyone knew that choice [about waged work] was no longer an option for ADC mothers."[40] And Blanche Bernstein, a prominent urban policy analyst and administrator, explained this development in 1973: "[I]t was the assumption at the time of the passage of the Social Security act [of 1935] that [needy] women could not, or perhaps should not, work." But, Bernstein stressed, "attitudes have changed."[41] Indeed, across the 1970s, the number of children with mothers in the workforce was approaching—and then surpassed—the number of children with mothers at home.[42]

When politicians, policy analysts, and ordinary people read in the morning newspaper about exploding welfare rolls and welfare costs, they questioned first of all whether all these women, paid with taxpayers' money to stay home, had any *value* in the home. Increasingly, the general public believed they did not.[43] Many Americans wanted to know how poor women had the right to stay home while such large numbers of other mothers went out to work. One group of analysts pinpointed the year 1970 as the moment when "exempting welfare mothers from employment when half of all mothers were working no longer seemed justified."[44]

Another new question that flared across the welfare landscape at this time was whether poor women should get to *choose* welfare over work if it turned out that they could do better financially on relief. Welfare expert Mimi Abramovitz has shown how, indeed, welfare "became an economically rational choice for some poor women" by the early 1970s, as the AFDC grant grew by 75 percent between 1960 and 1970, while an average worker's earnings rose by only 48 percent. By 1970, in many states, a woman on AFDC would have more money to support her family from the grant than she would make at a minimum wage job.[45]

Superimposed on all these ways of questioning the legitimacy of federal supports for poor mothers was the biggest question of all: Do welfare mothers have children in order to get welfare grants? Do they have additional children to get bigger grants? Many Americans were certain that this was the way poor, dependent (African-American) women generally calculated and exercised a bizarre kind of economic "rational choice"—

sex and pregnancy for federal funds. Daniel Patrick Moynihan, then domestic policy adviser to President Nixon, pointed out that members of the American middle class "would never dream of having another baby in order to get hold of an additional eight or twelve dollars a month." But, he wrote, these people "instantly conclude that out of depravity, cupidity, ignorance, or whatever, the poor would automatically do so."[46] Bearing out Moynihan's observation, two social welfare analysts found in 1974 that "popular, political, and professional support for the 'Brood Sow' myth seems to be common."[47] After all, between 1960, when the birth control pill came on the market, and 1973, when abortion was legalized, *Americans got used to thinking of pregnancy and childbearing in terms of choice.*[48] Pairing expanded access to AFDC money with motherhood-as-a-choice played a significant role in fixing gender on "welfare cheats." By the early 1970s, "chiseler" was becoming archaic; everybody recognized the Welfare Queen.

It is important to underscore that this new kind of thinking about women and welfare captured the poor mother as the symbol of *the dependent woman who makes bad choices.* When the typical recipient of public assistance had been the family headed by a poor white mother, likely a widow, *choice* was a limited category for the recipient, but not a bizarre category. A poor white widow was expected to make decisions about her role as a mother. In 1942 the federal Bureau of Public Assistance defended a mother's "right to choose aid," seconding the position of the War Manpower Commission, the agency charged with addressing labor shortages. According to one policy historian, "The bureau also criticized local welfare agencies for encouraging mothers of young children to look for jobs and called for higher assistance payments so they could stay at home where they were needed."[49] After World War II, the 1946 federal *Handbook of Public Assistance* defined the value of ADC, explaining that the grant should "make it possible for a mother to choose between staying at home to care for her children and taking a job away from home." The role of the public assistance agency, according to the handbook, was to "help the mother arrive at a decision that will best meet her own needs and those of her children." The important issue was to make it possible for this mother "to exercise some degree of choice."[50]

As soon as childbearing was linked with choice, however, and African-American women became eligible for benefits, "choice" acquired a bad odor in the world of welfare. As one analyst put it at the dawn of the era of choice, "The free choice these [ADC] mothers once had is now being eroded . . . The extent of the pressure on the mother [to work] measures the diminution of her freedom to choose."[51]

One welfare mother, a Detroit-area welfare rights activist named Mamie Blankley, responded in the early 1970s to the plethora of accusations against her kind and their putative bad choices as poor mothers. Note that this woman took on the ubiquitous comparison with middle-class mothers in her own way. She said:

> Let us talk a minute about a one-parent family. That woman has to be . . . mother and father . . . Why do we presume that [she] does not work? Raising a family is probably the hardest job around—and it certainly takes more than forty hours a week. No one talks about the middle-class woman who hires household help so she can go to Vic Tanny's or play bridge and returns home in time to cook frozen dinners . . . But the ADC mother is always pictured as unconcerned with her children's needs. And if she stays home to raise her children herself, she is lazy.

Insisting that even a poor mother on welfare was a legitimate mother and a valid choice maker, this woman argued, "Only a mother knows if her family will run reasonably if she is gone fifty hours a week. She should never be forced to work away from home."[52]

FOCUSED HOSTILITY: THE "WELFARE NIGHTMARE" IN THE 1970s

Mamie Blankley was defending poor mothers to a public largely convinced in the early 1970s that women like herself were responsible for the behemoth welfare mess that bedeviled Congress and the states and was said to be bleeding the taxpayers dry. A contemporaneous description of the "continuing frustration" of the members of the House of Representatives Ways and Means Committee demonstrates how elected officials experienced the "welfare mess" in this era: "*Disappointed* in the effects of the 1962 provisions [focusing on rehabilitative services], the

Committee concluded five years later that its approach to social services had proved a *failure*, and it recognized instead the need to prepare AFDC clients for work. But in 1970 it affirmed, and in 1971 reaffirmed its *disappointment* with the results of the work experience efforts" (italics added).[53]

The committee's disappointment and frustration were understandable: the WIN (job training and work incentive) program that was supposed to "stem the welfare tide" in the late 1960s and early 1970s did no such thing.[54] In fact, between mid-1969 and mid-1971, the AFDC caseload swelled by one million cases.[55] Middle-class, white Americans, grappling with the accomplishments of the civil rights movement, with antiwar activism and cultural upheaval, with inflation, rising unemployment, and then with oil shortages in the early 1970s, did not have a chance, or the motivation, to get used to "welfare justice" before the experts began to say that the welfare system had spiraled into a welfare nightmare.[56]

Demoralization in Congress during this period was a shadow of the demoralization—the craziness—on the front lines, where "wall-to-wall people" showed up in welfare offices every day for help. Administrators and caseworkers described a bureaucracy that drove employees and clients to distraction and beyond. A New York worker described how, in the early 1970s, client records "were being stored in stacks of beer cartons."[57] In Detroit, an eligibility examiner explained how she fielded frantic calls and anxious clients one after the other all day while facilitating address changes, rent verification, budget computations and changes, newborn additions to grants, restoration of utilities, deposits for utilities and shelter, lost check affidavits, food orders, home repairs, eyeglasses and dental estimates, supplements to cover increased needs, transportation for medical reasons, and questions about real estate. In addition, the examiner noted, "This does not include service provided to the client in initial contact necessary to refer them to a social worker, or the eligibility reinvestigation," the only duties the worker was actually credited with each month.[58]

Welfare workers carried out this vast array of duties in a bureaucratic hell. One Atlanta worker complained of the red tape she had to deal with: "[T]o process one client for eligibility for public assistance requires as many as twenty-seven forms."[59] Another, in New York, using despairing syntax to match the situation, explained, "We have so many overlapping procedures that come to us constantly and sometimes in my center you don't even have the procedure." Summing up the pervasive sense of bureaucratic breakdown, an official said in 1972, "So what it all boils down to is this: under existing law we can make rules, plead for compliance, document the chaos, and pay the bills—that's it."

Not surprisingly, clients found contact with the welfare bureaucracy unbearable. As one person in the system observed, "clients come in [and] find out there is no dignity in the center, no dignity in the program."[60] For starters, the system did not attempt to communicate with clients in a way they could comprehend. One study in the 1970s found that "about 75% of the AFDC clients possess reading skills of, at most, an eighth grade level. Yet . . . only about one in ten [of the forms, notices, and pamphlets] is comprehensible to an eighth-grade reader, while over one-third [of the welfare materials a recipient must read] require the reading skills of a college student."[61] Given this situation, clients often failed to return forms promptly or fill them out accurately.

In addition, welfare programs and their work demands on clients were often very poorly conceived and implemented. A Brookings Institution study in the early 1970s found, for example, that women who participated in the WIN program and subsequently failed to get a job—a group that included the vast majority of participants—ended up more resigned to welfare and less confident of themselves than when they entered the program.[62] Historian James Patterson described the utter failure of WIN in these terms: "Of the 2.8 million welfare recipients eligible for WIN in 1967, only about 700,000 were deemed by local authorities to be 'appropriate for referral.' The rest were ill, needed at home, considered untrainable, or without access to day care . . . [Eventually] only 52,000 or less than two percent of the total pool, actually were employed—at an average wage of around two dollars an hour."[63]

The profound frustrations associated with living in poverty and dealing with the bureaucratic and programmatic ineptitudes of the welfare system contributed to client eruptions that made headlines and defined recipients for the public. Less well publicized were physical attacks on welfare recipients looking for help in welfare centers. When welfare rights activist Theresa Funiciello faced Daniel Patrick Moynihan (by then a senator from New York) across a hearing table in 1978, she explained what some recipients faced: a kind of "brutality" that might include not receiving the check you'd been promised and also "getting your teeth kicked in." Funiciello said, "We have documented [this]. We have tried to give it to the politicians. We have tried to give it to administrators. The administrators are not believing it, or interested in it."[64]

Welfare workers in New York and elsewhere described how their totally inadequate training and the prevailing system of no set caseload and no set appointments left them completely unprepared for dealing with ordinary, well-behaved clients and especially with the extremely frustrated ones. Workers catalogued incidents where clients used derogatory language "that cannot be found in any dictionary," and where clients did worse, coming to centers brandishing weapons, threatening and even attacking workers.[65] The director of the Department of Social Services of Wayne County, Michigan, put the situation bluntly at a congressional hearing: "Due to the problems we have in terms of the number of clients, the limited staff, the proliferation of directives staff must follow, and the frequent changes in policies, rules, and regulations, [the system] is fast becoming a nightmare."[66] Such intense frustration on the part of legislators, administrators, service providers, and recipients in the period of welfare expansion demanded a scapegoat.

The general public couldn't have agreed more, as politicians, analysts, and bureaucrats oversaw a welfare system hurtling out of control. The public found its scapegoat in the national welfare rights movement that began to "stake its claims before local welfare agencies and before the Supreme Court" in the mid-1960s.[67] With the rise of a "rights" movement and cadres of vocal spokespersons, the public now had trouble imagining the "traditional," shamed, docile, single mother as a humble supplicant receiving benefits at the discretion of local government. Now many Americans woke up to mothers claiming—speaking loudly in public about—human dignity and "welfare rights."[68] Women were standing up in public and talking about how poor mothers were *owed* welfare benefits. As historian Deborah Grey White has written, "In defining themselves and in meeting their needs, organized black feminists and women on welfare defined black women to the nation."[69]

Indeed, by the end of the 1960s, most cities were home to visible groups of welfare mothers who were seeing their own circumstances through new eyes. Many of these women shaped their new perspectives into activist groups and into alliances with the National Welfare Rights Organization.[70] An African-American mother in Minneapolis, for example, described the changes she was going through this way: "A couple of weeks ago [a group of welfare recipients] went down to the welfare department because I wanted some money for a new bed." First there was a "hassle," and then, the woman said, "My eligibility technician . . . threw a big pile of papers at me and said I would have to sign [them]. I told her I didn't like her attitude and asked to see her supervisor. I can't imagine myself doing that two years ago."[71]

Another Minneapolis woman, Edna Eberly, explained why she and other recipients realized they "needed to band together" in the mid-1960s: a local legislator accused these women of trading their children around so that each mother could collect more benefits. The mothers simply got sick of being put down, degraded, and defined out of the human race because they were poor and needed help. They also had the example of the civil rights movement and its successes to inspire their own welfare rights activism. Banding together, pooling resources and information, made them feel more dignified, much stronger, and more capable of defining and defending themselves. One woman described how belonging to a welfare organization changed her: "My husband says I'm very militant now . . . I know a lot more things than I used to . . . People outside or on TV say, 'This is happening; this is the way it's supposed to be.' I'll sit there and say, 'That's a goddamn lie.' "[72] (Academics at the time validated this woman's perspective, finding that "welfare participants who are familiar with the local welfare rights organization are less likely to feel stigmatized than are others.")[73]

Welfare workers were quite well aware of what was happening with these groups. One "income maintenance specialist" noted that since recipients began to join "these groups . . . that are telling clients what their rights are . . . sometimes they can quote your procedure better than you can." She was not happy about the fact that women showed up at her office now with an attitude like, "You are supposed to have this and that, and you go to the center and demand it." Another worker complained that the "client action groups" were teaching women to "come to us and say they are entitled." These groups, she said, inform the client "that they're entitled to this, that, and the other thing," and "they come in here and they seem to know, and if you check it through you find out they were correct. They are correct." Summing up the problem, a welfare worker declared in 1972, "They feel it is their right. They come in and say, 'I want my money.' That is the way they tell you. 'I want my money and you're going to give me my money before I leave this center.' "[74]

When the media covered welfare mothers' militancy and their demands—their insistence on participating as decision makers in their own lives—Americans who already opposed welfare "handouts" had "strong reactions."[75] For one thing, during this period of welfare expansion and the formation of welfare rights organizations, the American public went from believing that the government spent "too little" on welfare to believing that the government was spending "too much."[76] In the late 1960s, with about 25 million Americans still living in poverty, 71 percent of the public believed that "many people getting welfare are not honest about their needs."[77] At about the same time, a University of Texas survey showed that 84 percent of Americans resented the average monthly welfare payment of $65.72 to single, poor mothers and their children because they believed "too many people who should be working are on relief."[78] Showing how wrong academic observers can sometimes be, one researcher looked at the activist poor and predicted that Americans would admire them for the effort.[79]

The fact that welfare had become so thoroughly racialized—so typically associated with people of color—despite the fact that most recipients were white, matched old racist convictions that Blacks lacked commitment to the work ethic and didn't deserve help. Media expert Martin Gilens points out that the Americans who mistakenly believed that most recipients were Black were more likely to believe that welfare recipients were "the undeserving poor."[80] They were also more likely to suggest that the solution to poverty was to put Blacks to work. (Interestingly, when "viewers" in a study of attitudes about poverty and race were shown a story about poor whites, they "were more likely to suggest societal solutions [to poverty] such as creating more low skilled jobs or reducing interest rates.")[81]

When Richard Nixon, running for president, described the United States between 1963 and 1968 as a country "deluged by government programs for the unemployed, programs for cities, programs for the poor," he was invoking an image most Americans recognized as the land ruled by the Welfare Queen. This was, for Nixon and his constituency, a reign identified with "failure across the land."[82] (Recently released Oval Office tapes of Richard Nixon and his aides discussing welfare pick up the president: "We're going to [place] more of those little Negro bastards on the welfare rolls at $2400 a family . . . Let people like Pat Moynihan and Len Garment and others believe in all that crap. But I don't believe in it . . . Work, work, throw 'em off the rolls.")[83]

As the era of the civil rights movement (and welfare expansion) had begun, public policy experts and others had identified objectionable African-American mothers as matriarchs—a breed of women defined by their unnatural strength and sometimes by their inexplicable ability passively to *endure*. Coming out of the civil rights era, the matriarch, with the assistance of the federal government, had acquired *agency*, a (false or deluded) sense of her rights and entitlements: she had become the Welfare Queen.

In one of the era's most intimate, familiar, richly detailed—fulsome—portraits of the Welfare Queen, the strongest emanation is the absolute sham of the recipient's sense of entitlement. Susan Sheehan, a journalist with a special interest in the lives of poor women, found a perfect subject in 1975: a New York–dwelling Puerto Rican mother of a number of children sired by a number of different men.[84] "Mrs. Santana's" life, as presented, surely seemed bizarre, out of control, and parasitical to the middle-class and affluent readers of the *New Yorker*.[85] The portrait draws on all the aspects of the welfare nightmare that middle-class Americans confronted regularly in the media.

As a classic Queen, Mrs. Santana's sense of entitlement here is a symptom of pathological dissociation. In reality, Mrs. Santana commands nothing. As Sheehan puts it, this woman "makes little real effort to dominate circumstances; though she likes to draw up plans and gives every appearance of intending to carry them out, they are soon forgotten." Mrs. Santana's general lack of command is related to her infantile relation both to time ("She is at ease with time, which is to say that she pays as little attention to it as possible . . . it would never occur to her to turn the time to her advantage by reading or sewing") and to money ("Mrs. Santana has never subscribed to a magazine, owned a car, a rug, or an air conditioner, or bought insurance, but she and her [nine] children love clothes and spend about two thousand five hundred dollars a year to dress themselves in the latest styles").[86] Sheehan makes it clear that a Welfare

Queen is a child, playing dress-up in an ill-fitting, ill-begotten grown-up costume: Mrs. Santana spends great chunks of her day watching TV cartoons. She is "an ardent fan of 'Bugs Bunny,' 'The Flintstones,' and 'Huckleberry Hound.' "

Mrs. Santana's reality is so sharply dissociated from the true reality of ordinary folks, like *New Yorker* readers, that she is "unaware of the resentment felt by many taxpayers against people living on welfare." According to Sheehan, Mrs. Santana doesn't "feel embarrassed or degraded" by welfare. The reader could easily conclude that she takes welfare "matter-of-factly" since she believes that people like herself have "the right" to public support. Surely most distressing of all to the reader is Sheehan's description of Mrs. Santana's casual attitude toward committing welfare fraud, or what Sheehan calls "cheating." Sheehan writes, "Mrs. Santana has no qualms about 'cheating on the welfare.' Almost everyone she knows cheats on the welfare." Her friends and relations cheat by living, off the record, with employed though often very poorly paid fathers of their children, or by working themselves, selling cosmetics door-to-door, for example.[87]

Mrs. Santana, as portrayed by Susan Sheehan, was a specimen of what Ronald Reagan called a "pig at the trough."[88] She was the epitome of the grotesquerie many Americans claimed had been created by—and was now presiding over—the equal opportunity state of the 1970s. Reagan, U.S. Representative Martha Griffiths of Michigan, and many other politicians argued that the law—federal welfare legislation together with recent Supreme Court decisions that created new rights for poor people and protected existing rights—enabled the emergence of the Welfare Queen. As Griffiths put it in the early 1970s, "The law is breaking up the home. This is all coming straight out of Washington . . . The law is saying . . . leave your husband because then we will pick you up on welfare."[89] Griffiths argued vociferously, again and again, that since the federal government allowed the states to provide different levels of welfare assistance, people moved around the country looking for the best welfare deal. Poor people were lazy and opportunistic, according to the congresswoman, but the law supported their behavior.[90]

Many critics of welfare and of the Welfare Queen believed that women like Mamie Blankley, the welfare rights activist in Detroit, who resisted "slave labor" jobs at wages nobody could live on, "let alone a family," were bad women, bad mothers, the products of bad laws. When Mamie Blankley argued that welfare mothers should be able to decide for themselves whether they were "more valuable at home or on the job," many Americans believed this was an expression of the central delusion that the welfare system imparted to Welfare Queens.

WELFARE FRAUD IN THE 1970s

Americans read accounts of Welfare Queens like Sheehan's Mrs. Santana and they saw a massed phalanx of poor women of color freely choosing to cheat the government, the welfare office, and the taxpaying public. In 1976, 85 percent of the respondents to a Lou Harris poll agreed that "too many people on welfare cheat by getting money they are not entitled to." According to the analysts John Gordiner and Theodore Lyman, "exposés of welfare queens," the new emblem of the inauthentic, scamming poor, began to "overshadow" all discussion of the causes of poverty and shape the content of welfare policy.[91]

By the early 1970s, the public and its legislative representatives were remarkably focused on conjuring up and bringing down the Welfare Queen, despite the fact that many experts admitted (still) knowing almost nothing about the true extent of fraud. To a startling degree, the lack of good data about fraud did not stop commentators from defining the system and its recipients as drenched in fraud. In San Francisco, a welfare worker reported in 1971 that she and her colleagues had been instructed to accept no pregnancy verifications from the Black Women's Free Clinic and other clinics because welfare supervisors claimed too many pregnancy reports were "frauds." The welfare worker remarked, "Nothing in my experience verifies [this charge]."[92] Lawrence Mead, the New York University urban policy specialist who was frequently invited to testify before Congress about the ills of welfare, opined in this general period (while providing no data), "[T]he main objection that ordinary voters and citizens have about welfare is not the cost . . . it's the abuses they perceive to be involved in the system, fraud and abuse . . . especially nonwork."[93] A 1974 congressional staff study affirmed that welfare policies created incentives for poor families to break up, for poor women to have babies, and for poor mothers to avoid work. The study could not show that actual persons took these actions in order to obtain benefits. But the main thrust of the report, "Welfare in the 1970s: A National Study of Welfare Benefits Available in 100 Local Areas," was to "leave little doubt" that actual persons behaved immorally or made very bad choices in order to collect AFDC.[94]

Again, with no data to back up the portrait, U.S. Representative Frederick Richmond of New York described how the Welfare Queen began her fraudulent career, as "a woman, a young girl with no job . . . a high school dropout [who] has only one easy out and that's to have a child." According to the congressman and to millions of Americans, this resourceless innocent makes rational if bad choices as she launches her life of dependency. The congressman continued, "Now in all likelihood that young girl didn't want to leave her family's house. She isn't really ready for the responsibility that comes with having a child. Basically she was just unhappy with her life. She couldn't read, she couldn't write, she wasn't trained for a job. She figured her only future was to go ahead and become the head of her own household so that she could go on welfare. Now, we all know these facts."[95]

A U.S. representative from North Carolina claimed in 1977 that his constituents were deeply suspicious of welfare recipients and probably rightfully so. "In my part of the country where the per capita income is very low, I find that the chief concern about welfare is the belief that there are people drawing it who are ineligible. Now that may not be true. But people working hard for a living see other people driving up in big automobiles to pick up food stamps, and they see welfare recipients buy steaks when they know they cannot afford these things themselves."[96] This was, of course, an old theme. In the 1930s, "any luxury suggested either hidden assets or misuse of relief monies. Anecdotes circulated of women on relief getting permanent waves and of relief recipients picking up their food orders in cars. The farmers adjacent to Muncie, Indiana, protested that relief recipients bought cigarettes and malt."[97] In this vein, President Reagan proposed new laws in 1981 that would enable states to send investigators into homes of welfare recipients to ensure that there were "no signs of excessive wealth."[98]

Prominent social scientists did write and speak out against the public's vision of the scamming queen, but to little effect. One study produced for Congress in the early 1970s found that AFDC did not have an impact on "the format of female-headed families, age of marriage, marital status, or the stability of marriages in either the white or the non-white populations . . . [or on] illegitimacy rates."[99] One of the authors of this report, Phillips Cutright, a prominent family sociologist, endorsed this against-the-grain assertion: "If the past AFDC program has not produced a clear-cut effect on marital behavior for three decades, it seems unreasonable to believe that a future program . . . [would]."[100]

Politicians rarely cited such studies, even when the studies had been prepared for them. Most politicians seemed to prefer the sensational queen, whose existence was typically proved by vague, agentless, even obscure observations such as this one: "Although the intricacy and subjectivity of welfare policies have so far prevented accurate measurement of the rates of ineligible and incorrect payments, estimates run high."[101]

Mildred Rein, a welfare analyst writing in the early 1970s, argued that policy makers focused on fraud at this time because fraud was a less controversial way of winnowing the rolls than instituting effective work requirements. Kicking people off for cheating the system was less costly than creating jobs or elaborate work incentives or paying wages that were higher than welfare benefits. Most important, a focus on fraud was acceptable to both liberals and conservatives.[102] When Ronald Reagan, as governor of California, invoked the Welfare Queen ("The other day a woman died in Sacramento. She had been on welfare for fifteen years—and we discovered after she died that she had $88,000, owned a couple of pieces of property . . ."), Americans responded.[103] Americans also responded to Representative Martha Griffiths, who held hearings on welfare around the country in the early 1970s. At every hearing, Griffiths, conflating public opinion, welfare myths, and real life, posed versions of this question over and over: "Well, let me ask you, one of the things that evidently everybody . . . resents the most is that there are some people apparently on ADC, living in air-conditioned houses with swimming pools. How do they do it?"[104] Over time, convincing Americans that welfare fraud was rampant was crucial to the argument that welfare allocations could be cut without hurting the truly needy.[105]

One way Americans responded to "rampant fraud" was by creating "fraud control units" in major cities—New York set up its unit in 1971. Washington, D.C.'s Department of Human Resources announced at the beginning of 1972 that it would hire forty-five new investigators. The department had to answer to welfare rights activists about how these new workers would be deployed. Etta Horn, the president of the D.C. Welfare Rights Organization, reflected recent history and expressed the fears of welfare recipients when she told Joseph Yodell, the district's newly hired welfare administrator, "We want no surveillance of our homes, no searches and seizures, nobody looking under the beds, no questions of the neighbors, no degrading questions, and no Gestapo tactics." And Yodell showed the status that welfare rights activists had achieved in some quarters (if not in the minds of most Americans) when he promised Horn that there would be "no return to the day of investigators looking under beds." He also promised that he would not make final decisions about how the investigators would be deployed "without further consultation with Mrs. Horn's group and other interested parties."[106]

With or without the approval of welfare rights activists, however, departments of public assistance in most cities dedicated massive resources in the early 1970s to identifying fraudulent claims. Welfare activist and scholar Richard Cloward claimed that "for every dollar that is disbursed by local departments, it costs them twenty-five cents because of the enormous paperwork and investigatory procedures, the enormous pressure they're under to detect cheating."[107]

At this time, the dawn of the age of bureaucratic computer applications, major sums for information systems were underwriting efforts, as Governor Hugh Carey of New York put it, "to increase our ability to detect fraud."[108] Generally, states reported more fraud as better computer systems were installed.[109] A 1977 government report indicated that "cases of potential fraud climbed dramatically" between 1971 and 1975, but acknowledged that the rise "appears to be more a reflection of increased detection efforts on the part of the states than . . . increases in the actual incidence of fraud." In fact, this report (like others) concluded, "the real extent of fraud in the AFDC Program is basically unknown."[110] But again, politicians knew that "fraud" served them well. The governor of Illinois, Dan Walker, for example, "made big headlines and received widespread media coverage when he announced a massive computerized crackdown on welfare cheats" in 1973. One Chicago journalist explained what Walker accomplished with this "computer crackdown," even though it turned out that his claims had almost no factual basis, or at least none that Walker's investigators turned up: "While

Walker's crackdown story made a big splash, five months later only seventeen cases in Cook County [Chicago] had been acted on. One story appeared then, but months went by without further follow-up. So the public's final impression was not that the government might have been making a sensational pitch for its own purposes, but that the poor were ripping off the taxpayer again."[111]

The Department of Health, Education, and Welfare convened a national conference on fraud in 1978. The computer expert who ran a session called "The Role of Computer Technology in Fraud Detection" observed, "The situation in late 1978 in regard to the use of computers for detecting fraud can be best described as immature adolescence."[112] This may have been a generous appraisal, considering how wildly different computer-assisted estimates of fraud were in the 1970s. Computers in the New York City Department of Social Services, for example, estimated that the city's welfare fraud rate was between 2 and 4 percent, while the New York State bureaucracy calculated the city's rate at 20 to 30 percent. In late 1971, the state's newly appointed welfare inspector general, George F. Berlinger, hired to "weed out corruption, fraud, and inefficient administrative practices," raved about the "extent" of fraud in the city. But Robert F. Carroll, an official in the city's Human Resources Administration, denied Berlinger's charges and said the Inspector General was merely casting "doubt and suspicion on the poor." Carroll said, "During the six months since the creation of [Berlinger's] office, not a single fraud case has been referred to the District Attorney and only nineteen unsubstantiated cases were referred to the Department of Social Services, five of which were child abuse cases, having nothing to do with fraud."[113]

Figuring out how many Welfare Queens were out there remained depressingly difficult. But one welfare bureaucrat in Detroit at the time showed why precise information was so important when he expressed his optimism about Michigan's new computer system in these terms: "It is going to be very helpful in changing the attitudes of many people who now react on the basis of opinion. [With the new computer system,] we can base decisions on fact."[114]

When the new computer systems at fraud control units in New York City and elsewhere started spitting out data in the 1970s, the nature of that data may have surprised some, like Lawrence Mead, who were thoroughly convinced that "nonwork" was the big problem ("If more of the poor were working the major public upset with welfare would be alleviated").[115] In fact, the data were revealing that the scammers were people like the twenty-nine-year-old mother of three who worked as a clerk at the Police Department, the five women employed as aides, clerks, and paraprofessionals at the New York City Board of Education, and the therapy assistant at Brooklyn's Kingsbridge Veterans Hospital. All of these were mothers of young children, all working a substantial number of hours each week for public agencies, and all paid wages that did not enable these employees to support their families.[116]

Jet magazine described the plight of one such working mother, "who said she was only trying to make ends meet" by collecting welfare at the same time that she had a job as a clerk. This mother of four, facing up to fifteen years in prison for fraud, explained that her salary of $169 a week was not enough to survive on, so she figured out a way—albeit illegal—to get enough welfare money to cover the rent and "family needs." Fully aware of how the public would evaluate her and her "scam," this woman "dismissed the idea that all those accused of bilking welfare use the funds to buy luxuries." She said, "A lot of these people aren't driving fancy cars." The sympathetic journalist for *Jet*, a magazine aimed at the African-American community, noted that "like her, many other working single mothers are getting welfare and they're taking that extra money and buying their kids shoes. They're trying to feed their children."[117]

Early computerized welfare fraud studies (designed to match the names of welfare recipients and public employees) enabled the media to show that many scammers were also workers. But politicians and others pushed on with the project of associating welfare with lazy, fraudulent queens.[118] They talked about welfare cheats and proposed ways of catching them. In the mid-1970s, some states established toll-free hot lines to solicit tips from people claiming to have information about fraudulent activities.[119] One was set up in Illinois—a state where "front page headlines and TV and radio news blare[d] WELFARE COSTS SOAR 20 PERCENT, WELFARE ROLLS DISPLAY HEFTY HIKE, WELFARE QUEEN ARRESTED."[120] A welfare worker in Atlanta described how she encouraged clients to check up on each other and let the office "know if something is amiss." For example, she said, a client might call her up and say, "Mrs. Brown lives down the street and her husband lives there and they are both working and they have two Cadillacs out in the yard." This worker acknowledged that "often these are just quack calls." Another Atlanta case manager, when pressed about how much fraud she saw, reported that she knew of only one case—where a father said that his kids were with him part-time, but in fact the mother had full custody.[121]

The Massachusetts state commissioner of welfare was similarly disturbed by the "overemphasis on fraud" at a time when his state reported an "AFDC error rate of 4.1%—and the Internal Revenue Service reported an error rate of 18%." This state official argued strenuously before Congress that trying to reduce fraud was "very cost ineffective," and also reflected a poor sense of priorities. "We will spend more money trying to get down to . . . [a] low . . . error rate than we do on the entire employment and training program in Massachusetts or the WIN program nationally. I really think," the commissioner added, "it is a totally misguided effort."[122]

Most Americans imagined the alleged welfare scammer in the 1970s as a tricky African-American single mother with "too many" children, and few newspapers or public officials challenged this version with alternative facts. Instead, the media was a central force in promulgating news and solidifying attitudes about the Welfare Queen and welfare fraud. In April 1973, for example, *Business Week* published a two-panel cartoon under the headline "How Welfare Keeps Women From Working." On the left was a picture of a slim, well-dressed woman shopping alone. She was holding a modest-sized paycheck in her hand, looking mildly discontent. The panel on the right depicted a fat, happy, garishly dressed mama in the grocery store. The mother was pushing a shopping cart that was labeled AFDC and crammed with five little kids, food, foodstamps, and housing subsidies. She was holding a huge "welfare benefits" check in her pudgy hand.[123]

Melba Blanton, a reporter for an alternative newspaper in Oklahoma in the same era, provided a tutorial regarding how newspapers broadcast the worst impression of fraud-prone welfare recipients:

When newspapers publish an account describing some flagrant abuse by a welfare recipient, check the dateline. Did this happen 1,500 miles from Oklahoma in a community you have never visited and where you know no one (and where you have no way of checking the situation yourself)? One incident of welfare abuse is instantly picked up and carried by major newspapers countrywide; it has news value not only because it is rare, but also because it reinforces the "scape-goat" "prostitute" image that is desirable to many.[124]

Given this situation, it makes sense that the National Welfare Rights Organization and the Black Feminist Organization—which together had complex agendas focusing on workers' rights, reproductive rights, health care, education, and job training—gave "day care and the media's portrayal of black women [top] priority."[125]

But few other Americans were willing to defend an unpopular figure associated with the "rip-off of the rest of the nation by Black people." Members of the first generation of nationally prominent Black politicians, such as Mayor Richard Hatcher of Gary, Indiana, did speak out in defense of welfare recipients, but it was a lonely job. Hatcher noted "that the same people who have fits about welfare fraud have very few fits about equally illegal and much more egregious fraud in the Defense Department or in the professional, corporate, and business side of life." More pointedly, Hatcher complained that after investigative columnist Jack Anderson uncovered hundreds of millions of dollars of military-related government waste, he didn't hear "an outcry equal in volume to that which one hears when someone is labeled by the press a 'welfare queen.' " Hatcher suggested a solution: "Maybe we need to add our 'welfare queens' to our 'military hardware kings' to right the balance a little."[126]

To be sure, in the 1970s and beyond, it was difficult for the average American to assess what was going on, good or bad, in the welfare system. The public statements of politicians and administrators and others were typically contentious, contradictory, and highly ideological. In the 1980s, President Reagan and his congressional allies regularly associated poor women with fraud, for example by championing a national data bank to ferret out welfare cheats.[127] In 1982, along with National School Bus Safety Week and Alzheimer's Week, Congress resolved to establish National Welfare Fraud Prevention Week.[128] Government officials argued broadly about who was responsible for the welfare mess—the federal government, the states, the cities, the welfare bureaucracy, or the

Welfare Queen. They also argued more narrowly about whether the system was most beset by fraud or by the errors of welfare workers. How the media—and then the average American—came to resolve these questions had consequential implications for a country struggling with issues of race and gender equality and a nascent antistatist conservatism.[129]

It simply made sense to more than 80 percent of Americans that the Welfare Queen was cheating because she could get away with it in "a chaotic do-it-yourself system" that was "cheating the whole nation."[130] In addition, as one journalist observed, media enthralled with the queen have "funneled energies away from investigations dealing with the quality of welfare programs and their ability to help people."[131]

WHY AMERICANS BELIEVED IN THE WELFARE QUEEN IN THE 1970s

For a number of reasons (in addition to historical ascriptions), the Welfare Queen made sense to most Americans in the early 1970s as a way to explain the "welfare mess" and the role that welfare played in creating national problems, local chaos, and personal grievances. And in the early 1970s, the sense of multilevel malaise and helplessness was pervasive.[132] In an early, sour response to the political and cultural upheavals of the 1960s and the economic stagnation of the 1970s, many Americans identified poor women and the system supporting them as the sources of the ills besetting the country. One commentator noted, "Inflation, high taxes, large deficits, even an impoverished national defense [were] all laid at the doorstep of excessive welfare expenditures." Conservative politicians began to style "tax-and-spend" liberal politicians as the court ministers of Welfare Queens. They claimed liberal politicians overfunded social spending, thereby robbing taxpayers and destroying work incentives for the poor. Liberal politicians were also accused of aiding and abetting and ultimately supporting a local apparatus that amounted to a fully staffed entourage for Welfare Queens. The apparatus encompassed VISTA offices, clergy, Community Action Programs, Model Cities, OEO legal services, other urban coalition-style organizations, and radical students all engaged in an effort to preserve and extend the welfare state, a place identified as the home address of the Welfare Queen. For increasingly bitter middle-class Americans, "social spending could be reduced to welfare, and welfare to welfare queens."[133]

The iconic Welfare Queen may have been, first of all, an expression of white America's anger about race, about the successes and continuing threats of the civil rights movement. By the early 1970s, many white Americans believed that the government had done enough. New laws, policies, and Supreme Court decisions had acknowledged and ameliorated historical racial prejudice in the United States, many argued. If, after all this accommodation, so many—in fact, a growing number—of mothers and their children were still claiming need, it made sense to assume these people were, one way or another, cheating.

In a way, most often unacknowledged, poor mothers claiming "welfare rights" were the shock troops of what was left of the street-level civil rights movement by the early 1970s. To the extent that welfare mothers had a public voice, they were using that voice to demand welfare provision as a badge of citizenship for poor, often minority women and their children.[134] Sociologist Susan Hertz, in her study of welfare rights activism in Minneapolis in this era, has pointed out that members of that city's welfare rights organization began to refer to themselves in the late 1960s as "citizens," especially as "first-class citizens," as a way of stressing publicly that "welfare mothers should be regarded as people entitled to the full privileges and enfranchisements of their nation."[135]

But the resourcelessness and "dependency" of poor (and iconically Black) mothers raised the question whether these women lacked the independence required of citizens. This is, of course, an old theme in American sociopolitical thought. Eric Foner reminds us in his study of the history of "freedom" in the United States that from the beginning of this nation, only two groups were denied the right to become citizens: European aristocrats and nonwhites. Foner explains what these two categories had in common: "Both were viewed as deficient in the qualities that made freedom [or independence] possible: the capacity for self-control, rational forethought, and devotion to the larger community."[136] The epithet "Welfare Queen," with its solid identification with Black women, was perfect—it merged the two groups of excluded ones.

Hertz also notes that members of welfare rights groups were eager to be recognized as mothers, women dedicated to the "full-time bearing and raising of children," their own children.[137] Members were interested in stressing that they occupied and had the right to occupy the dignified status "mother," despite the fact that claiming rights or dignity through motherhood had not, historically, been a likelihood for poor African-American women.

Welfare recipients had to stand up to the charge that they had babies for money and that they were more prostitute than mother. They also had to deal with the charge that collecting welfare was genetic—inherited, like royal status. An Ohio representative in Congress, Clarence Brown, explained in 1977 how this biologically deterministic syndrome worked: "People are on welfare and their children are on welfare and when the old folks pass away there's another generation of the same family that moves into the welfare pattern." Representative Brown described welfare recipients not as mothers but specifically as members of a "caste situation."[138] If welfare recipients' claims to dignified maternity were mocked as delusional by the icon of the Welfare Queen, they were also mocked as delusional for another reason: in the early 1970s, the Welfare Queen mocked African-American and African nationalist aspirations and the feminist aspirations of many women of color. The icon pictured a Black woman head of state as the ultimate travesty-sham.

In fact, the Welfare Queen spoke to the way many politicians, policy makers, and others characterized women in general as out of control in the early 1970s. From this perspective, one notices immediately that the figure of the Welfare Queen effaces its referent's association with motherhood, patriarchy, marriage, and domesticity. The application of the epithet to any woman or a group of women enforced the idea of women's alienation from these traditional and foundational aspects of female life. Further, the Welfare Queen pictures a grasping female, one taking more than her share—the very opposite of the self-sacrificing woman that the culture had constructed and embraced and that many people feared was dying in the eddies of cultural change.[139]

Lawrence Mead argued that federal policy created an "exempt" status for Blacks (a status, he stressed, that was more harmful than racism), the most prominent example of which was the status of the Welfare Queen, who believed herself exempted from finding a wage-earning husband, exempted from working herself, and exempted from performing as an adequate mother.[140] Relative to the last exemption, women of all sorts, middle-class and poor, sustained this charge, both those who held wage-earning jobs and those who did not. But one Republican representative to Congress managed to tar poor mothers who did either with one brush stroke: "Increased day care funding is of marginal use if the real problem is [mothers'] ignoring their children."[141] Through the icon of the Welfare Queen, the American public cast poor mothers as radical, man- and child-hating "women's libbers." They associated public assistance–receiving mothers with the second-most hated female icon of the era. (For many, the "women's libber" was an even more fearsome female than the Welfare Queen, since for many she was a lot closer to home.)

The figure of the Welfare Queen embodied rejection of everything that most Americans wanted to associate with womanhood. It also fully embraced attributes that many feared in the early 1970s would characterize liberated women, all women, in a hideous future. Probably chief among these attributes were "free sex" and "free choice," behaviors closely associated with the 368,000 unwed mothers newly eligible for welfare between 1969 and 1971. When thousands of these women made "the welfare choice," they were maneuvering in terrain that polls indicated most Americans now believed was off-limits for poor mothers. The earlier, first generation of poor, white mothers eligible for federal assistance had been, as we've seen, presumed to be choice makers about important matters such as whether to stay home with their children or go out to work. But the iconically minority recipients dominating public consciousness in the 1960s forward were associated with making choices inappropriately and badly. And public policy became explicitly associated with the effort to "constrict [a recipient's] choice."[142]

Representative Martha Griffiths told a story in Atlanta that she assumed would resonate with her audience, a panel of welfare administrators, because it was about a welfare mother who was a genuine prostitute and an unwed mother—a couple of female role violations many Americans worried about in the early 1970s. She said, "I was talking with a young man[143] the other day who told me that the woman right across the street from him had six kids and was drawing AFDC. Every morning at eight o'clock she put all six kids out in the yard, locked the doors, and they were not permitted back in until suppertime because she spent the day prostituting." Griffiths, disclosing that this story almost caused her to faint, conveyed how likely she found it when she asked the case managers in the hearing room with her what they did when they heard about this type of behavior in their area.[144]

Reflecting contemporary uneasiness about women pouring into the business world, Welfare Queens were said to be making rational, if immoral, economic and "lifestyle" choices when they took welfare, just as they were described as having made a "calculated economic decision to leave their husbands."[145] Historian Michael Katz has noted that in this era, "Both [Senator Daniel Patrick] Moynihan and most of his critics assumed that black families increasingly were female-headed by choice."[146]

Since most women were not paid well by their employers, a Congress member argued, a woman with three children on welfare was making "a career choice" to do better.[147] Women in Detroit who wanted to live in attractive subdivisions were accused of choosing welfare to facilitate their dreams. According to Martha Griffiths, one of her endless supply of informants told her that she believed that "at least 95%" of the houses in the 800-house development the informant lived in "were occupied by women drawing ADC and at least 50% of them had a man living in the house, with an income other than [welfare]."[148] This story, like Griffiths's many others, was offered off the cuff as emblematic: "This is what Welfare Queens do. This is how they beat the system."

In the midst of fevered claims about a teen pregnancy "epidemic," young welfare mothers, presumably beneath the age of rational choice, were described as making the inexplicable choice to be poor.[149] A New York Times editorial writer explained, "an increasing number of unmarried Black teenagers are choosing poverty by choosing to become mothers."[150] And in the midst of intense national concern about the rising incidence of divorce, a group of welfare officials in the 1970s agreed that the following scenario was not at all uncommon: "There are many fathers who, when contacted are only too happy to pay for supporting their children, but are furious that their [ex-]wives are drawing aid to dependent children. But [his] money practically has to be thrust upon the [ex-] wife. She doesn't want it coming from him. She prefers her own [welfare] check so that she doesn't have to waste time with the [ex-]husband, apparently."[151] Like other such scenarios, this one was offered apparently on the spur of the moment, data-free, and certainly without reference to relevant public information. In this case, pertinent to evaluating the divorced woman's need for welfare would have been the fact that, at this time, prominent studies showed that only one in four divorced fathers was in full compliance with his court-ordered support obligations.[152]

To reiterate, in the 1970s the Welfare Queen was the symbol of dependent women making bad choices. The figure of the Queen stood for a woman who made the kind of choices that caused other women, working people, the oppressed middle class, and all good Americans to resent her and even hate her and to see her as the member of a reviled caste. Ronald Reagan spoke the mind of many Americans when he pointed to the Welfare Queen and said, "You know here's a woman who is demanding her right to be supported by the working people, and she is saying to millions of other people who are chambermaids in a hotel or maids in homes—she is insulting them and saying that somehow they're beneath her and that she will only work if you can guarantee that the job will be at the executive level."[153]

WHAT THE ICON HIDES

The Welfare Queen, like the Back Alley Butcher, is a capacious symbol. The Welfare Queen has absorbed and reflected a bitter clutch of ideas about who poor women are—and how they got poor. And most of these ideas, of course, have to do with a belief that poor women are poor because of their own bad choices, their own weak-minded and weak-willed behavior. The Welfare Queen has been such a powerfully convincing symbol that invoking it has effectively blotted out alternative claims about women in trouble. Most important, when the Welfare Queen is in focus, we cannot see past this symbol. The Welfare Queen blocks our ability to imagine the social and economic forces that have created hardship, especially intractable poverty, for millions of women and children in the United States.

In fact, powerful social and economic forces have been far more responsible for driving women into the welfare system than the *behavior* of any given poor women or the *behavior* of poor women in general. A short list of these forces must include the multiple effects on women of deindustrialization; the rise of low-paying, non-benefit-bearing service jobs; the lack of a national day care policy and inadequate provision for day care; poor educational opportunities for poor people; inadequate child support and child support enforcement; and welfare policies that have mandated that poor people must be destitute and remain destitute to receive government assistance. These macrofactors, among others, were responsible for the fact that over the course of the 1970s, the number of female-headed families living below the poverty line rose about 40 percent. The bad behavior of an individual Welfare Queen may have been grist for a sensational feature story in the morning paper. But the big, faceless macrofactors were what caused "the feminization of poverty" and pushed an exploding number of women onto federal assistance.[154]

The Welfare Queen obscured the real consequences of the government's social welfare efforts in the 1970s, when most Americans were apparently getting fed up with women on welfare. First, as we've seen, the actual incidence of welfare fraud was indeterminate but almost surely amazingly small, particularly relative to the looming figure of the Welfare Queen. Second, invoking the Welfare Queen became a very effective way of distracting attention from the fact that welfare expansion and other government antipoverty efforts in this era did not hurt the country's economic growth, did not deepen social problems, and did not undermine the work incentive of poor people. In fact, the government's social welfare efforts were impressively successful in the short period they were permitted a vigorous life.

Michael Katz, historian of poverty and poverty policy, has shown that "between 1960 and 1980, the proportion of Americans living in poverty declined by 60%." Without AFDC and other "transfer payment" programs, poverty would hardly have declined at all. Regarding the work incentive issue, Katz points out, "During welfare's expansionary phase, unemployment grew very slowly, and employment rose faster during the period of welfare's greatest expansion than during the preceding fifteen years."[155]

The iconic figure of the Welfare Queen has not only blotted out a consideration of the real causes of poverty in America and the real accomplishments of government social welfare efforts. The Welfare Queen has silenced the real voices of real poor women struggling to care for their families on welfare. This is a considerable and circular tragedy. Since most Americans have no way of hearing or reading about how poor mothers describe their own lives or define their own selves, most Americans have no reason to give up the Welfare Queen.

When poor women were given—or took—the space to speak out about their predicament in the 1970s, they often self-consciously spoke against the grain, against the characterization imposed on them. For example, many welfare mothers and welfare mothers' groups introduced themselves to the public through newsletters and public statements as *mothers*. This was, of course, the central feature of welfare recipients' lives that was effaced when people called poor mothers Welfare Queens. When a rights group in Minneapolis chose a name for its newsletter, they emphasized their relation to mothering: "The Cradle Rocker Crier."[156] And a Michigan welfare rights activist wrote to Congress stressing the important role even poor women play as mothers: "Children need their mothers in the home." A former recipient tried to get her middle-class audience to understand how crucial welfare mothers were to their children's lives by reminding her listeners, "These children have already lost one parent." Recognizing that many Americans believed that a welfare mother was an inadequate mother, this woman explained the public policy consequences of such a belief: the mother is pushed into the workforce to earn a pitifully small wage, and the government-subsidized baby-sitter who comes to take care of that woman's children is paid at a higher rate than the working mother. "Why," she asked rhetorically, "would the government be willing to pay a baby sitter more than the mother makes?"[157] Many poor mothers could find no child care workers at any price. Demonstrating how threatened welfare recipients were and how determined they were to keep and be mothers to their children, one crowd of welfare rights activists shouted at a Mother's Day event in 1968, "The welfare officials want to break up our families . . . We refuse to be separated from our children one by one like puppys [*sic*] being separated from their mothers."[158]

Some poor mothers, when they got the chance, spoke out about how hard they struggled to be good mothers. They focused on how much *work* it was to be a mother in poverty. Trena Downey from Berkeley, Michigan, got a chance and described the kinds of calculations that defined her life as a mother: "Each person in the household is allowed eighty-three and a half cents per day for food . . .; fifty cents of that is needed for milk per child, leaving thirty-five cents. If the mother takes a bus anywhere and back, she has spent two and a half times that amount for one bus trip to apply for a job."

Another woman spoke about the emotional struggle of poor mothers: "Our children watch TV and see that there are other children in America that are being well-fed, clothed and housed, and they say to their mother, 'Why can't we have the same?' All that mother can do is drop her head and cry because she doesn't have an answer to give that child."[159]

Sometimes welfare workers who had frontline contact with poor mothers did speak out about the tough time their clients had being mothers. A worker in Atlanta in the early 1970s spoke of the thousands of mothers his office had discovered to have "serious medical problems" because of poverty.[160] Representatives of the East Harlem Interfaith Community in New York City in the 1970s tried to bring public attention to the fact that welfare mothers in their area were reduced to scavenging to feed their kids. A survey of seventy-nine families including 278 people showed that "welfare recipients have been waiting around the schools in East Harlem for the garbage to be sent out so they can go through the bags, pick out halves of sandwiches and whatever else the kids have thrown out."[161] And James Bennett, director of the welfare agency in Fannin County, Georgia, told a congressional committee that he was really angry about the stereotypes people used to describe the poor. He said, "The myth of the welfare Cadillac is a savage distortion that makes me furious every time I hear it. The average welfare client in Fannin County has NO transportation."[162]

This kind of public support was so occasional and specific that many welfare mothers believed that only they could speak in defense of recipients. Olia Calhoun, a member of Westside Mothers, a welfare rights organization in Detroit, expressed how many welfare mothers felt: "You know, people shouldn't talk about things that they don't know, only a A.D.C. mother knows." AFDC mothers were, in fact, especially concerned about speaking in defense of recipients as good, everyday choice makers faced with impossible choices. Olia Calhoun, for example, explained how she chose to take care of her children, even though the choice made her poor: "I worked [when] the children were small, but as they grew, I found out that they needed me more than that job needs me." (Calhoun also talked about how "welfare" pressured her to get a job and leave the care of her children to others. She observed in 1972, during an acute period of layoffs in Detroit, "Who are they fooling, there are no jobs.")[163]

Another recipient, one with two small children, who characterized herself as "desperate" for money, described the impossible choice she rejected: "I'd have gone out and sold my body if I knew how—or thought I could get anything for it"; and the impossible choice she made: not to report to her welfare worker a small amount of income she had earned. The day this woman was sentenced in court for the bad choice she'd made, she was given a stiffer sentence as a first offender—a Welfare Queen—than the judge handed out to an armed robber, a man who had committed an assault with a deadly weapon, a drunk driver who had hit and nearly killed a ten-year-old, and a fifth-time-offender pimp.[164]

Kathy Baker, in Annapolis, Maryland, described how after she and her three children escaped in a snowstorm from her violent husband, she had no money, no home, no job, and the ordinary expenses of a family. Her trips to the welfare office were horrible. She said, "I began to feel like my integrity was doubted—like I was just lying to get money." But she was determined: "[M]y children deserved these benefits so I kept on." That was a major choice, but then on an everyday basis, impossible choices presented themselves to Kathy Baker. For example, as a welfare mother, she was well aware that she had to calculate how to present herself in public so as to stimulate the least possible opprobrium: "[People say] 'why is she on welfare if she is dressed so nicely,' but when I had on jeans and a T-shirt, it was, 'why does she dress so sloppily?' "[165]

A Boston welfare rights activist, Doris Bland of Mothers for Adequate Welfare, did not hesitate to claim her right to choice outrageously in 1968: "Ain't no white man going to tell me how many babies I can have, 'cause if I want a million of them, and I can have them, I'm going to have them. And ain't nobody in the world going to tell me what to do with my bod, 'cause this is mine, and I treasure it."[166]

In 1973—the year "choice" became respectable for some women in the United States—psychiatrist Robert Coles spoke out in the voice of a welfare mother asking the kinds of questions that bedeviled the lives of so many poor women and that made it likely such women would be damned for whatever "choices" they made: "Why do I have to stay away from my husband in order to get welfare money?; I mean, he can't find a job, and I have children to feed, and isn't it a job taking care of children, bringing them up, so why do they come here, the welfare people, and make me feel like two cents, and my kids, too? Why do they tell me one thing about my child and then another, call him 'sick' or 'a severe delinquent,' then take him away, then bring him back?"[167]

In fact, again, when welfare mothers got the chance, they spoke in public in the fiercest terms about how they did everything they humanly could to manage their children and their households, how they *did* work, and how they were eager to get decent wage-earning jobs. (A welfare official in Detroit who'd seen a lot by 1972 supported these efforts, pointing out that poor people he knew managed their meager welfare money better than "most of the people in society.") One welfare mother explained that she "managed" her household all right, but ended up feeling like a "cheat" in her own terms, as many welfare mothers probably did. "We all cheat because when our children need a pair of shoes, or a pair of pants, a dress or coat, we take money from the food budget, the light bill and the gas bill to buy them. That is the only way we cheat." This is what the same woman had to say about the other kind of cheating, the kind attributed to Welfare Queens and investigated by folks who operated without budget constraints: "I feel like we have been punished for too much now. To have someone that doesn't know what it was like to be poor spend half a million dollars to investigate something that isn't there is very cruel. Unless you are poor you don't know what it is like to live on less than a dollar a day like I do."[168]

Among welfare recipients who spoke out in this era about motherhood as work was Suzanne Murphy of Boston, whose husband abandoned her and their three small children. Murphy described her welfare choice this way: "It was either go on welfare or see my children go hungry." After she "chose," this woman felt pressed very harshly to justify her life, which she did by identifying herself as a skilled worker: "I would just like to say that it is time for our society to wake up and recognize [the] truth. I am a professional. I am a mother and motherhood is the most honorable and revered profession this world has ever known. It is also a position that is deserving the utmost respect."[169]

When they got a chance to speak out, a group of welfare rights activists in rural St. Clair County, Michigan, similarly stressed that mothers' work was really work. Focusing on the government's interest in separating poor mothers from their children by sending the woman out to a low-paying job and putting her kids in day care, they protested, "Rather than support the mother, [the government wants] to pay someone to act like a mother." They asked a crucial question: "Do the activities of a woman become more valuable because they bear the label of a 'job'? . . . Why do we judge a poor woman unable to discern the advantages and disadvantages of working for her family?"[170]

Many welfare mothers were aware of the public pressure on their kind to go out to work, as so many mothers of all economic classes were doing by the early 1970s. And many were eager to do so. A survey conducted in the early 1970s showed, indeed, that AFDC recipients had essentially the "same attachment to the work ethic" as other adults.[171] The fact was, many welfare mothers were not unemployed by choice. According to a 1976 front page article in the *New York Times*, "The stereotype of the shiftless, procreating welfare recipient—a stereotype replete with overt and covert traces of racism—persists despite innumerable studies and statistical analyses showing that the vast majority of those receiving aid are either virtually unemployable or simply can't find jobs in today's frayed economy."[172] Sadie Mobley, a Washington, D.C., woman whose husband left her and two daughters after fifteen years of marriage, revealed her attachment to the work ethic when she said she planned to go on public assistance only for as long as it took her to find a steady job. With only a seventh grade education, however, Sadie Mobley had a hard time finding this job. She, like many other welfare mothers, described herself this way: "I am trying to work. I am doing the best I can, but I am not receiving any help."[173] She, like Willie Blackmon in Michigan, was clear-sighted about what welfare mothers needed—and didn't need—to achieve gainful employment. As Blackmon put it, "What is needed is more jobs, more job training programs, more day care centers, transportation to jobs—not forced labor and threats to cut off income or to remove children from their parents."[174]

These welfare mothers did not see themselves as exploiting the system. They did not see themselves as anything like Welfare Queens. Despite the assistance they needed, they were invested in their own dignity, and expressed their interest both in resisting jobs that exploited their vulnerability and in securing high-quality day care for their children. In the 1960s and 1970s, day care was extremely hard to secure, which was one reason jobs programs such as WIN always failed to place many mothers of young children in "job slots." In 1967 the director of a child welfare organization reported, "We have day-care facilities (after many years of trying to increase the program) for approximately seven thousand children in all of New York City with approximately the same number of children on the waiting lists because there are no facilities. Their mothers want to work. They cannot work because there is no program for their children."[175] A county welfare director in California in the mid-1970s explained the similar situation in his area: "We have approximately 12,000 mothers receiving AFDC. We do not have child care for more than about one-third of that group. Therefore, we aren't going to stress that those 12,000 mothers go to work."[176] In other parts of the country, welfare mothers who secured jobs were not able to have a say in the day care placement of their children. One recipient described how welfare mothers were "stepped on" in this regard: "She has no choice in day care for her own child and no say in how her child should be cared for."[177]

Not surprisingly, some prominent policy analysts and politicians, particularly those who promoted public acquaintance with the Welfare Queen, discounted the day care crisis while they verbally flogged poor mothers for failing to get jobs. Lawrence Mead reported that jobs program staffers told him that, typically, mothers who demanded day care from the program were trying to avoid participation; those who wanted to work arranged day care for themselves.[178] Martha Griffiths, who excoriated poor mothers for staying home, scoffed at a welfare worker in Georgia who claimed that in her area, there wasn't anywhere near sufficient day care for working mothers. Griffiths said, "It's a worldwide phenomenon that women don't like to put their children in day care centers"; they prefer, she said, "to make their own arrangements."[179]

The figure of the Welfare Queen, so vibrant and powerful in the minds of so many Americans in the 1970s (and beyond), lent support to Mead's and Griffiths's disregard for the day care problem. After all, the Welfare Queen was the symbol of aggressive women who despite their poverty, or because of it, could make whatever arrangements suited them. The great irony here is, of course, that every time politicians and others invoked the symbol of the Queen, explicitly or implicitly, they contributed to effacing the voices, the power, and the self-determination of real, poor women. They helped create the predicament we continue to live within: real, poor women have to struggle very hard for visibility and voice in a culture that imagines them and attacks them as Queens.

One welfare rights activist in the 1970s gives us a hint of what it took to speak in her own defense. She stood in public and said, "I am an ADC mother. I'm one of those ADC mothers who have finally crawled out of the woodwork and come forward, and I have sworn to speak before groups."

Another 1970s recipient-activist, Joycelyn Hubbard of Pontiac, Michigan, spoke out at a welfare reform "leadership conference" in January 1972. Hubbard not only had visibility and voice at this event. She had a powerful analysis to offer the audience:

> I am an expert on poverty. I have been poor all my life. I was born poor and Black and unless things change a lot in this country, I'm going to die the same way. Everyday I live with this knowledge. Everyday I see, feel, taste, smell and touch the poverty of my people and my community. Everyday I live with the knowledge that you want us poor—just in case you need your bedpans emptied, your shirts ironed, your yards mowed, your houses cleaned and your children tended—and just in case General Motors should need some cheap and temporary help. You brought my people to this country to use our men for labor and our women for housework and pleasure, and little has changed. Today my caseworker denies me help with my college expenses because she says I have a job skill and need no more education. I understand that—after all, who will empty the bedpans when I become a nurse? . . . I know how you have used me and my people and I know you intend to continue to use us.[180]

I imagine, a full generation after Joycelyn Hubbard spoke on January 17, 1972, how the bureaucrats and politicians at the leadership conference responded to this speech. I imagine their discomfort, embarrassment, even anger growing as Hubbard delivered her powerful historical analysis about the ways that welfare policy, labor force needs, sexism, and racism interact. Then I can imagine the bureaucrats and politicians quietly and firmly folding Joycelyn Hubbard into the figure of the Welfare Queen.

Joycelyn Hubbard felt the full measure of public scorn as a poor woman. And she expected that women in her position would continue to be under the thumb of welfare caseworkers, used as "cheap and temporary help," and disrespected by the institutions of society far into the future. In Chapter 6 I review the attitudes of many politicians and others toward poor women that shaped welfare reform debates and policies in the 1990s. At the end of the century, Hubbard's predictions were borne out.

CONSUMERIST CONCLUSIONS

The brilliant law professor Dorothy Roberts has pointed out that the welfare mother occupies such a degraded status in the United States because "an individual's entitlement to welfare benefits [has come to] depend on [the recipient's] relationship to the market . . . As unpaid caregivers with no connection to a male breadwinner, single mothers are considered undeserving clients of the welfare system."[181] This observation captures a core characteristic of the Welfare Queen. The Queen has no role in legitimate market relations; she has no status as a consumer, but consumes anyway, as a parasite consumes. This is what made the welfare mother into the Welfare Queen, in the public's opinion: her illegitimacy as a citizen-consumer.

Tragically and ironically, at just the time when many African-American women were cast so harshly and enduringly as Welfare Queens, this demographic group was, in fact, emerging as a distinct and desirable market segment. Historian Robert Weems has shown how advertisers began to target African-American consumers in the 1960s; Weems quotes from a 1966 article, "How to Sell Today's Negro Woman," which warns advertisers and marketers about her differences from the "blue-eyed suburban housewife," and cautions against referring "to the Negro woman as 'Negress or Negresses,' a phrase guaranteed to produce an unfavorable reaction."[182] Welfare recipients understood this development and formulated their 1968 "Winter Action Campaign" and other events as "consumer rights" actions.[183]

Some antipoverty programs and government functionaries actually accorded welfare mothers status as consumers at this time.[184] Programs managed by the Office of Economic Opportunity in the late 1960s included "consumer action" initiatives and credit unions to "extend low-cost credit to low-income people, who would otherwise not enjoy this [opportunity]."[185] At a congressional hearing in 1972, the director of the Wayne County (Michigan) Department of Social Services explained, "Our department has made serious attempts to establish meaningful dialog with the consumer of our services. Consumers are involved with the social service board and welfare rights groups who meet monthly with the department representatives." The official was clearly associating "consumer" with dignity and citizenship status.[186]

But most Americans were convinced that poor African-American women were not authentic consumers and were materially harming the real, deserving, taxpaying consumer. Americans expressed their rage about sham consumers by taunting welfare mothers and calling them Welfare Queens. They also expressed themselves by singing songs about the absurdity and obscenity of casting welfare recipients as consumers. Several songs making this point circulated in the early 1970s. One, "Welfare Cadillac," was a favorite of Richard Nixon's. The president once asked the band at a formal White House event to play it for his guests. One verse went like this:

> We get peanut butter and cheese and, man,
> They give us flour by the sack
> 'Course them welfare checks, they meet
> Them payments on this new Cadillac.[187]

Dorothy Roberts's observations about welfare mothers place poor women in a category separate from and beneath other Americans, especially other women. Welfare rights activist Johnnie Tillmon, on the other hand, in an essay first published in 1972, placed welfare mothers quite differently. Tillmon catalogued the long list of "lies that male society tells about welfare mothers"; then she observed, "If people are willing to believe these lies, it's partly because they're just special versions of the lies that society tells about all women."[188] In Tillmon's formulation, welfare mothers suffered from "inclination[s] firmly rooted in female life."

Historian Elaine Abelson's study of the kleptomaniac, first cousin to the Welfare Queen, is illuminating here. Abelson describes the advent of the category of middle-class shoplifters in the nineteenth century. She explains that shoplifters constituted a tiny fraction of all women shoppers, but the type was quickly accepted. Experts in many fields rushed to elaborate the type, defining her as "inherently unstable," a kind of consumer-pervert, biologically inferior, afflicted by a "mania" for consuming, highly susceptible to the temptation to steal. Fundamentally, the experts argued that all women were potential shoplifters, just as in the 1970s, Tillmon argued, "society" believed that all women were potential scammers and all mothers on welfare were Welfare Queens.

Abelson finds that the "unrestrained behavior" of the kleptomaniac—the aberrant consumer—was perceived as an obnoxious challenge to dominant values. She argues that this behavior "seemed to imply a kind of moral chaos and to raise questions about the fundamental understanding of class and gender."[189] The aberrant, inauthentic, or perverse female consumer could do that in the nineteenth century via the kleptomaniac and in the second half of the twentieth century via the Welfare Queen. In the wake of the civil rights movement, when welfare eligibility and rolls expanded, the welfare mother was generally cast as an emblem of cultural and political chaos and a challenge to dominant, if fraying, American values.

When *Life* magazine published an article in 1967 about female shoplifters in the United States, the author of the article merged these nineteenth- and twentieth-century models of aberrant, female, consumer behavior, describing the motivation of inauthentic consumers in the 1960s as "justifiable retaliation."[190] The article did not focus on poor women, certainly not on welfare mothers. Shoplifting was portrayed as something any kind of woman might do. Any woman might feel that she was a victim then, so why shouldn't she steal? This is precisely the calculation most Americans imagined was in the heart of the most aberrant female consumer of all, the Welfare Queen.

Whether the welfare mother was cast as different from other American women or as an exemplar of female perversion, the Welfare Queen was out of line as an American citizen. By the late 1960s, the core identity of the American citizen may have been a consumer identity. By this time, the core problem poor, single mothers represented may not have been that they didn't have husbands or that they raised the specter of nonwhite women and their hordes of babies taking over the country. The main problem may have been that such women had no jobs and therefore no money. Americans may have been most hostile to welfare mothers because they were not legitimate consumers. Since that time, many Americans have been increasingly unwilling to acknowledge the rights, the motherhood status, or the citizenship status of poor mothers. Instead, most have chosen to support public policies designed to be ever tougher on incorrigible women bent on taking the taxpayer for a ride.

MOTHERHOOD AS CLASS PRIVILEGE IN AMERICA

A PUBLIC POLICY PROJECT

———

The entire difference between being dependent on society and being independent of society is expressed in having or not having a legal right.   —A. Delafield Smith[1]

In September 1969, lawyers for Kathleen Ramos, a fifteen-year-old member of the Rinion Band of Mission Indians, attempted to convince a panel of judges in San Diego that their client should not be removed from her home and placed in foster care. As the lawyers put it, this "case tells the sad story of the by-product of poverty." Kathy Ramos, they argued, "has never hurt anybody. She loves her family and they love her, but she faces removal from her home and placement in a foster home with strangers, perhaps in a strange community."[2] The documents describing the circumstances that led San Diego officials to threaten Kathy's removal—essentially, too many absences from school—indeed tell a "sad story."

Five months earlier, the Juvenile Department of the Superior Court of California, County of San Diego, had designated the girl a ward of the court. Kathy, then a sophomore at Escondido High School, was "habitually truant" according to the California Education Code. That meant she had been "absent or tardy without valid excuse for more than five days within the present school year."[3] Kathy and her mother could not afford to have a lawyer to represent them at the hearing. Nor were they given the opportunity to have counsel at the expense of the county. Nor, in fact, were they provided with written notice of the nature of the proceedings or informed of their rights and responsibilities before the hearing.

As a ward of the court, Kathy was permitted to live with her grandparents, Delia and Joe Morales, and directed to spend the summer of 1969 in school. In late August, however, the court found that Kathy hadn't attended and completed summer school "successfully." As a result, the girl and her family were notified that the probation office planned to "request her removal from her present family environment and her placement in a foster home."[4]

Kathy Ramos's mother, Marcella Mason (Kathy's father had died some years earlier and Marcella had remarried), begged the probation officer in charge of the case not to take Kathy away from her. She said that Kathy had "done nothing wrong." She tried to explain that Kathy had missed school because of her chronic bronchitis and because the school was so far away, four and a half miles. Mrs. Mason told the probation officer that the family's car, a broken-down 1959 stationwagon, always had something wrong with it. The family was too poor, she said, to buy a new car or to pay for repairing the old one. The other problem, she said, was that the county provided no alternative transportation to summer school. A Mrs. Cavey, the school district's representative at the hearing, responded directly to Mrs. Mason's claim that the problem was largely about Kathy's transportation to school. She said that the girl "should be put in a home where there was a car which could get her where she wants to go." When Kathy's lawyers tried to prevent the state from removing the girl from her family, they pointed to Mrs. Cavey's dictum as a "firm indication that, indeed, the poverty of Kathy's family is to blame for her troubles."[5]

These sad but illuminating facts about Kathy Ramos's troubles triggered but were not central to the case that Kathy and her mother pursued to the U.S. Supreme Court regarding where Kathy lived and whether her own mother should get to take care of her. The core issue in the case that came to be called *Ramos v. Montgomery* was whether it was reasonable for foster parents to get a grant of $105 a month to take care of Kathy while Marcella Mason, a mother on AFDC, was allotted only about a third that amount to cover the same child's needs. In her own defense, Mrs. Mason wrote in an affidavit, "If I could have the money which the county would pay to strangers to take care of my [daughter], I know I could do a much better job."[6]

Mrs. Mason and her lawyers were not alone in the late 1960s and early 1970s in claiming that the foster care system was unfair because it transferred children from poor mothers to better-off, though still subsidized, families. This practice was so robust at the time that some experts called it a "growth industry."[7] A prominent study explained the role of poverty in creating opportunities for foster families: "inadequate financial resources comprise an underlying factor which is present to one degree or another in almost all cases in which children are in foster care."[8] Another study described the class dynamics of foster care explicitly as "a system in which middle-class professionals provide and control a service used mostly by poor people, with upper-lower and lower-middle-class parents serving as intermediaries."[9] Differential child support rates like those that plagued Kathy Ramos's family reinforced the class dimensions of foster care across the country. New York Family Court judge Justine Wise Polier pointed out in the 1960s that a mother on AFDC received less than a dollar a day to support a child; a foster family got about seven dollars a day, and an institution up to fourteen dollars a day. She said, "The further the child is removed from his family, the more we are ready to pay for his support."[10]

In these years, the foster care system exploded partly because many frontline social welfare workers and the bureaucracies they worked for judged poor parents quickly and harshly. A California study found that "a special problem . . . for poverty-stricken families appears to be that because of the differences in socio-economic class attitudes toward parental competence, children may be removed from the home too soon."[11] Another child welfare study described the capriciousness of bringing neglect charges and actions for removal against a parent: such actions depended "on the personal 'neglect threshold' of the individual social worker," or even on whether or not the mother was on welfare.[12]

These prejudices were evident at many levels of the child welfare system. A scholar at Michigan State University warned in the 1970s that health care workers were removing children "without all the facts." She gave the audience at the first national conference on child abuse and neglect a perspective on why this practice was so common: "[W]henever a group has been designated as being different in culture, color, or behavior . . . the group then becomes associated with lowly or evil things," such as behavior justifying child removal.[13]

A 1973 essay in the *Harvard Education Review* reported that the courtroom was a dangerous place for poor biological parents whose custody of their children had been challenged. According to this study, a judge in such a case typically decided that "parental behavior was immoral, and without any systematic inquiry into how the parental conduct damaged or was likely to harm the children, the judge then determined the children to be neglected and removed them from their home." Neglect proceedings were "highly informal." As in Kathy Ramos's case, "few parents and far fewer children [were] represented by counsel." Typically, "hearsay evidence of all sorts" was admissible and "specific findings" were absent. Judges removed children from mother-headed homes because the mother had sex without being married or had an extramarital affair, was a lesbian, kept a dirty home, had unconventional religious beliefs, had written bad checks or "mismanaged" money, had been seen drinking in a tavern, or had allowed "a friend or neighbor to care for a child without official state sanction."[14]

But probably the most common and grievous violation a mother could be accused of was poverty. A 1970s "class analysis of foster care and adoption" by Betty Reid Mandell described the "welfare witch hunts" conducted periodically by public officials who held the threat of child removal over the heads of women on AFDC. Mandell explained that these mothers felt "that to lose their children is to lose the only wealth they have, and sometimes to lose their only reason for living." A contemporary-sounding list of actions taken against poor women because they were mothers in the early 1970s includes threatening to cut or actually cutting the public assistance grant if the women had more than one out-of-wedlock child, threatening to place any out-of-wedlock child in foster care or an adoptive home, and forcing AFDC mothers to work at cheap labor. These actions were mandated "under the guise of 'protecting the children,'" but to Mandell it appeared that the litany of pressures separating a poor mother from her children was simply "the litany of poverty."[15]

In a period when the courts downgraded the notion of "parental rights" in favor of "the best interests of the child" as the guiding principle in family and child welfare cases, poor mothers faced deepened disadvantages.[16] In the nascent "era of choice" (birth control pills became widely available in the early 1960s and some states began to relax restrictions on abortion in the late 1960s), poor women who had children could be tagged as bad choice makers, as "morally depraved," and targeted for child removal. That is what a Reagan-sponsored program in California aimed to do in the early 1970s. Governor Reagan's seven-member Social Welfare Board caused an uproar when it took actions suggesting that the children of poor women were simultaneously too expensive and valueless. The director of the Los Angeles County Department of Adoptions described the board's plan as a proposal to "take large numbers of minority children from their mothers, to be brought up in foster homes at tremendous expense to the taxpayer and probably at great harm to the child."[17] In California and elsewhere, race, poverty, and unmarried childbearing could disqualify a woman from claiming parental rights—and from status as a legitimate choice maker. According to Robert E. Mitchell, the chairman of the state's welfare board at the time, choice was a central concern. He said, "a woman does not have the right to have as many illegitimate children as she chooses."[18]

A poor mother who became enmeshed in the child welfare system might well lose her child.[19] Plus, despite the fact that foster care placement was supposed to be temporary, and social workers were supposed to help "natural parents" regain custody, most studies showed that "in the 'natural parents–child–foster parents' triad, the natural parents receive the least attention from social workers."[20] A typical study showed that 70 percent of the "natural parents" had "no relationship" with the agency responsible for removing the child. Such child welfare agencies claimed they had "no time for the kind of continuous work with the parents . . . which could effect the rehabilitation of the home."[21] One social agency worker reflected bluntly on another stumbling block to reconciliations: "We were able to offer very little help with one problem that emerged during many discussions [with the natural parents], i.e. the difference in living standards between the foster and parental homes."[22]

Ignored by social workers, poor mothers who had their children taken into foster care reported being treated as "a necessary evil" or like "dirt" by the foster parents.[23] They reported that foster parents didn't invite them, or even tell them about, special occasions in their child's life, such as a school graduation ceremony. They complained that foster parents didn't consult them about important matters that required parental decisions. And most bitterly, they complained that "the foster parents were sometimes guilty of the same actions which had resulted in their child being removed from the home; yet the foster parents were permitted to care for the child and were paid for doing so."[24]

This last was, of course, similar to Marcella Mason's complaint and the basis of the "agonizing dilemma" she faced. Marcella loved her daughter and wanted to hold her family together. Yet if she refrained from fighting the removal order of the department of social services and simply acquiesced as her mother status was breached, then Kathy would be transferred to a better-off (and more generously recompensed) household. Kathy could be a teenager with "a more adequate material standard of living."[25] Marcella Mason, Kathy Ramos, and their legal advocates pressed their case, however, because it so strongly suggested that "all AFDC families will be threatened by loss of their children to foster homes by reason of the family's poverty so long as California law provides more than twice the amount of AFDC to foster homes for the care of children than parents or relatives receive."[26]

In Kathy Ramos's case, the U.S. District Court for the Southern District of California in San Diego acknowledged that "some children must of necessity be placed in foster homes due to the financial inability of parents to provide a suitable home." But the court concluded, in a decision that seemed to suggest (with no evidence provided) that poverty was a less likely cause of removal than bad parenting, that it was not unreasonable to pay foster parents more than poor biological parents to take care of the same child.[27]

Why was it that so many public officials, at so many different levels in the welfare, educational, correctional, and judicial systems, agreed in the 1960s and 1970s that poor mothers like Marcella Mason should be tagged as bad mothers and disqualified from motherhood? I have tried to show in this book and elsewhere that the early outcomes of midcentury liberation movements—the civil rights movement and the women's rights movement, the contraceptive movement and the abortion rights movements—which aimed in various ways to establish the personal autonomy and citizenship status of marginalized people, were complicated, especially for relatively resourceless mothers.[28] Young mothers, poor mothers, and mothers of color were marked early on, in the dawn of the era of personal choice, as bad choice makers and poor prospects for becoming or raising good citizens.[29]

After 1960, many policy makers, politicians, and social service providers began to strongly associate pregnancy with *intent*. Many took the attitude in this era that poor females who could have prevented pregnancy but had an illegitimate child instead were bad choice makers who did not deserve welfare payments and perhaps did not deserve to be mothers at all.[30] In the midst of the civil rights movement, Congress made illegitimacy a federal matter for the first time. Revisions in the Social Security Act of 1967 allowed states to move children into foster care if their home environments were poor. Illegitimacy became the chief marker of a poor home environment.[31]

Going even a step further, the state of Louisiana explicitly tied the poor choice making of "illegitimate mothers" to the denial of citizenship rights when the legislature said that women with out-of-wedlock babies could not vote.[32] Since legislators associated "illegitimacy" with African-American girls and women, this was a bald effort to deny a segment of the state's African-American population the citizenship right that was the central focus of the civil rights movement.[33] This act was also a harbinger of a perverse, continuing, and nationwide association of poor mothers with a nasty invocation of the civil rights movement: mothers of color who did not benefit from the "guarantees" of the civil rights movement and remained poor were marked as bad choice makers. Tragically, many Americans pointed to the unrealized goals of a liberation movement to show that bad women perpetually making bad choices were not living up to their new rights.

The rights claims of the women's rights movement were also marshaled at this time to stigmatize poor mothers as bad choice makers. Those women—poor and young, and especially poor and young and of color—who appeared to behave reproductively as if biology were (still) destiny and had "too many" children, were targeted as retrogressive by population controllers and by politicians interested in exploiting hostility to welfare recipients. According to the critics, these females were irresponsibly backward because they were nonusers or ineffective users of birth control. They were also accused of violating the first principle of modern womanhood—*rational exercise of choice*.[34] The attacks marginalized poor women in general as aberrant. They also deepened the alienation between white middle-class women and those with fewer resources. Middle-class women were in the process of *defining* their reproductive "right to choose" motherhood as distinct from a biological imperative. At the same time, poor women were often *being defined* as resisting their alleged *duty* not to choose motherhood.[35]

Another core feminist goal in the late 1960s and early 1970s—equal rights for women in the areas of employment and economic opportunities—also turned into a threat against poor women and women of color and their "choices" by the mid-1970s. It is a well-known postwar phenomenon that rather than "returning home" after stints as war workers, hundreds of thousands of women a year streamed into the workforce in the 1950s. This trend continued and accelerated across the postwar decades. It was fueled by feminist claims regarding women's employment rights, by the growing need for female workers in the newly burgeoning service economy, and by the need for two-income families as the purchasing value of paychecks began to decline in the early 1970s.[36]

Most women workers in the United States, however, did not achieve economic self-sufficiency by earning a salary.[37] Most women earned two-thirds what men did, and most women workers were stuck in "pink ghetto" jobs. Decent wages and self-sufficiency (and adequate child care) were particularly elusive for women who entered the workforce poor. Women who worked but remained poor or didn't achieve self-sufficiency—especially the growing number of single mothers—were increasingly confronted by these loaded questions: Can you afford to be a mother? Can you afford to exercise choice? Do you have the right to be a mother?

With the fall of the biological imperative, social commentators increasingly defined still-poor mothers—even if they were employed—as having made deliberate though bad choices to become mothers: such women couldn't afford motherhood. In the past, these women would have been called simply the "irresponsible poor." Now they were defined as more complex failures. They ignored their release from the biological imperative, plus they failed to capitalize on women's new economic opportunities to achieve personal liberation and economic self-sufficiency, the qualities that increasingly defined legitimate mother-

hood. As it turned out, the escalating rates of women's workforce participation became a justification for stigmatizing and disqualifying poor
women as mothers. Women who earned enough at work (or who had
husbands who did) were the ones who earned the right to choose motherhood. Despite the fact that women of color had always had higher
workforce participation rates than white women, those who did not earn
enough, or earned nothing at all, were blameworthy, since "economic
opportunity" was now women's right.[38] Lacking resources, such women
did not merit the right to choose motherhood. By 1980, motherhood was
a contingent right that only good earners could choose.[39]

Now many Americans had an apparently race-neutral way of stigmatizing poor mothers. They simply compared poor women to highly skilled
and educated modern, middle-class, choice-making women and found
the former deeply inferior. Many believed that poor mothers were so
flawed as mothers that their failures could be predicted, especially their
failure to carry out the traditional civic function of raising future citizens
who would be assets in a democratic society.[40] In the not-too-distant
past, policy makers had believed that even poor mothers, many of them
immigrants, "were capable" of serving the country by raising good children "under proper guidance."[41] But in the midst of the civil rights
movement, in the nascent "era of choice," public policy reimagined the
functions of poor mothers altogether. Public policy, notably the 1967 Social Security Amendments, which mandated work requirements for poor
mothers, were particularly palatable at the time because so many Americans had come to accept the proposition that poor mothers were "inadequate mothers."[42]

As "inadequate mothers," these women were pressed in the late 1960s
and early 1970s to give up their traditional child-caring functions as
well. Policy expert Grace Ganz Blumberg noted in 1973 that "welfare
mothers, who are generally understood to be a burden on the economy,
are seriously told that they are better off, *financial considerations aside*, if
they go out to work and leave their children in day care centers. Politicians and social workers and government economists advise each other
and welfare mothers [to this effect]."[43]

One such expert defined the purpose of "intensive day care of the
'headstart' type" as providing "values to the child that the marginal
mother cannot provide."[44] A social work analyst with a more complex

view of poor mothers regretted at the time that "too often the response of professionals who come into contact with such children is to 'save' the child from [his mother.]" This writer described policy makers as overly fixated on the "product," that is, "cognitive gains for the child," and as disrespectful or rejecting of the "mother who is perceived as less than adequate."[45] (Not surprisingly, experts often saw the day care issue through a class-tinted lens, finding, for example, that while day care might not be good, emotionally, for middle- or upper-class children who would suffer for being separated from their mothers, the stability and enrichment features of day care would definitely help the children of poor and inadequate mothers.)[46]

Scholar and policy analyst Sheila Kamerman wryly noted in 1973 that "the legitimation of day care could not have come at a better time. Here is a socially acceptable mechanism for getting welfare recipients back to work, and at the same time for transferring the care of their children to 'better hands.' There is no group that reads women's liberation on day care with greater pleasure than [welfare] administrators."

Kamerman recognized how unlikely it was that jobs would be found for most poor mothers; she believed that most government policy makers realized this too. So, she observed, policy makers who crafted the early work-for-welfare programs "took refuge in a much more ambiguous and hard-to-measure promise of educating and improving [poor] children." Kamerman imagined proponents of institutional day care arguing first, "Isn't it good to get poor children out of rat-infested tenements for eight hours a day?" Then, Kamerman added, proponents would probably argue that the government should have the right "to coerce [poor] mothers into placing their child in day care centers."[47]

These ideas and policy initiatives dealing with poor mothers and their mothering functions reflect one powerful response to the liberation movements of the 1960s and 1970s: deep middle-class ambivalence—even hostility—toward the "liberation" of poor mothers, a group often cast as illegitimate beneficiaries of reproductive rights, civil rights (including welfare rights), and women's rights. In a society especially worried in the 1960s and 1970s about the relationship between rights, individuality, selfishness, and depravity, poor mothers became the emblem of what could go wrong when a particular population segment was inappropriately associated with rights. Public regret about this turn of events was expressed, as we have seen, in the construction of the Welfare Queen, and also in Swiftian proposals to take poor children from "lazy, improvident" mothers and give them to "adoptive parents who are not lower class" or put them "in an orphanage."[48] They were also expressed as warnings that poor mothers are not unlikely to exploit their own children.

We are already familiar with the charge that poor mothers exploited motherhood to begin with by having children as an income strategy. But legal scholar Thomas Ross points out how, in an important 1971 U.S. Supreme Court case testing whether an AFDC mother in New York City had the right to refuse a welfare worker's inspection of her home, Justice Blackmun "cast the dispute as a conflict between the child's needs [for inspection and protection of his physical, mental, and moral well-being] and what the mother claims as her rights." Ross finds that Justice Blackmun—and many Americans—assumed the "propensity" of poor mothers "to act contrary to the interests of [their] children."[49]

Throughout the liberationist periods of the 1960s and 1970s, public policies and public policy proposals incorporated efforts to limit the impact of poor mothers, in part by separating them from their children. Additional efforts aimed to remake poor mothers as limited, rational choice makers. By the end of the 1970s, a roster of public policies aimed to differentiate poor women as constituting a suspect class of mothers whose choices must be limited. It is illuminating to consider that, to an important degree, the 1970s were a decade when populations were differentiated demographically by their normative relationship to "choice" and "rights." Specifically, by the end of the 1970s, fathers were recognized as having rights, fetuses were granted rights, and "children's rights" were newly and broadly acknowledged. Women, on the other hand, were accorded only "choice"—or what I call "rights lite"—by the end of the decade.[50]

In the Reagan-Bush era politicians and policy makers not noted as champions of women's interests were outspoken about their belief that women controlled the future of the republic. But in the 1980s, when politicians ascribed such power to women, they weren't referring in the traditional way to women's soldierlike willingness, through childbirth, to risk their

lives for the country. Nor did the references point toward women's traditional nation-sustaining work as "witnesses for peace," or even to their
role as "the only bulwark between chaos and an organized and well-run
family unit."[51] Rather, in the 1980s, when women's behavior was publicly
associated with the future health of the polity, speakers were most likely
referring to the ruinous impact of Welfare Queens, illegitimate mothers,
or poor mothers having too many costly children. Gary Bauer, a key social policy aide to President Reagan, described the dreadful impact that
women making what he called "reckless choices" were likely to have on
the future of the United States: "[T]here will either be no next generation, or [there will be] a next generation that is worse than none at all."[52]

Despite the fact that the birthrate for unmarried black women fell
13 percent between 1970 and 1980 (while the rate rose 27 percent for
white unmarried women), public policies targeted poor, unmarried, black
mothers as unworthy and intensified efforts to define these mothers as
poor choice makers, individually responsible for their "dependent" condition.[53] Few Americans who were not on welfare could calculate the impact of factors beyond the control of these women that pushed them to
accept public assistance. These factors included the lack of appropriate
jobs that paid a living wage and the lack of affordable day care, coupled
with the fact that welfare benefits grew in the early 1970s faster than
wages.[54]

Nevertheless, in the 1980s, after the real value of the welfare check
began to plummet, conservative politicians and public policy experts attacked poor mothers with vigor, claiming that their receipt of welfare
benefits—their welfare dependency—was built on choices that reflected
irresponsibility, even depravity. Lawrence Mead, the politics professor,
drew a thick bottom line in defining "welfare mothers" during a congressional hearing in the mid-1980s. "I wanted to comment," he said, "on
the presumption that the poor are like the rest of us." This, Mead argued, was a misconception. Unlike "us," the poor are "remarkably unresponsive to . . . economic incentives." He found their behavior "a
mystery," but suggested an interpretive key: welfare recipients were
"semi-socialized." Unable to make sensible choices, they became wholly
dependent on welfare.[55]

The purpose of policy, Mead argued, is "not to expand the freedom of
. . . recipients. It is, in fact, to constrict their freedom in necesssary

ways."[56] In other words, poor women could not and should not exercise choice. Mead and others in the policy arena were emphatic: when poor, unemployed women made unconstrained choices for themselves, the consequences were awful. Gary Bauer acknowledged in a 1986 report to President Reagan that he could cite no statistical evidence to prove that these unemployed women decided to have babies in order to collect welfare. "And yet," he claimed, even the "most casual observer of public assistance programs" could perceive this motivation.[57] Revitalizing this thirty-year-old charge depended on convincing the citizenry that dependent women were deliberate malfeasants or compulsive miscreants. Either way, their choice to have babies and to stay home with them was pathological. Many argued that compounding this bad choice was another, though lesser bad choice: the unnatural decision to give birth to babies who would not have proper fathers.[58]

Basically, these charges against poor, unemployed mothers made sense to many Americans because these women did not have paying jobs.[59] Economic dependency, caused by bad choices and leading to more of the same, was now seen as the core problem of poor, unemployed mothers, not racism or sexism or the effects of deindustrialization, or even the absence of a husband, all of which did create powerful constraints on the opportunities of poor women. Lawrence Mead, Gary Bauer, and Charles Murray met a warm reception in Washington after 1980, when they claimed that eradicating dependency involved aborting the bad choices of poor women, including their choices to have too many children.

While increasing the military budget, granting corporate tax relief, and investing in the private sector, the Reagan administration aimed to "break the cycle of dependency" by reducing the number of choices a poor, unemployed mother could make. For example, the administration eliminated the Comprehensive Employment and Training Act (CETA) and diminished appropriations for the Vocational Education Act, which had provided jobs and training options for poor mothers. The U.S. Civil Rights Commission noted early in the Reagan era that "Federal support for employment and training programs has decreased dramatically, and therefore, special efforts will be needed to provide alternate sources of skills training for poor women unable to gain access to currently available resources. If not, they may find themselves trapped in poverty in spite of their best efforts to avoid or overcome their dependency."[60]

The administration also crafted policies that eliminated a significant amount of public housing stock, raised rents, and reduced federal subsidies for new construction and rehabilitation of dilapidated housing stock. It slashed fuel assistance programs for low-income households and made it much more difficult for poor women to obtain free legal representation. Very significantly, the administration cut allocations for day care programs at the same time that 36 percent of low-income women and 45 percent of single mothers said they would work if child care were available. For example, Title XX of the Social Services block grant, a major source of day care funding, was cut 21 percent in 1981.[61] Finally, Reagan's policies continued the process of reducing the real value of the average AFDC check—between 1970 and 1985, the real value of these benefits declined 33 percent—and began aggressively pushing mothers with younger and younger children into the workforce.[62]

As housing, employment, and training options and day care programs were liquidated or hobbled in the 1980s, the Reagan administration and state-level politicians also focused considerable attention on policy initiatives that would directly punish unemployed, poor mothers for the double-barreled bad choice they were accused of making: having a baby and not having a job. (In this climate, Lawrence Mead would suggest that "Congress might wish to consider differentiating between married and unmarried mothers, the latter to face more immediate work obligations.")[63]

The results of Reagan-era policies were very quickly grim. Between 1980 and 1984, the incomes of the bottom one-fifth of American families, a quintile that included 43 percent of African-American families, dropped by 9 percent. At the same time, income rose 9 percent for the top quintile, a segment that took in only 7 percent of African-American families.[64] The Congressional Research Service reported that 557,000 people became poor because of cutbacks in social programs that Congress approved at the request of President Reagan during the first years of his administration. This was on top of the 1.6 million people who became poor in 1982 because of the economic recession.[65] In these same years, the percentage of children who were living in poverty rose from 16 percent to 20 percent, a development that brought the number of children in the United States living in households subsisting at or near poverty levels to one in four.[66]

This politics of reviling and punishing poor mothers for being unemployed, while at the same time making it more difficult for them to receive the education and training necessary to secure family-sustaining jobs, was a hallmark of the Reagan years. President Reagan himself complained that people unhappy with this policy paradox were simply "sob sisters" unwilling to face reality.[67]

President Reagan's epithet—"sob sisters"—perfectly captured the conservatives' firm determination in the 1980s to clarify welfare as an issue associated with weak women. Opponents of tough (masculine) Reagan policy were cast as emotional, irrational partisans, wallowing in expensive and destructive sentimentality. Also, Reagan administration attacks on "sob sisters" (welfare mothers and others who spoke out in support of these women's needs) were calculated to salvage traditional gender and race ideologies that had been battered by a generation of liberatory legislative, judicial, and policy innovations and mass movements.[68]

Having lost significant battles in the effort to maintain male supremacy and white supremacy in the generation between 1954 and 1980, Reagan-aligned politicians and policy makers were waging one of their fiercest battles over considerably diminished terrain: the definition of poor women. Many entered this battle as if the fight to constrain the misbehavior of unemployed, poor mothers was the last great legitimate effort of government, and as if winning this battle was crucial to restoring the health of American society.

Looking back on this era, it is striking how pointedly public policies in the 1980s aimed to revive strategies from the 1950s that denied women reproductive rights while insisting on special qualifications for motherhood. Douglas Besharov of the conservative American Enterprise Institute kindly referred to this revival as "help[ing] these women make choices about having children."[69] Lawrence Mead spoke more directly: "[I]t would not be true to say that choices are really being offered to [poor mothers]. There is a strong element of guidance here—an element of direction, public authority."[70]

Poor women experienced their new, constrained relation to choice—and childbearing—as they encountered rules and programs that replaced reproductive rights with the reproductive duty to refrain from reproducing. Poor women now encountered policies and proposals offering payoffs for using long-acting contraceptives and regulations that singled out pregnant drug users for punishments, such as incarceration, that non-pregnant drug users did not face.[71] Poor women experienced public pressure to constrain their reproductive choices when politicians such as U.S. Representative E. Clay Shaw of Florida spoke out about the need for "sterilization of some of these women." Shaw said that it couldn't be compulsory, "but when they start having these babies one after another, and the terrible thing they are doing to the next generation . . . something has got to be done to put a stop to it."[72]

Poor mothers also experienced the public will to use the welfare system to constrain their choices in the 1980s, another revival of a 1950s strategy. Through the welfare system and other mechanisms, vulnerable mothers found themselves once again targeted for child removal. In the Reagan-Bush era, this meant encouraging white single mothers to give up their children for adoption—a practice that had declined dramatically since the early 1970s—and fueling a resurgence of foster care placements for the children of poor mothers of color. (Foster care placements plummeted in the late 1970s, but quickly accelerated during the Reagan years.)[73]

By the mid-1980s, only about 7 percent of unwed mothers—still mostly white—placed their babies for adoption, and the administration made strenuous efforts to convince unmarried young women that mothers who chose adoption fared better than those who kept their babies.[74] The Adolescent Family Life program aggressively promoted adoption, and the Office of Population Affairs in the Department of Health and Human Services produced an "adoption resource directory" and an "adoption information guidebook" to facilitate the process.[75] Throughout the Reagan-Bush era, adoption was promoted as a cure for child poverty and a way to reduce welfare costs.[76] When congressmen discussed adoption, they assumed that the best thing the government could do for the child of a poor, single mother was to transfer him or her to wealthier parents. They assumed that poor mothers should not, properly, become mothers. Christopher Smith, a Republican representative from New Jersey, spoke for himself and many others when he explained the virtues of adoption: "It provides a child who might otherwise face a bleak or less than positive childhood [with a poor mother] the prospect of having loving parents, a stable home, a higher standard of living, and enhanced career opportunities as the child matures into adulthood." Smith provided data to prove his point: "In fact, according to the 1982 National Survey of Family Growth, only 2% of adopted children live in poverty, compared with almost 62% living with [poor, unmarried] mothers . . . We must make it easier for these children to find families."[77] Many Americans embraced a logic that denied poor women a legitimate mother and family relationship to a child they could not afford to raise on their own. Many seemed to desire a financial test for motherhood in the United States.

Policies facilitating both adoption and foster care in the 1980s and beyond were characterized by an eagerness to free the child as quickly as possible from an inappropriate mother. When Marcia Robinson, a lawyer for the Children's Rights Project of the American Civil Liberties Union, complained during a 1991 congressional hearing about this determination to cut mother-child bonds swiftly and cleanly, Jim McDermott, a Washington Democrat, explained, "the real issue here is let's act before [the poor mothers] change their mind."[78]

A few years later, at another hearing, Patricia Newell, a foster parent, was horrified—she said a chill went up her spine—when legislators and testifiers showed eagerness to terminate parental rights quickly so that children could break their association early with resourceless mothers. She said, "I just actually panicked, and I thought: that is a harsh, harsh [plan] . . . What I thought about was that if [my foster child's] mother's rights had been terminated within one year, she would not be at home with her son . . . today." Newell went on, aware of the presuppositions of her congressional audience, "I really need to say that before I met my [foster child's] mother, I probably thought I was a better parent for him than she, and I based that in large part because I knew that I had resources that she did not have." Patricia Newell was offering a public policy perspective when she concluded her testimony this way: "probably in my forty years of living, I have never done anything more decent and humane and dignified than to help this woman get her child back."[79]

It seems likely that by some point in the Reagan-Bush era, the majority of white, middle-class Americans believed that women who had resources had won the "right to choose" whether and when to become mothers. For them, choice became a capacious, empowering emblem of liberation from the tyranny of biology. "Choice" also became a symbol of middle-class women's arrival as independent consumers. Middle-class women could afford to choose. They had earned the right to choose motherhood, if they liked.

According to many Americans, however, when choice was associated with poor women, it became a symbol of illegitimacy. Poor women had not earned the right to choose. As dependents they could not afford to choose. As dependents they were categorically excluded from good choice making. The specter of poor women illegitimately exercising choice stimulated middle-class Americans to think about constraints and punishments and strategies for transforming choice into duty. The rest of this chapter will be concerned with juxtaposing pairs of late-century policy initiatives to show how policy discussions have drawn on these different views of choice to justify a mostly unspoken but widely accepted proposition: that motherhood should be a class privilege in the United States.

Kathy Ramos's case in 1970 raised sharp questions about whose mothering (and whose biological motherhood) society values and rewards with public funds, and whose society finds less valuable or worthless. In the same way, later policy paradoxes are important indicators that Americans are defining the good mother in class terms today.

The first group of policies surfaced almost simultaneously in the late 1980s and early 1990s: policies promoting what U.S. Representative Patricia Schroeder of Colorado called "family-building activities" for middle-class families (allocating public funds for adoption and infertility treatments) on the one hand, and what might be called the curtailment of family-building activities among the poor (family cap legislation) on the other hand.

When Representative Schroeder introduced legislation promoting family-building activities in the late 1980s, she identified health insurance plans covering federal employees as the place to start. Through these plans, the government could endorse and underwrite "medical procedures necessary to overcome infertility . . . and necessary expenses related to the adoption of a child."[80] In 1988 Schroeder explained why this legislation was so crucial in a democratic country: "It is important that all families be treated equally, and they are not. There is certainly an awful lot of economic discrimination if you don't start your family in the way that has been traditional."[81]

From the first day of the hearings on the Federal Employee Family Building Act of 1987 (H.R. 2852), class issues played the central role in all discussions about opportunities for "family building." What is so striking about these hearings is the way that the middle-class participants speak boldly and resentfully about class or financial barriers to adoption and infertility treatments—both are so expensive. When participants suspend class-specific language, they speak in universal terms, referring to the very broad and deep desire of many people, regardless of class, to become parents. In both cases, though, participants are silent about the class and financial barriers poor women face as they try to keep their own children, or when they find themselves suppliers of babies for better-off people.

One man, who admitted to a very comfortable annual income, spoke during the hearings about his inability to pay for his wife's repeated infertility treatments and about how desperately she and other women wanted to have babies: "I have seen them alternate between crying their hearts out, pleading with God, and doggedly pursuing medical and adoptive procedures, refusing like the Biblical Rachel to be consoled." The director of reproductive endocrinology at Yale University agreed and catalogued the terrible impacts on women unable to be mothers: "They mourn the loss of personal growth, there is tremendous personal growth associated with having children, and these people are denied that . . . [and there is] tremendous loneliness because of the lack of companionship of having children." Another medical infertility expert asked if it was fair that her patients, "who felt less adequate than dogs and cats who can mate and have offspring," could not have children simply because they were not rich enough.

While many speakers at the hearing recognized and resented the means test for middle-class parenthood, they did not address the way the means test constrained women whose resources did not meet middle-class levels. Linda Brownlee, a Virginia woman who had not been able to conceive, described her sadness in terms eerily similar to the terms birthmothers have used to describe their loss: "I remember feeling empty arms imagining what my child would have looked like. I'll never know for certain what he or she would have been like . . . There is no funeral for our dreamchild, no sympathy card, no outward marking of the emptiness we feel."[82] Another woman asked audience members at the congressional hearing to imagine whether they "could . . . in good conscience tell someone, no, you can't have [a baby] because you don't have enough money to pay for it to happen?"[83] Again, this speaker was addressing only the middle-class dilemma, even though her words seemed to embrace precisely the plight of many poor mothers in the 1980s. Kim Gore, an adoptive mother and fourteen-year employee of the Department of Defense, spoke plainly about why she supported the Federal Employee Family Building Act: "because it seems like adoption is only going to be available to the rich." And, she added, "you know, you don't have to be rich to be a good parent."

A pro-adoption administrator expressed the most pragmatic hope for the family-building legislation: "The desire to procreate and raise the next generation should be a choice. [This legislation] would open possibilities for some to bear children and others to create families through adoption."[84] This speaker referred to, but did not acknowledge, that the act would, of necessity, build families for some by encouraging others—resourceless mothers—to surrender their children. (Conservative policy commentator Robert Rector of the Heritage Foundation remarked in these years that many children born out of wedlock need to be moved away from their mothers and, via adoption, placed "into alternative and superior forms of care.")[85] In fact, an adoption agency director identified successful strategies to achieve just this goal: using "public service announcements, radio and TV spots, paid advertising in ethnic newspapers and Yellow Pages, establishing liaisons with schools, hospitals and maternity shelters." The goal here was pointedly financial—and reinforced the shared, though unspoken perspective that motherhood was a status that should be reserved for middle-class women: to target young women who "can go on with their lives without going on public assistance. Their infants are then adopted without going through the public system and at no cost to the government and to tax-payers."[86]

Only one person at these hearings in 1987 and 1988 acknowledged how vulnerable women can be when they are resourceless and babies are in such hot demand. Barbara Eck Manning, founder of Resolve, an organization focusing on the rights and needs of infertile people desiring children, said, "I think we can all agree that if this were a perfect world, there would be no unwanted babies and no babies given up for adoption. Those of us who build our families through adoption must realize that the very fact that babies are available reflects society's failure in providing education, in providing access to family planning, in providing access to medical services and in providing support for young single mothers." Manning added, "It is spurious to discuss ways to increase the numbers of healthy white infants available for adoption, since the only way this could be done is to deny the constitutional rights of women to elect abortion . . . or to coerce them into surrendering their babies after birth."[87]

When Representative Pat Schroeder and others revived a focus on adoption, they were, in part, addressing a concern that "too many" single women in the United States were having babies and too few of them were giving up the babies for adoption. (In 1962, about 702,000 illegitimate children were adopted; these babies accounted for 80 percent of the children adopted in the United States by nonrelatives. In 1969, over 360,000 babies were born to unmarried women; approximately one out of four was placed for adoption. By the end of the 1980s, about a million babies a year were born to single women; fewer than one out of twenty-five was surrendered.)[88] Schroeder and other adoption-advocates in the late 1980s and early 1990s were also concerned about the needs of people such as the ones who spoke at the government hearing on family building. These were people who wanted to find babies but couldn't because surrendered babies had become such a scarce and dear commodity.

Many conservatives in this period expressed frustration about this situation. Particularly frustrating was the fact that "authorities" were no longer able to set and enforce the conditions of motherhood, as various authorities had been able to do in the past.[89] Typically they used harsh language and proposed harsh measures to disqualify poor, single women from motherhood. They mainly stressed the interests of children and potential middle-class adopters while degrading or effacing the interests and motherhood status of poor women. Charles Murray put it this way in 1992: "If need be [the government should] spend lavishly on adoption services and lavishly on orphanages. But the government will no longer try to help the innocent child by subsidizing the parents who made them victims."[90]

Again, effacing poor women as valid mothers and stressing how important class—or possession of financial resources—was to legitimate parenthood status, a Missouri representative to Congress described adoption as a "win-win" situation. He said, "Everyone knows . . . that the child's life expectancies and hopes go up by thousands of percent if the adoptions occur."[91] In the same period, Representative Clay Shaw described adoption as "universally regarded as good," a proposition many birthmothers would surely dispute. The politician indicated what he believed birthmothers, as resourceless mothers, had never been able to offer: "Throughout history, communities have found that adoption is an exceptionally effective way to ensure that children are reared in loving, attentive homes."[92] Hillary Clinton, too, joined the anti–poor-mothers adoption crusade when she endorsed a tax credit for adopting families with incomes up to $75,000. "We should," Clinton said in 1996, "make it possible for thousands more children to be adopted by Mother's Day next year."[93] Public officials and policy advisers implied that poor biological mothers were unfit for Mother's Day commemorations and that public funding should reflect that position. Clinton and supporters of the 1996 Contract With America believed the government should subsidize the transfer of babies to parents with incomes large enough to make hefty tax breaks useful. One can imagine mothers like Marcella Mason trying once again to make the case that with this kind of substantial financial assistance from the government, a poor mother, too, could be an exemplary parent.

Another kind of family-building activity singled out for public funding in the late 1980s was infertility services for middle-class, heterosexual couples. By the late 1980s, a number of technologies had been successfully employed to facilitate pregnancy in women previously unable to conceive. The media and many interested couples were paying close attention to these developments. Many sought infertility services. In 1988, infertility-related expenditures hit one billion dollars, a figure that included payments for more than 1.6 million office visits, up from 600,000 office visits in 1968, despite the fact that there had been no increase in the incidence of infertility.[94]

As with adoption, doctors, infertile men and women, and their advocates spoke forcefully in class terms as they argued for government money to help middle-class Americans pay for expensive family-building treatments. Again, Representative Pat Schroeder introduced the subject of class fairness in the 1987 hearing she chaired. She said, "Although couples of lesser means have a higher incidence of infertility, it is only the well-to-do who can pursue treatment. This bill will correct this inequity by bringing family building within the reach of all working couples." A man who worked for the federal government referred to the dilemma middle-class couples faced as "a cruel choice" and "an emotional nightmare" because they were forced to decide between paying for infertility treatments and owning a house. The government should help people in this situation, he said, since this is "a society that has prided itself on its advances in equal opportunity and treatment of all its citizens."[95] Class references and civil rights–inspired language made a strong argument for federal support for anyone who needed financial assistance to build a family.

Yet few advocates acknowledged that the highest rates of infertility occurred among African-American and Latina women, poor women, unmarried women, and women enrolled in Medicaid.[96] Few referred to the fact that infertility treatments—which according to a government study cost between $2,055 and $22,000—were geographically remote from and financially inaccessible to these groups and likely to remain that way.[97] A researcher for the Reproductive Laws Project at this time noted that by law, government-supported family planning services "are supposed to treat those wanting to conceive as well as those who do not." But, she found, women without "adequate resources" were unlikely to locate a clinic willing to help them conceive.[98] At a government hearing on these matters, Dr. Robert Windom, assistant secretary for health at the Department of Health and Human Services, was pressed to acknowledge that while twenty-five states and the District of Columbia "defined their family planning services under Medicaid to include the provision of fertility services and drugs, [a] recent informal survey suggests that the incidence and cost of these services and drugs has been minimal."[99] In fact, the federal government's Office of Technology Assessment reported in the late 1980s that it had been unable to identify any state program that had paid benefits to any woman on Medicaid seeking in vitro fertilization.

At this time, fertility technologies were unpopular with most health insurers, not only with Medicaid administrators. Group health plans tended to omit coverage of "fringe" services, such as in vitro fertilization (IVF), that were perceived as experimental or as engaging certain moral or ethical concerns. IVF, in particular, was, according to a government report, perceived in the late 1980s as a "procedure of uncertain benefit to a few at the expense of the many." Insurers described IVF and other in-fertility treatments as lacking "a societal consensus."

Nonetheless, in 1987, the state of Delaware decided to cover all state employees for IVF, and so did Maryland, followed by a small group of other states, which like Maryland typically excluded Medicaid sub-scribers from this benefit. According to a 1987 study by the Health In-surance Association of America, more than 40 percent of the general insured population was actually covered for most of the services asso-ciated with IVF, even if various health policies did not cover IVF by name. Many federal workers—there were approximately three million workers covered by government health insurance in the late 1980s—had government-supported insurance policies issued by Aetna, for example, or Blue Cross–Blue Shield, companies that excluded IVF by name but in fact paid for infertility services on a case-by-case basis with public money.[100] Far from causing a public uproar or even public uneasiness, when the government spent public money to support middle-class family-building activities, it was, according to two policy experts, "the subject of very little public debate."[101]

Most middle-class Americans, including policy makers and politi-cians, seemed to agree that it was a "tragedy" when a middle-class woman could not have a baby. The president of a pharmaceutical com-pany that manufactured fertility drugs spoke to a large constituency in the late 1980s when he defined "fundamental rights to life" as including "access to infertility therapy."[102] Yet many people seemed to draw the line at applying these principles to the family-building urges of poor women. Most Americans agreed that motherhood was "a source of self- and community esteem" for middle-class women, "of family life, of conti-nuity, and of loving relationships."[103] Most agreed "that the desire to raise a family is a fundamental human longing for most adults, and to be denied that experience is a denial of the right to choose."[104] Yet when women with few resources had the desire to have a child or to build a family, many Americans freely and quickly applied a financial test for motherhood and found such women inappropriate candidates for moth-erhood. As we have seen, many argued that for the poor, motherhood was a source not of self- and community esteem or loving relationships but of dependency and even depravity.

During the same season that some members of Congress were promoting middle-class family-building activities, federal and state politicians were engaged in plans and fantasies to give governmental authorities greater power than ever before to control how resourceless women made fertility-related decisions, and to control the arsenal of punishments leveled against a poor woman who made the "wrong choice."[105] In the late 1980s, in Michigan and other states, politicians were working to cancel Medicaid funds that had given poor women the choice of abortion, at roughly the same time that Pat Schroeder introduced the bill mandating insurance coverage for middle-class infertility cures. On the federal level, President Bush approved big cutbacks in the WIC program—covering nutrition and health care for infants and their low-income mothers—while Pat Schroeder and some of her colleagues spoke piously to the middle class about the basic human right to create family and the joys of tending one's children.[106]

But the most dramatic and perhaps the most popular effort to restrict family building among the poor was the introduction of "family caps," a mechanism for uncoupling the size of poor families and the amount of the welfare check. For about forty years or more by this time, politicians had been claiming that poor women who collected welfare had sex—and so babies—for government money. The first success in passing a law to squelch this alleged form of prostitution was a Georgia bill passed in both houses of the state legislature and signed by the governor in February 1951. The legislation, which the federal Social Security Commission pressed Georgia state lawmakers to repeal before it went into effect, would have denied welfare grants to "more than one illegitimate child of a mother."[107]

For more than a decade following the Georgia effort, the federal government actively discouraged states from trying to constrain poor women from having babies using this kind of law. In 1960, a prominent government report on illegitimacy and its relation to the welfare program counseled state legislators and others: "An additional child may mean an increased [welfare] payment to meet part of the cost of the child's care. For the mother, no 'profit' is involved. Rather, an additional child adds to her responsibilities and in many instances, means spreading her income a little thinner."[108]

By 1970, however, signs of change in the government's attitude were apparent. When Maryland passed a law capping the maximum welfare grant at a figure fixed for a family of six, the state claimed it was providing incentives for family planning. In *Dandridge v. Williams*, the U.S. Supreme Court affirmed Maryland's welfare plan, and the majority opinion spoke disapprovingly about poor women having babies.[109] According to legal scholar Thomas Ross, *Dandridge* constructed a poor mother's choice to have another child as "a choice to put her entire family in an even worse position." Ross points out that when the Supreme Court accepted Maryland's family planning argument, it accepted the charge that for a poor mother, becoming pregnant is an act of "moral weakness."[110] Ross suggests that to understand how this decision "draws on the theme of the moral weakness of the poor," we might "imagine the popular response to a similar, hypothetical state action directed against wage-earner families [that deduct dependents for tax liability–reducing purposes]."[111]

National attention was focused on the "family cap" as an effective way to get poor mothers to stop having children when Wayne Bryant, a "wealthy, patrician lawyer," the highest-ranking African-American legislator in New Jersey—he was the Democratic assembly leader—introduced family cap legislation in the spring of 1991. Bryant's plan denied increased benefits to mothers on welfare if they gave birth to additional children while they were on public relief. The proposal garnered so much attention in part because Bryant was African-American; many white politicians and others felt that a black insider was finally willing to stand up and speak the truth about his own people.[112] (Bryant apparently found it necessary to defend himself against the charge that he was prejudiced against his own people; when he appeared before the U.S. Senate, he said, "Let me state from the outset, sir, this is not a David Duke.")

The New Jersey family cap proposal also created sparks because of Bryant's timing: almost twelve years into the Reagan-Bush era, the majority of middle-class Americans had embraced the truth of the Welfare Queen and was eager for strategies to dethrone her, particularly during the economic recession of the early 1990s. Lawrence Mead accurately described just how hot the family cap plan was when he testified before the Senate in 1992: "There has been great interest in this. In fact, I spent much of the last two months on the phone talking to reporters about these proposals. I even got a call from *Glamour* magazine. When *Glamour* wants to write about welfare, then you know it's on the front burner."[113]

Throughout late 1991 and early 1992, states applied to the Bush administration for permission to bypass federal welfare guidelines and institute family cap regulations based on the New Jersey model.[114] Presidential candidate Bill Clinton, making a political calculation, spoke out in favor of the New Jersey plan in May 1992 after having opposed the plan previously.[115] Meanwhile, in New Jersey, the combination of the family cap and state funding of abortions for poor women apparently steered, and may have coerced, poor women to have abortions instead of children.[116] When the U.S. Supreme Court affirmed New Jersey's family cap regulations in C.K. v. Shalala, the majority claimed that this legislation could have "an ameliorative effect" on poor women by curtailing "family instability" and other social ills resulting from poor women having children.[117] Legal scholar Linda C. McClain argues that this court decision "seems to carry the further message that an important and legitimate way to end poverty is to end procreation by poor people."[118] Longtime New York senator and family poverty specialist Daniel Patrick Moynihan acknowledged how far Americans had come since the human rights era of the 1960s in accepting the proposition that public policy should constrain the reproductive choices of poor women when he said in 1992, "Twenty-five years ago [the New Jersey family cap regulation] would have caused howls."[119]

But by the early 1990s, the years of anti-poor, anti-welfare rhetoric beamed across the country had had what Cynthia Newbille of the National Black Women's Health Project called "a devastating effect on the public's perception of [poor] women."[120] In these years, conservative writers and policy makers frequently invoked frightening images of poor mothers and sometimes used these images to justify transferring their babies to middle-class couples or curtailing public support for these mothers altogether. Conservative analyst Heather MacDonald characterized a poor mother in 1994 as one "who has been beating her children, or failing to feed and bathe them." MacDonald discouraged funding for rehabilitative services because she doubted that such a woman could be rehabilitated. Instead, she championed child removal as the best solution for saving the children of poor mothers. Marge Roukema, U.S. representative from New Jersey, also championed removal because, she said, "ultimately . . . Americans and the Congress will not countenance children being raised in abusive drug-infested households or going hungry in the street."[121] Neither woman provided statistics or citations to bolster their characterizations.

Not surprisingly, Charles Murray and many Republican politicians who looked to Murray for policy guidance drew on these scary images of poor mothers—and on the uneasiness of many Americans responding to the news that their tax dollars were being thrown at these women—to trumpet a dramatic policy initiative based on the premise that poor women should not be mothers. Newt Gingrich and the conservative firebrands in Congress began to tout a plan to send children of poor mothers to orphanages.[122] This plan, they confidently claimed, would solve the illegitimacy problem and the welfare problem, and would finally convince poor women that the government was serious: no more help for their kind.[123] Tony Blankley, Gingrich's press secretary, explained why he thought this initiative captured so much attention. "Orphanage," he said, "is a term that communicates very well."[124] Numerous polls at the time showed that most Americans did not support the orphanage initiative, but Republicans continued promoting the idea.[125] One close observer commented, "Raising the specter of orphanages was viewed as a means to persuade unmarried mothers and welfare-dependent women into controlling their reproduction."[126] In an essay with a title that captured perhaps the most important domestic policy debate in the 1990s, "Do Poor Women Have a Right to Bear Children?," sociologists Christopher Jencks and Kathryn Edin characterized the Contract With America crowd as "welfare bashers [who] would like to prevent the poor from having children."[127]

Some critics pointed out that "welfare bashers" wanted to institutionalize the children of poor mothers simply because of "the absence of jobs for mothers willing to work" or the absence of jobs that paid a living wage.[128] Legal scholar Dorothy Roberts emphasized that policy makers were identifying a group of women—iconically Black—who were "less entitled to be parents." In various venues, Roberts asked Americans to consider the proposition that "denying someone the right to bear children deprives her of a basic part of her humanity."[129] Katha Pollitt, columnist for the Nation, argued that the "Murray-Gingrich orphanage proposal" did not simply threaten poor mothers. Rather, the proposal was an example of "symbolic politics" that aimed to teach Americans "to think of children who have living parents as 'orphans' just because those parents are young, female, unmarried and poor." Pollitt went on, "We are . . . being taught to see those mothers as having no rights and nothing to contribute—as being, in effect, dead."[130]

Someone sympathetic to the plight of poor mothers invited Clarissa Pinkola Estes, author of the enormously popular book *Women Who Run With the Wolves*, to speak at a congressional hearing on the Contract With America in 1995, when conservatives were promoting orphanages and other means of punishing poor mothers. Pinkola Estes, whose speech caused intense, partisan applause in the hearing chambers, echoed Marcella Mason's sentiments. She said, in part, "[T]he money that it takes to fund [orphanages and maternity homes] would more properly go directly to the recipients . . . As a woman myself who when I was eighteen years old had my first child—as a teenager—I think that most of us, even though we had made a mistake, does not mean that we are stupid." Fundamentally, Pinkola Estes argued that being young and being poor did not disqualify her or other women from motherhood.[131]

Politicians were largely uninterested in, or disagreed with, this argument as they pushed on toward "welfare reform" in the mid-1990s. In fact, the welfare reform bill that won bipartisan support in 1996, commonly called the Personal Responsibility Act (PRA), encoded a deeply negative assessment of poor mothers into law. Over and over in the introductory material appended to the PRA are "findings" that strongly suggest only women with proper and adequate resources can or should be mothers. The "findings" also indicate that poor mothers are illegitimate mothers, produce poor-quality children, and must be stopped from reproducing.

In the wake of the PRA, other government and community agencies have followed Congress's lead, adopting programs and slogans designed to convey (and enforce) this message: "Don't become a parent until you are truly ready to support a child."[132] In November 1999, the *Baltimore Sun* reported that some anti–teen pregnancy groups had adopted the slogan, "A baby costs $474 a month. How much is your allowance?"[133] These financial test/reality-testing messages mask a profoundly important set of issues about who can or can't "afford" to be a mother in the United States. The fact is, using the affordability test reveals that millions of girls and women cannot afford to become mothers because of circumstances beyond their own control. Jencks and Edin point out that "in

1989, a single working mother with two children needed about $15,000 worth of goods and services to make ends meet. Less than half the 25-to-34-year-old women [the demographic group with the fastest-growing number of single mothers] who worked in 1989 earned that much."[134] Using 1997 data, a study called "Equal Pay for Working Families" found that if women got equal pay, the annual family incomes of single working mothers would increase $4,459 on average—reducing poverty rates for this group by half, from 25.3 percent to 12.6 percent.[135] (Also important here is the fact that almost half of the children on welfare were born to women who were married at the time they gave birth.)

The most important point Jencks and Edin make is that economic policy in the United States creates and depends on sustaining a pool of low-wage workers, including women who make salaries too low to enable them to "afford" motherhood. The sociologists put it this way: "As long as America remains committed to competitive labor markets, open borders, and weak labor unions, most marginally employable adults will need some kind of public assistance if they have children."[136] In other words, using a financial test for motherhood would exclude millions of women in the United States from having children because their employers pay white women 73.2 percent and minority women 63.7 percent of what white men earn.[137]

These data seem never to make an impression on politicians. Nor have politicians and policy makers been moved by the data, available both before and after "welfare reform" was enacted, that many poor mothers have been stymied in their efforts to earn enough to "afford" their children because of the absence of day care opportunities. In 1994, Illinois had 34,000 families on a waiting list for day care, California families had a two-to-three-year wait, and thirty-three other states reported substantial waiting periods as well.[138] In 1999, a study by the U.S. Department of Health and Human Services found that 82 percent of New York families eligible for government-subsidized child care were not receiving it, and that nationally the figure was even higher.[139]

In a brilliant study of poor mothers—their work and survival strategies—Kathryn Edin and Laura Lein emphasize the point that the financial test for motherhood would exclude millions of women through no fault of their own. Edin and Lein find that what poor mothers lack is "a living wage," not values or worthiness. They reject the personal attacks on poor mothers as dependents and bad choice makers and say, instead, that poor mothers' problem is a "labor-market problem." Poor mothers in their study "had made repeated efforts to attain self-sufficiency through work but the kinds of jobs they could get paid too little, offered little security in the short term and provided few opportunities over time. Meanwhile," they found, "mothers who chose to work were even worse off in material terms than their welfare counterparts."[140] Judging by the level of support for "welfare reform" rhetoric, most Americans would look at the bank balances of both the mothers on welfare and the ones at low-paying, dead end jobs and determine that neither group had the right to be mothers because they couldn't support children adequately on their own steam. By inference, it seems, most Americans embrace a proposition that is profoundly problematic in a democratic society, that motherhood should be a class privilege. Motherhood is appropriate, it seems, only for women with enough money to meet the financial test.

A quite nasty development in late twentieth-century America was the enthusiastic willingness of "policy experts" to ignore factors such as wage levels and child care availability when they excoriated poor women, crafted public policies to punish them, and defined them as not-mothers. Charles Murray, whose ideas have had such a powerful impact on the opportunity of poor mothers to care for their own children, claimed that it "makes little difference" why poor single mothers lacked steadfastness, maturity, and competence. Perhaps the cause was youth, he said, or "drug addiction, low ability, an unjust social system, or defective character."[141] But Murray's refusal to incorporate or consider findings such as Edin and Lein's denied his work "empirical respectability," even while it reserved him "a seat at the right hand of power."[142]

Throughout the 1990s, Murray encouraged and teamed up with others who like himself ignored evidence and eschewed empathy as they mounted scurrilous attacks on poor mothers. These women comprised a group Lawrence Mead classified as living by "impulse," as "self-destructive," as "immature and uncommitted."[143] Another analyst likened a poor single mother, categorically, to a heroin addict and approved public policies that raised "the spectre of starvation" for such people. Only looking starvation in the face would move poor mothers into the workforce, this man claimed.[144] Prominently in the 1990s, influential conservative spokesmen such as William Bennett called for restigmatizing the status of poor single mothers as another way of persuading poor women to meet their social obligation not to reproduce.[145] A statement issued in 1994 by the Progressive Policy Institute, an arm of the Democratic Leadership Council, called for renewing the stigma and declared, "It is wrong—not simply foolish or impractical—for women and men to make babies they cannot support emotionally and financially."[146]

Such spokesmen were, apparently, unconcerned with providing evidence for their damning assertions. They were also rarely willing to admit or consider at all the perspectives of poor mothers themselves. When one rare exemplar, Tandi Graff, was invited into a congressional hearing room to testify about her experiences as a welfare mother, she swiftly turned the tables on the members of Congress before her. Graff told them that their Contract With America proposals would have destroyed her as a young poor mother. "Your plan wants to cap the very [assistance] that helped me to succeed," she said. Trying to teach the lawmakers several commonsense lessons at once, Graff boldly challenged them "to hand in your pay checks for one month and live on welfare. You will discover that it is not a luxurious lifestyle." Graff added, "I knew I was a better mother during those times when I wasn't worried about paying for my basic survival." Finally, Tandi Graff posed the question that she believed was at the heart of the "welfare reform problem": "Are you trying to get people off welfare by solving problems or are you punishing them for the choices that you disagree with? If you are trying to solve the problem," Graff advised, "go back to the drawing board, and listen to people like me."

But since people like Tandi Graff were rarely allowed in places where the consequential decisions were being made, lawmakers continued to titillate each other and miseducate Americans with horrifying recitals of the behavior of poor mothers. Representative Jim Nussle of Iowa delivered a typical recital, casually, anecdotally, without proper evidence, in fact without any evidence at all, in the halls of Congress in 1995: "Let me give you the option that appears to be out on the street right now for a lot of mothers, and that is throwing their babies in a dumpster as opposed to giving an opportunity, whether it is an orphanage [or not] . . . some kind of placement for the protection of that child . . . What would be your advice? I mean if the only opposition is dumpsters versus orphanages, what option would you choose?"[147]

In the end, lawmakers crafted "options" they defined as more practical, to remove children from the "decisively, profoundly negative" effects of living with their single poor mothers.[148] They enacted legislation that forced mothers with infants as young as twelve weeks into the workforce and the babies into child care situations. After the PRA became law, more and more states developed work rules that approached the midcentury Georgia regulation that forced all "able-bodied mothers with no child under one month of age" to work for wages.[149] Edin and Lein stressed the obvious when they observed, "For parents who have sole responsibility for their children . . . [e]very hour spent in the workplace is an hour children must spend without their parents."[150] In the mid-1990s, a bipartisan and overwhelming majority of lawmakers endorsed this separation, but only for the poorest mothers and their children, as we shall see.

Lawmakers embraced the PRA with a lick and a prayer and a lot of confident talk about restoring the work ethic and fortifying the American family. But in fact they could not refer to studies showing that the provisions of the PRA would yield what they hoped. Nor did they have data showing that the new policies would not harm target populations. In fact, it is striking how confidently Congress imposed "welfare reform" on poor women and their children, when they actually knew so little about the effect of welfare on poor people or the likely impacts of welfare reform. One prominent scholar described the state of the research upon which new policies were built as "generally so flawed methodologically and so narrowly conceived that no study has succeeded in credibly isolating either the impact of welfare on family structure or the causes of social failure."[151] Another group of scholars expressed their frustration directly in 1996: "It is infuriating that weak and often contradictory images of the impact of welfare are allowed to dominate public discussion and suggestions for the improvement of the welfare system."[152]

At the time the PRA became law, researchers did not know what the impact would be on young children in very poor families to have their only active parent go to work twelve weeks after giving birth.[153] They did not know if poor mothers pushed into the workforce would find subsidized, quality day care for infants and young children, or what consequences babies and toddlers would suffer if the government did not choose to provide the "massive increase in the resources [for] early childhood education and high quality day care" that would be necessary under the new regime.[154] It was not at all clear to researchers that sending poor mothers into the workforce could lift poor families out of poverty. Researchers readily admitted this uncertainty, but politicians did not.[155]

Strangely, as the PRA became law, the information that *had* been gathered by researchers about hardships that brought poor mothers into welfare offices (desertion, domestic violence, including histories of sexual abuse, low-paying jobs, lack of education, being born into poverty), the brief periods most families stayed on welfare (less than two years), and the small number of children most poor mothers were raising (1.9), was not widely available or generally accepted. When studies showed that welfare mothers placed high value on child rearing and were worried about how their very young and school-aged children would be supervised while mothers worked, this type of information was not published in mainstream venues.[156] Nor were data showing that mothers on AFDC were more likely than other mothers to be caring for a child with a chronic health problem, but these mothers were more likely to have jobs that didn't carry sick leave benefits or other paid leave or flexible work arrangements.[157]

Maybe most consequential, politicians, policy makers, and ordinary Americans did not discuss the findings of contemporary studies showing that among poor mothers, the ones who fared best as parents were the ones with more resources, such as higher levels of literacy, more years of schooling, and greater social supports. Instead, welfare reformers and their champions pushed policies that ignored the fact that resources, not constraints and punishments, are what help a woman, any woman, take good care of her children.[158]

Arguably, the PRA's most important cultural accomplishment was to mark ever more sharply the separation and difference between middle-class mothers and poor mothers in American society. The PRA announced that poor mothers would, from now on, pay for being poor in two humiliating and punishing ways: (1) public policy generally cut off the access of poor mothers to choice making, thus alienating them from the very hallmark of modern womanhood; and (2) public policy specifically excluded poor mothers from making choices that other mothers may make—whether to take care of their children or to work for wages, and if the latter, how soon after giving birth and for how many hours a week. All that was now prescribed for poor mothers.

In a weird twist, just following the government's enactment of welfare reform, Congress held hearings about the matter of giving tax credits to middle-class mothers so they could choose to stop working outside the home. It must be stressed here that when the government achieves social goals through tax policy, such as giving tax credits to one group or another, the effect is similar to the impact of giving or withholding welfare. Both policies make some people more or less wealthy. So when Congress explored tax credits for middle-class mothering in the same general period as it dramatically curtailed the possibility of mothering by poor women, this was notable.[159]

The 1998 hearings on "Caring for America's Children" were characterized by powerful claims that "non-family care of very young children tends to be damaging." Danielle Crittenden, a spokesperson for conservative think tanks, presented the case of mothers appealing to Congress to reduce their family tax burden so they could afford to stay home. She said, "No amount of Fisher-Price geegaws and cheerfully painted walls and chirping, brisk day-care workers trained in sensitivity can replace a mother's love and attention. Nor can putting our children in these surroundings ease our maternal fears for their well-being and our aching longing for their company."[160]

Senator Paul Wellstone of Minnesota dropped in on this hearing in time to hear Crittenden and others speak about the glories of maternal child tending and the dangers of day care centers. He made the connection few others were willing to make: "As long as we are talking about the importance of a parent staying at home and how much we value that, I think . . . we better revisit . . . what is happening to the welfare bill . . . what is happening to [poor] children, where they are and what kind of child care they are getting, because [in the case of poor mothers], there is no option to stay at home . . . We have somehow kind of put that in parentheses and turned our gaze away from it, and it is a pretty frightening picture."

Helen Blank, director of child care policy for the Children's Defense Fund, backed up Wellstone. Blank provided data showing the large number of poor children in the United States with single, working mothers who did not have the kind of tax liability that could be reduced by a tax credit. This scheme, she showed, would not help poor mothers stay home. Blank described the 34 million women who worked at hourly jobs, half of them for a wage of $7.90 an hour or less, as people who work because they "have no choice."[161]

Wellstone and Blank did not succeed during this hearing in their attempt to match and merge the interests of poor and middle-class women. In fact, they spurred other speakers at the event to stress the differences between these mothers, especially how the size of income separated these mothers definitively as mothers.[162] Maggie Gallagher, a scholar at the conservative Institute for American Values, spoke sharply to this point: "Most married homemakers that I know do not believe and do not appreciate being seen as cognates of dependent welfare mothers."[163] Gallagher and Senator Dan Coates of Indiana underscored the reason for this: middle-class, married women who take care of their kids, they said, are good mothers, whereas poor mothers, mostly single, are "destructive."[164]

In addition to distinguishing mothers by class or income, these speakers were equally willing to endorse different arrangements for children, depending on their class. Poor children should go to day care centers, even while we know, according to Senator Coates, "that the children's development is best enhanced, we are . . . giving the child the best chance for the future, by recognizing that the emotional attachment to the mother and to the family in raising them . . . is better for the child than the alternative." Danielle Crittenden and her conservative colleagues supported the provisions of welfare reform that mandated that poor mothers work for wages and send their children to child care. But at these hearings, Crittenden called these innovations "creepy" because they tried to connect working mothers with their children in day care via the Internet, or allowed breast-feeding on the job. These innovations were "creepy" because they were such feeble attempts to make up for the lack of real mother care. Deploring how work separated middle-class mothers from their children, Crittenden asked, "The New York animal shelters will not let you adopt a cat or dog if you work full time. Why should our attitude toward children be any less?" For the most part, participants in this event were firm about the fact that the impact of work and child care on the poor was simply a "separate policy question." The point of the event was to focus on "healthy, functioning families and their needs."[165]

U.S. Representative Patsy Mink of Hawaii was not present at "Caring for America's Children," though elsewhere Mink spoke directly about the class-determined visions of motherhood and mother care that shaped this event. She said, "The desire to have women work is limited to only poor women with dependent children so as to teach responsibility. For non-poor women the need to remain in the home to nurture their children into wholesome maturity is still the social ethic of our time."[166]

At about the same time that Mink spoke about motherhood and class, a Santa Fe woman following welfare debates in Congress wrote a letter to the House Ways and Means Committee that chastised lawmakers for dividing mothers and their rights, responsibilities, and privileges, by class. This woman asked, "Why is it that a woman who, because she is of a privileged economic class, chooses to stay home and raise her children is performing the most important job in the world, but a poor woman is a lazy, no-good cheat? You preach family values, but is it only for a privileged class?"[167]

When Marcella Mason tried to claim her mother rights to her own child in 1970, even though she was poor, the winds were blowing ill for women like her. And over the next generation, the ill winds blew stronger. Many Americans were unhappy in the 1970s that even so dependable a cultural figure as Mother had blasted apart into unfamiliar new forms. Many Americans were uncomfortable contemplating feminist-careerist mothers and second-income mothers with full-time jobs and kids in day care. Even more troubling to many were "welfare mothers" and the explosion of single mothers in the United States.[168] At the same time, the "traditional" stay-at-home, take-care-of-the-kids image of motherhood was seriously tarnished. According to the First Women's State of the Union Address, delivered in 1977, "*The Dictionary of Occupational Titles* published by the Department of Labor classifies mothering and homemaking skills in the lowest possible skill code; the occupation of dog trainer is given a higher numerical rating."[169] Reflecting these trends, a young woman attending a meeting on the family at Tulane University, also in 1977, was reported in the *New York Times* as plaintively asking the panel of experts before her, "I just want to get married and have a child. Is that still okay?"[170]

Modern American women were supposed to build new relationships to work and money and to sex and reproductive control in the 1970s. These prescriptive, new relationships did breathe potency into the idea that "choice" was the sine qua non of modern womanhood. Having been freed from laws and taboos governing contraception, abortion, single motherhood, welfare, and job eligibility, a great deal of women's behavior now appeared to be governed solely by individual choices. Many girls and women in the United States benefited from social and cultural changes that allowed them more control over their own lives. But many Americans were not prepared to associate choice making with a traditionally dependent population: women.[171] This uneasiness gave rise to persistent questions, such as: What kind of woman chooses to leave her children for a job? What kind of woman doesn't? What kind of woman chooses an abortion? What kind of woman chooses to have too many children? In an era of redefining motherhood, "choice" became a very useful concept for sorting out good women from bad, responsible women from irresponsible women, independent women from dependent women.

As Americans started in the 1970s to struggle with the reality that most women were making open, consequential choices about work and money and about sex and reproduction, there were a number of early signs that what many women considered "choice" was viewed as self-indulgence, or worse, by others.[172] The dissenting Supreme Court justices in *Roe v. Wade* were clear on this matter. They associated "the power of choice" with women's "convenience," "whim," "caprice," with women willing to "exterminate" their pregnancies "for no reason at all" or because of their "dislike of children."[173] Bioethicist Ruth Hubbard matches the rise of "choice" with the decline of the "image of the selfless mother who sacrifices her need to those of her family." In its place, we got "the selfish mother who puts her own needs first and pits her interests against those of her fetuses and children."[174] Many Americans were not happy to see women apparently slighting their "maternal instincts" to follow untrustworthy, individualistic impulses—especially if the individualists were poor women.[175]

But increasingly over the last decades of the twentieth century, Americans interpreted reproductive "choice" to refer to individualistic, marketlike behavior, and not surprisingly, motherhood became an economic status. As one welfare reform advocate put it, "The most important concept that . . . Congress can enact is that of an economic safe harbor for children. A child needs to be in the custody of that parent who is most financially capable of caring for him."[176] Politicians, policy experts, social commentators, and many ordinary Americans agreed: poverty and motherhood are incompatible. Common wisdom today insists that children deserve parents with appropriate bank balances. Charles Murray spoke aptly for this perspective when he said, "A great many [poor girls and women] have no business being mothers."[177]

Since the 1970s, the emergence of the public concept of "choice" has stimulated people in the public policy arena to argue that community norms are no longer powerful enough to sort out the good choice makers from the bad, the appropriate mothers from the women "who have no business being mothers." We need, they have argued with increasing vigor, policies such as the PRA to disqualify or punish the latter. As these kinds of policy intentions have evolved, they have yielded some very troubling policy intentions regarding the lives of resourceless women.

For the past two decades, many congressional and state politicians have worked hard to ensure that few poor women would have abortions paid for with public funds. At the same time, many of the same politicians have overseen cuts in welfare benefits, including day care subsidies, and have worked to impose "family caps" and stimulate public censure of "excessively fertile" women. Many Americans have had a hard time understanding how these apparently contradictory policy initiatives can simultaneously serve our national interests. Some feminists and others have adopted the slogan "Life begins at conception and ends at birth" to express their frustration with the impact of these contradictory policies. But for an *explanation* of how politicians—and a large segment of the American public—resolve the apparent contradiction or live comfortably with the paradox, one may look at the revitalized relationship between dependency and choice. Today many Americans are convinced that poor women as dependents do not and cannot make good choices. This conviction tends to apply categorically, whether a poor woman chooses to get an abortion that she does not have the money to pay for herself, or if she chooses to have a baby while she is poor. Policy makers insist that these pregnancy and motherhood choices of poor, dependent women, *whatever the choices are*, are immature, reckless, selfish, and bad. When poor women appear to exercise choice regarding pregnancy and motherhood, they are blamed and blocked, and finally excoriated as bad mothers.

Pregnant teenagers, of course, face similar policy paradoxes. Many of the same politicians and policy makers determined to block this group's access to sex education and safe, effective contraception also champion parental consent laws to constrain the abortion choices of teenagers. And these are often the same folks who lament teenage pregnancy and lambaste poor, teenage mothers. Again, many Americans live comfortably with apparently contradictory policies that are resolved not by a real belief that dependent girls will stop having sex, but by the conviction that they can be stopped from making choices.

The role that the dependency-choice antithesis plays in making sense of these paradoxical policies illustrates the powerful relationship between welfare politics and reproductive politics today. Far from simply referring to the separate arenas of welfare and abortion, dependency and choice vibrantly interact, depend on each other for meaning, and together shape and justify punitive and constraining public policies, including eugenically based definitions of motherhood.

Historian Linda Kerber has shown how, in the Revolutionary era, "a liberal language of independence and individual choice could accommodate white women as full participants in the life of the state."[178] This language located women's worth in mothering activities: acting as custodians of civil morality, facilitating political socialization, teaching civic culture.[179] All of these activities, of course, were performed in the service of raising the next generation of good citizens. By the end of the twentieth century, however, notions of "civic morality," "political socialization," and "civic culture" were drowning in the market-oriented culture that swamped all human activities, including childbearing and child rearing.

The idea that a mother's most important job was to rear good citizens has always been complicated in a country where children of color and their mothers have had incomplete citizenship rights.[180] In the last decades of the twentieth century, Americans enlarged that tradition of exclusion by defining poor mothers categorically as unqualified for the job. Recent public policy commitments to alienate poor women from "choice" have given us a national policy that aims to establish a financial test of consumer readiness for motherhood. Women who fail the financial test—who cannot afford to give their babies "advantages" but have babies anyway—are targets of public judgment, public name calling, and punitive policies. When Kerber considered the role of mothers in the early years of this country, she associated the task of mothering most strongly with "responsibility for maintaining public virtue."[181] Today the idea of "public virtue" is just about nonexistent as a cultural attribute or as a goal of child rearing. Possibly the most vibrant training up that goes on in the contemporary American family is consumer training. In this family, the mother is blamed and found wanting if she isn't qualified to train up good consumers—that is, if she is poor.

That is the problem with choice. In theory, choice refers to individual preference and wants to protect all women from reproductive coercion. In practice, though, choice has two faces. The contemporary language of choice promises dignity and reproductive autonomy to women with resources. For women without, the language of choice is a taunt and a threat. When the language of choice is applied to the question of poor women and motherhood, it begins to sound a lot like the language of eugenics: women who cannot afford to make choices are not fit to be mothers. This mutable quality of choice reminds us that sex and reproduction—motherhood—provide a rich site for controlling women, based on their race and class "value."

The ways we use the idea of choice—distinguishing good choice makers from bad choice makers—lead us straight to a clutch of crucial questions: What qualifications do Americans want to establish for motherhood in the United States? Do we want educational qualifications, age, ethnic, racial, marital, financial qualifications? Do Americans want motherhood to be a class privilege? A life experience only available to middle-class women? Do Americans want the federal government and the states to answer these questions for us? Should the government or the community enforce qualified, credentialed motherhood in the United States? (Can reproductive "choice" coexist with "credentialed" motherhood?) For many women who participated in the reproductive rights struggles to gain female autonomy and racial equality, these questions constitute something like a recurrent nightmare. At its best, the reproductive rights movement revealed that women's bodies and their fertility have repeatedly provided rich political opportunities in the United States for politicians and policy makers determined to preserve male supremacy, white supremacy, and the privileges of the middle class. Contemporary questions about reproductive "choice" and qualifications for motherhood suggest that female fertility continues to provide rich political opportunities.

Today, the politics of choice has—unfortunately and unexpectedly—shaped the problematic ways we think about fertility, reproduction, motherhood—and women's status in society. First, "choice" degrades a woman's decision about whether to become a mother by tightly associating that decision with the most essential consumerist concept of our time: choice. It turns out that in this country, women's special guarantee is a consumer protection. To make that protection worth anything at all, a woman has to be a "legitimate consumer," a person with sufficient resources to enter the (reproductive) marketplace.

Second, "choice" has effectively blocked cross-class coalitions of women supporting each other's reproductive dignity, as Americans have come to strongly and stubbornly associate financial "independence" with legitimate choice making. It is worth remembering that "free white men" ultimately rejected a property qualification for male voters in the nineteenth century. Yet many Americans want to apply an analogous financial test for motherhood at the beginning of the twenty-first century.

Third, and most fundamentally consequential: "choice" has, for the past generation, underestimated the basic relationship between reproductive autonomy and citizenship status. We have seen that reproductive autonomy—that is, the right to decide whether and when to become a mother and the right to decide whether or not to raise one's child—requires more than the class-and-race-inflected guarantee of "choice." After a generation of practicing "choice," it is clear that all women—regardless of race and class—can achieve the status of full citizen in the United States (and around the world) only when reproductive autonomy is a full-blooded *right*, not merely a consumer's "choice." Achieving the status of full citizen, then, is an unfinished project of the twentieth century for the women of the United States.

NOTES

1: CHOICE IS A MOVING TARGET

1. Thomas Ross, *Just Stories: How the Law Embodies Racism and Bias* (Boston: Beacon Press, 1996), 74.
2. January 22, 1973, *Television News Index and Abstracts, A Guide to the Videotape Collection of the Network Evening News Programs in the Vanderbilt Television Archive* (Nashville: Vanderbilt Television News Archive, 1973), 138.
3. See, for example, "The Abortion Revolution," *Newsweek*, February 5, 1973, 66.
4. Marian Faux, *The Crusaders: Voices from the Abortion Front* (New York: Birch Lane Press, 1990), 5.
5. Sarah Weddington, *A Question of Choice* (New York: Putnam, 1992), 149, 152, 169, 171.
6. Ninia Baehr, *Abortion Without Apology: A Radical History for the 1990s* (Boston: South End Press, 1990), 7–18.
7. Quoted in Kristin Luker, *Abortion and the Politics of Motherhood* (Berkeley: University of California Press, 1984), 97.
8. Suzanne Staggenborg, *The Pro-Choice Movement: Organization and Activism in the Abortion Conflict* (New York: Oxford University Press, 1991), 51.
9. *Television News Index*, 138. The term "freedom of choice" was not a new one on the landscape of American politics. Throughout the 1960s, school systems in the South were under court order to engage in "the free choice method of desegregation." The U.S. commissioner of education called "freedom of choice" in this arena "illusionary," and the U.S. Commission on Civil Rights attributed "the slow pace of integration" to the "so-called 'free choice plans' " because "such plans did not eliminate the racial identity of the schools and placed the burden of change upon Negro parents and pupils who were often reluctant to assert their rights for fear of harassment and intimidation by hostile white persons." When the general counsel to the civil rights commission remarked on whites' strategies to maintain segregation in the workplace, he

showed the utility of this bogus concept: "We seem to have heard some testimony that if signs are taken down from restrooms, colored and white signs . . . and if the employees happen to continue using the restrooms that they have always used, well, that is freedom of choice." It appears that "freedom of choice" could no more establish the educational rights of resourceless African-American children or the Title VI rights of African-American employees in the 1960s than it could establish and protect the reproductive rights of resourceless women in the 1970s and beyond. *Southern School Desegregation, 1966–67* (Washington, D.C.: U.S. Commission on Civil Rights, July 1967), 3; Hearings before the U.S. Commission on Civil Rights, Montgomery, AL, April 27–May 2, 1968 (Washington, D.C.: U.S. Commission on Civil Rights, 1968), 473.

10. Baehr, *Abortion Without Apology*, 39.
11. See Will Saletan, "Electoral Politics and Narrowing the Message," in Rickie Solinger, ed., *Abortion Wars: A Half Century of Struggle, 1950–2000* (Berkeley: University of California Press, 1998), 111–23, for a related discussion of calculated language strategizing in the 1980s.
12. "Abortion: What Happens Now?" *Newsweek*, February 5, 1973, 66.
13. Rickie Solinger, *Wake Up Little Susie: Single Pregnancy and Race before Roe v. Wade* (New York: Routledge, 1992); Deborah Gray White, *Ar'n't I a Woman?: Female Slaves in the Plantation South* (New York: Norton, 1985), and *Too Heavy a Load: Black Women in Defense of Themselves, 1894–1994* (New York: Norton, 1999); Christine Stansell, *City of Women: Sex and Class in New York, 1789–1960* (New York: Knopf, 1986).
14. *Roe v. Wade*, 410 US 113 (1973).
15. Linda Gordon, *Women's Bodies: Women's Rights: Birth Control in America* (New York: Penguin, 1990); James Mohr, *Abortion in America: The Origins and Evolution of National Policy, 1800–1900* (New York: Oxford University Press, 1978); Leslie J. Reagan, *When Abortion Was a Crime: Women, Medicine and the Law, 1867–1973* (Berkeley: University of California Press, 1997). See Rickie Solinger, " 'A Complete Disaster': Abortion and the Politics of Hospital Abortion Committees, 1950–1970," *Feminist Studies* 19 (summer 1993): 241–59, for many examples of psychiatrists and others who assessed women as psychologically ill when they tried to make choices for themselves in the postwar decades.
16. Elizabeth Pope, "Is a Working Mother a Threat to the Home?" *McCall's*, July 1955, 29.
17. "Abortion on Demand," *Time*, January 29, 1973, 47.
18. Teresa Amott and Julie Matthaei, *Race, Gender, and Work: A Multi-Cultural Economic History of Women in the United States* (Boston: South End Press, 1996), 300, 301, 306.
19. Kenneth W. Kammeyer, Norman R. Yetman, MeKee J. McClendon, "Family Planning Services and the Distribution of Black Americans," *Social Problems* 21 (June 1974): 674–89.

20. Loretta Ross, "African American Women and Abortion," in Solinger, ed., *Abortion Wars*, 176.
21. Social Security Act, Title XX, section 2001; United States Code Annotated Section 1397 (West Supp. 1977). See also "Family Planning, Contraception, Voluntary Sterilization and Abortion: An Analysis of Laws and Policies in the United States, Each State and Jurisdiction" (As of October 1, 1976 with 1978 Addenda), prepared by the Alan Guttmacher Institute, DHEW Publication No. (HSA) 79-5623, U.S. Department of Health, Education and Welfare, Public Health Service, Health Services Administration, Rockville, MD, 1978, 5 (hereafter referred to as the Guttmacher Report). See generally Donald T. Critchlow, *Intended Consequences: Birth Control, Abortion, and the Federal Government in Modern America* (New York: Oxford University Press, 1999).
22. See, for example, Robert Kistler, "Women 'Pushed' Into Sterilization, Dr. Charges: Thousands Victimized at Some Inner-city Teaching Hospitals, Report Claims," *Los Angeles Times*, December 12, 1974, 1, 3, 26–28.
23. Elena Rebecca Gutierrez, "The Racial Politics of Reproduction: The Social Construction of Mexican-origin Women's Fertility," unpublished Ph.D. dissertation, Sociology Department, University of Michigan, 1999, 204.
24. The court's decision is quoted in the Guttmacher Report, 8. For information about sterilization of poor women just before *Roe*, see Vaughan Denton and Gerald Sparer, "Ethnic Group and Welfare Status of Women Sterilized in Federally Funded Family Planning Programs, 1972, *Family Planning Perspectives* 6 (fall 1974): 224–29. Also see *A Health Research Group Study on Surgical Sterilization: Present Abuses and Proposed Regulations* (Washington, D.C.: Public Citizens, 1973). For insight into the government's byzantine policies regarding sterilization (including promulgating and blocking efforts to regulate the practice), see the statement of Dr. Warren Hern, in "Quality of Health Care—Human Experimentation," Hearings before the Subcommittee on Health of the Committee on Labor and Public Welfare, U.S. Senate, 93d Congress, 1st sess., April 30, June 28–29, July 10, 1973, Pt. 4 (Washington, D.C.: U.S. Government Printing Office, 1973), 1496–1552.
25. The sterilization of the young, Black, poor Relf sisters of Montgomery, Ala., at this time was shocking and garnered national attention. For an excellent account of this case, see the statement of the Southern Poverty Law Center lawyer for the Relf family, Joseph Levin, in "Quality of Health Care—Human Experimentation," Hearings, 1496–99; also see letter regarding the Relf sisters to the committee by Dr. Cyril Crocker of the Freeman Hospital and Howard University, 1616–20. This volume also contains excellent material on the sterilization of Niel Ruth Cox in Plymouth, N.C., in 1965, and the American Civil Liberties Union's class action suit, *Cox v. Stanton et al.* See 1585–1600. The ACLU's "Statement of Claim" made this point: "over the years, the Sterilization Statute has been applied discriminatorily on the basis of sex, race, age, marital status, class or welfare status, and the "legitimacy" of children of the

person to be sterilized" (1597). When Niel Ruth Cox spoke for herself, she described her situation like this: "I was living with my mother and eight sisters and brothers. My father . . . is dead. My family was on welfare, but payments had stopped for me because I was eighteen. We had no hot or cold running water, only pump water. No stove. No refrigerator, no electric lights. It got cold down there in the winter. I got pregnant when I was seventeen. I didn't know anything about birth control or abortion. When the welfare caseworker found out I was pregnant, she told my mother that if we wanted to keep getting welfare, I'd have to have my tubes tied—temporarily. Nobody explained anything to me before the operation. Later on, after the operation, I saw the doctor and I asked him if I could have another baby. He said that I had nothing to worry about, that, of course, I could have more kids. [Now I know that was a lie and] I know now that I was sterilized because I was from a welfare family." Ibid., 1586.

26. "Jury Seated in Suit over Sterilization," *New York Times*, July 15, 1975, 13; also see "Court Sets a Sterilization Code for the Retarded in Institutions," *New York Times*, January 9, 1974, 9, and David E. Rosenbaum, "U.S. to Shift Rules on Sterilization," *New York Times*, January 22, 1974, 13, for Alabama sterilization cases; also see the Guttmacher Report, 97.

27. Harold M. Shmeck, Jr., "Court Curbs U.S. on Sterilization," *New York Times*, March 16, 1974, 1, 17.

28. P.L. 94-63, Act of July 29, 1975; 42 United States Code Annotated Section 300a.9 (West Supp. 1977). See Thomas B. Littlewood, *The Politics of Population Control* (Notre Dame, Ind.: University of Notre Dame Press, 1977); Thomas M. Shapiro, *Population Control Politics: Women, Sterilization, and Reproductive Choice* (Philadelphia: Temple University Press, 1985).

29. "HEW Bars Full Matching Aid for the Poor in Abortion Cases," *New York Times*, December 9, 1974, 18; also see "Manila Set Back on Birth Control," *New York Times*, December 15, 1974, IV, 7.

30. See Dorothy Roberts, *Killing the Black Body: Race, Reproduction, and the Meaning of Liberty* (New York: Pantheon, 1997), ch. 2. Also see Sheila M. Rothman, "Funding Sterilization and Abortion for the Poor," *New York Times*, February 22, 1975, 27.

31. Barbara Campbell, "City Blacks Get Most Abortions," *New York Times*, December 6, 1973, 94.

32. Richard Lincoln, Brigitte Doring-Bradley, Barbara L. Lindheim, Maureen A. Cotterill, "The Court, the Congress, and the President: Turning Back the Clock on the Pregnant Poor," *Family Planning Perspectives* 9 (September–October 1977): 210. Also see Rosalind Pollack Petchesky, *Abortion and Women's Choice: The State, Sexuality, and Reproductive Freedom*, rev. ed. (Boston: Northeastern University Press, 1990), ch. 4.

33. Weddington, *A Question of Choice*, 176.

34. *Doe v. Rose* 499 F.2d 1112, 1117 (10th Cir. 1974).

35. See "Abortion, Medicaid and the Constitution," *New York University Law Review* 54 (April 1979):124; and *Constitutional Aspects of the Right to Limit Childbearing: A Report of the United States Commission on Civil Rights* (Washington, D.C.: U.S. Government Printing Office, April 1975), 22.

36. Letter from Dr. Arthur Flemming, Chairman, U.S. Commission on Civil Rights, to the Honorable Charles H. Percy, responding to an invitation to comment on Senator Bartlett's amendment, reprinted in the *Congressional Record—Senate*, Vol. 121, Pt. 8, April 10, 1975, 9809, 9818.

37. *Congressional Record—Senate*, Vol. 124, Pt. 24, September 27, 1978, 31917. A study in the 1970s showed that before the Hyde Amendment, between 164,000 and 245,000 Medicaid-eligible women who needed or wanted abortions couldn't get them because of "restricted Medicaid practices and the lack of abortion services in most states." Lincoln et al., "The Court, the Congress, and the President," 211. Also see Willard Cates, "The Hyde Amendment in Action," *Journal of the American Medical Association* 10 (September 4, 1981): 1109–1112. Rosalind Petchesky noted in the early 1980s: "[the] Hyde [Amendment] aroused the apprehension of many feminists that poor women would be forced to bear unwanted children, to get unwanted sterilizations, or to risk death or injury from illegal abortions." Petchesky writes that as of the early 1980s, "these effects have not occurred. Rather, the immediate result of the Hyde Amendment was that an estimated 94 percent of Medicaid-dependent women needing abortions continued to get them." *Abortion and Women's Choice*, 160. Still, the specter of poor women's vulnerability continued to stimulate the concerns and the rhetoric of abortion rights proponents.

38. "Abortion, Medicaid, and the Constitution," 125. The trio of 1976 cases were *Beal v. Doe*, 432 US 438; *Maher v. Roe*, 432 US 464; and *Poelker v. Doe*, 432 US 519.

39. For a complete discussion of these matters, see David Garrow, *Liberty and Sexuality: The Right to Privacy and the Making of* Roe v. Wade (New York: Macmillan, 1974), ch. 9.

40. Michael J. Perry, "Why the Supreme Court was Plainly Wrong in the Hyde Amendment: A Brief Note on *Harris v. McRae*," *Stanford Law Review* 32 (July 1980): 1125–26.

41. Leslie Friedman Goldstein, "A Critique of the Abortion Funding Decisions: On Private Rights in the Public Sector," *Hastings Constitutional Law Quarterly* 8 (winter 1981): 339.

42. *Congressional Record—House*, Vol. 123, Pt. 16, June 17, 1977, 19698–19715.

43. Dallas A. Blanchard, *The Anti-Abortion Movement and the Rise of the Religious Right: From Polite to Fiery Protest* (New York: Twayne, 1994); Petchesky, *Abortion and Women's Choice*, ch. 7. For a contemporary analysis of the politics of the Hyde Amendment, see Joyce Gelb and Marian Lief Palley, "Women and Interest Group Politics: A Comparative Analysis of Federal Decision Making," *Journal of Politics* 41 (May 1979): 362–92.

44. See, generally, Martin Gilens, *Why Americans Hate Welfare: Race, Media, and the Politics of Anti-Poverty Policy* (Chicago: University of Chicago Press, 1999).

45. *Congressional Record—Senate*, Vol. 121, Pt. 8, April 10, 1975, 9813.

46. *Maher v. Roe* 432 US 500, Brennan for Marshall, Blackmun, dissenting.

47. *Harris v. McRae* 448 US 297. Also see Petchesky, *Abortion and Women's Choice*, 295–302.

48. *Congressional Record—Senate*, Vol. 124, Pt. 24, September 27, 1978, 31898.

49. *Congressional Record—Senate*, Vol. 121, Pt. 8, 9804. During this discussion in the Senate, Senator Edward Kennedy of Massachusetts responded to Bartlett's nonsense by citing the *Uniform Crime Report*, which indicated 51,000 female victims of forceful rape in 1973. Kennedy pointed out that the FBI considered rape a seriously unreported crime, that in fact 3.5 to 9 times the reported number actually occurred, and that "4% of these rapes produce pregnancies—which means as many as 18,000 a year" (9805, 9803).

50. *Time*, December 19, 1977, 12–13.

51. Susan Frelich Appleton, "Beyond the Limits of Reproductive Choice: The Contributions of the Abortion-Funding Cases to the Fundamental-Rights Analysis and to the Welfare-Rights Thesis," *Columbia Law Review* 81 (May 1981): 722, 758.

52. *Congressional Record—Senate*, Vol. 122, Pt. 24, September 21, 1976, 30988–89.

53. See, for example, Steven Polgar and Ellen S. Fried, "The Bad Old Days: Clandestine Abortions Among the Poor in New York City Before Liberalization of the Abortion Law," *Family Planning Perspectives* (May–June 1976): 125–27. The authors observe: "[V]irtually all of the women who have died from illegal abortions since the Supreme Court decisions have been poor and members of minority groups—80% of them were non-whites." Senator Javits pointed out on the Senate floor that in addition to expressing disregard for the lives of poor women, the new policies would be cost-ineffective: "HEW has estimated that if reimbursement for abortion under Medicaid were no longer legal, up to 250 deaths would occur yearly from women who would attempt to abort themselves, and up to 25,000 cases of serious medical complications from self-induced abortions, at a potential cost to the Government for these Medicaid recipients of between $375 and $2000 per patient for hospital costs alone." *Congressional Record—Senate*, Vol. 125, Pt. 8, April 10, 1975, 9812. Lincoln et al., in "The Court, the Congress, and the President," also predicted dire results, including elevated rates of mortality among poor women who can't afford abortions (213). Also see D. B. Pettiti and W. Cates, Jr., "Restricting Medicaid Funds for Abortions: Projections of Excess Mortality for Women of Childbearing Age," *American Journal of Public Health* 67 (1977): 860–62.

54. James Trussell, Jann Menken, Barbara L. Lindheim, and Barbara Vaughan, "The Impact of Restricting Medicaid Financing for Abortion," *Family Planning Perspectives* 12 (May–June 1980): 120.

55. Quoted in Ross, "African-American Women and Abortion," 186. Also see

Dorothy E. Roberts, "Punishing Drug Addicts Who Have Babies: Women of Color, Equality, and the Right of Privacy," in Solinger, ed., *Abortion Wars*, 145. Also see Sheila M. Rothman, "Sterilizing the Poor: The Medical-Welfare Complex," *Society* 14 (January 1977): 36–40.

56. *Maher v. Roe* 432 US 494–95, 498.

57. *Harris v. McRae* 448 US 316.

58. Remarks of Charles Grassley ("Medicaid for Abortions?"), reprint from the *Des Moines Register*, *Congressional Record—Senate*, Vol. 123, Pt. 25, September 29, 1977, 31673.

59. *Congressional Record—Senate*, Vol. 124, Pt. 14, September 27, 1978, 31900.

60. Stanley K. Henshaw and Lynn S. Wallisch, "The Medicaid Cutoff and Abortion Services for the Poor," *Family Planning Perspectives* 16 (July–August 1984): 171.

61. Lincoln et al., "The Court, the Congress, and the President," 211. The authors here point out that in the mid-1970s, in Mississippi, the average cost of an abortion was ten times higher than the monthly AFDC check and that thirty-seven states had lower AFDC payments than the cost of an abortion.

62. *Congressional Record—Senate*, Vol. 128, Pt. 8, May 21, 1981, 10684.

63. Senator Edward Brooke talked about pricing abortion "out of reach." See the *Congressional Record—Senate*, Vol. 122, Pt. 24, September 21, 1976, 30989.

64. *Congressional Record—Senate*, Extensions of Remarks, Vol. 122, Pt. 24, September 20, 1976, 31453.

65. *Congressional Record—Senate*, Vol. 124, Pt. 24, September 27, 1978, 31900. In fact, David Garrow cites "one major opinion poll [that] showed that 55 percent of Americans opposed public funding for abortions" in the late 1970s. *Liberty and Sexuality*, 629. But Senator Javits made the following excellent point: "on the argument . . . that we are expending Federal funds [for an unpopular purpose], I would like to see those opposed to the Vietnam war and whose taxes were used for the war—I would like to hear them on that subject . . . That was their argument and we voted them down time and again . . . if you are going to have the doctrine in this country of a selective right to pay taxes or to withhold taxes because you do or do not agree with a particular proposition, it is anarchy and chaos . . ." *Congressional Record—Senate*, Vol. 121, Pt. 8, April 10, 1975, 9812.

66. Laura Foreman, "Carter is Expected to Back Union Drive for New Labor Laws," *New York Times*, July 13, 1977, 1.

67. *Maher v. Roe* 432 US 494.

68. *Constitutional Aspects of the Right to Limit Childbearing*, 71.

69. George Cameron Nixon, "*Harris v. McRae*: Cutting Back Abortion Rights," *Columbia Human Rights Law Review* 12 (spring–summer 1980): 115.

70. See, for example, Lawrence R. Berger, "Abortion in America: The Effects of Restrictive Funding," *New England Journal of Medicine* 26 (June 29, 1978): 1474–77.

71. Trussell et al., "The Impact of Restricting Medicaid Financing for Abortion," 129 30.

72. Ibid., 120; also see *Abortions and the Poor: Private Morality, Public Responsibility* (New York: Alan Guttmacher Institute, 1979); Rachel Benson Gold, "After the Hyde Amendment: Public Funding for Abortion in FY 1978," *Family Planning Perspectives* 12 (May–June, 1980):134.

73. Trussell et al., "The Impact of Restricting Medicaid Financing for Abortion," 129.

74. "Indian Child Welfare Act of 1978," Hearings before the Subcommittee on Indian Affairs and Public Lands of the Committee on Interior and Insular Affairs, House of Representatives, 95th Congress, 2d sess., on S. 1214, "To Establish Standards for the Placement of Indian Children in Foster or Adoptive Families, to Prevent the Breakup of Indian Families, and for Other Purposes," February 9 and March 9, 1978 (Washington, D.C.: United States Government Printing Office, 1981), 69; 30 (rates are listed here for a number of states); 62. Also see Suzanne Letendre letter, regarding extremely high rates of adoption of Indian children in Boston and other localities in New England, 257.

75. Roberts, "Punishing Drug Addicts," 147.

76. See Melissa Fay Greene, "The Orphan Ranger: Adopting a Damaged Child," *New Yorker*, July 17, 2000, 38–45, for a typical example of this sort of treatment.

77. See Kay Johnson, Huang Banghan, and Wang Liyao, "Infant Abandonment and Adoption in China," *Population and Development Review* 24 (September 1998): 469–510; and Karin Evans, *The Lost Daughters of China* (New York: Jeremy Tarcher/Putnam, 2000).

78. Francisco J. Pilotti, "Intercountry Adoption: A View from Latin America," *Child Welfare* 64 (January–February 1985): 26; Barbara Joe, "In Defense of Intercountry Adoption," *Social Service Review* 52 (March 1978).

79. John Triseliotis, "Inter-country Adoption: In Whose Best Interest?" in *Inter-Country Adoption: Practical Experiences*, ed. Michael and Heather Humphrey (London: Routledge, 1993), 130.

80. "Refugees from Indochina," Hearings before the Subcommittee on Immigration, Citizenship, and International Law of the Committee on the Judiciary, House of Representatives, 94th Congress, 1st and 2d sess., April 8, 9, 14, May 22, July 17, 22, October 8, December 18, 1975; February 2, 1976 (Washington, D.C.: U.S. Government Printing Office, 1976), 48.

81. Rita J. Simon and Howard Alstein, *Transracial Adoptees and Their Families: A Study of Identity and Commitment* (New York: Praeger, 1987), 135–36.

82. Pilotti, "Intercountry Adoption," 27.

83. Mary Ellen Fieweger, "Stolen Children and International Adoptions," *Child Welfare* 70 (March–April 1991): 285–91. Sociologist Barbara Katz Rothman put it this way, "Poor countries export children to rich ones, black parents to white, poor children to better off." *Recreating Motherhood: Ideology and Technology in a Patriarchal Society* (New York: Norton, 1989), 130.

84. See generally "Romanian Adoptions," Hearings before the Subcommittee on International Law, Immigration, and Refugees of the Committee on the Judiciary, House of Representatives, 102d Congress, 1st sess., June 5, 1991 (Washington, D.C.: U.S. Government Printing Office, 1991); also see Holly Danks, "The Irrecoverables," *Oregonian*, March 10, 1991. Danks observes, "In a country of chronic food shortages, subsistence salaries, and antiquated medicine, babies were born underweight and sickly to malnourished mothers. Oppressed parents couldn't care for [their families]."

85. Ginger Thompson, "In Mexico, Children, Promises, Unkept," *New York Times*, June 2, 1999, A1, B4; also see Joseph P. Fried, "Women Plead Guilty in Baby Smuggling Case," *New York Times*, July 16, 1999.

86. Evans, *The Lost Daughters of China*, 244. Evans also comments on the commodification of children within China: "Some prosperous citizens today happily and routinely pay for the privilege of having a second, and even a third child. It's even become a bit of a status symbol" (237).

87. Triseliotis, "Inter-country Adoption," 121.

88. Ibid., 131.

89. Christopher Bagley with Loretta Young and Anne Scully, *International and Trans-Racial Adoption: A Mental Health Perspective* (Hants, England: Ashgate, 1993), 155.

90. Ibid., 154.

91. Thomas Malone, "Adoption and the Crisis in the Third World: Thoughts on the Future," *International Child Welfare Review* 28 (1976): 22.

92. See Fieweger, "Stolen Children and International Adoptions," 287.

93. Robert Lindsey, "Childless Couples Adopt in Mexico, Often Illegally," *New York Times*, November 13, 1978, 18.

94. *Sixty Minutes* transcript, "Romanian Adoptions," Hearings, 240.

95. Ibid., 185–86. The speaker is Romano L. Mazzoli, U.S. representative from Kentucky.

96. Fieweger, "Stolen Children and International Adoptions," 284.

97. Bagley, Young, and Scully, *International and Trans-Racial Adoption*, 177–78.

98. Ann Colamosca, "International Adoption: Considering all the Families," *Ms.*, January 1983, 97.

99. Bagley, Young, and Scully, *International and Trans-Racial Adoption*, 153.

100. "Romanian Adoptions," Hearings, 225.

101. Kathleen Hunt, "The Romanian Baby Bazaar," *New York Times Magazine*, March 24, 1991, 38.

102. Ibid., 53.

103. Anthony Lewis, "Helping the Vietnamese: Time for Action," *New York Times*, April 7, 1975, 31.

104. Letter to a State Department official from James F. Greene, Deputy Commissioner, INS, October 8, 1975, Refugees from Indochina, Hearings, 425.

105. "Romanian Adoptions," Hearings, 177.

106. Hunt, "The Romanian Baby Bazaar," 29.

107. "Romanian Adoptions," Hearings, 171.

108. "Refugees from Indochina," Hearings, 77–78.

109. Simon and Alstein, Transracial Adoptees and Their Families, 133.

110. Sixty Minutes transcript, "Babies for Sale," "Romanian Adoptions," Hearings, 235.

111. Margie Boulé, "The Orphans Who Weren't Really Orphans," Oregonian, April 30, 1991. Inter-country adoption proponent Elizabeth Bartholet, about whom I write more later in this chapter, acknowledges the prevalence and pivotal relation of the bribe to the adoption when she writes about an Italian mother who went to Peru to adopt. She obtained a baby, but after eight days was told she had to return the baby, who was "no longer available." Bartholet comments, "Some legal complications may have developed . . . The birth mother may have changed her mind. But I have learned by now to be suspicious of these stories about adoptions that have to be called off, children that have to be returned. In many cases the only problem is that someone in the system has not received a 'gift.' " Family Bonds: Adoption and the Politics of Parenting (Boston: Houghton Mifflin, 1993), 42.

112. Bagley, Young, and Scully, International and Trans-Racial Adoption, 190.

113. Pilotti, "Intercountry Adoption," 31.

114. "Romanian Adoptions," Hearings, 8, 96, 107, 213–14.

115. See, for example, A. Ingelman-Sundberg, photos by Lennart Nilsson, A Child Is Born: The Drama of Life Before Birth (New York: Dell, 1966).

116. For a recent example of how crucial the idea of "choice" has become in efforts to efface the interests and the person of resourceless women vis-à-vis the interests of their fetuses and children, see Linda Greenhouse, "Should a Fetus's Well-Being Override a Mother's Rights?" New York Times, September 9, 2000, A1. Disregarding the complexities of "choice" in contemporary society, John Robertson, professor of law and bioethics at the University of Texas, is quoted here: "A pregnant woman, if she chooses not to end the pregnancy, takes on a moral and perhaps a legal obligation to refrain from clearly harmful prenatal conduct" (italics added).

117. Bartholet, Family Bonds, 230.

118. "Romanian Adoptions," Hearings, 153. Elsewhere during this hearing, McNary does acknowledge the dicey side of foreign adoption, but his sympathy ends up with the victimized consumer-adopters: "The Service has found that there is a potential for foreign children to be stolen from their parents for adoption in the U.S. by unscrupulous individuals, and there is a market for fraudulent documents for children who are beneficiaries of orphan petitions. Arrangers entice clients by boasting that theirs is a faster, cheaper, and easier way to adopt children. Adopting parents have been exploited by being charged exorbitant fees and never getting the children or getting unhealthy children. Adopting parents have also been made parties to fraudulent acts." 167.

119. Colamosca, "International Adoption," 96.

120. Bartholet, *Family Bonds*, 44, 120, 135–36.

121. Claire and Andrew Astachnowicz, "From San Salvador to Hackney," in Humphrey and Humphrey, eds., *Inter-Country Adoption*, 20.

122. Warren Hoge, "Brazil Blocks 13 Adoptions by Americans," *New York Times*, October 11, 1981, 11. Also see Cheri Register, *Are Those Kids Yours?* (New York: Free Press, 1991), 39, where the author briefly assesses what the experience must be for the "surrendering" mother.

123. "Romanian Adoptions," Hearings, 123.

124. I explore this economic basis for defining who is qualified to be a mother in Chapter 6.

125. "Romanian Adoptions," Hearings, 191.

126. Triseliotis, "Inter-country Adoption," 131.

127. "Romanian Adoptions," Hearings, 94, 101.

128. Ibid., 142.

129. Bartholet, *Family Bonds*, 142, 163, 234.

130. Triseliotis, "Inter-country Adoption," 132.

131. Holly Danks, "And Love Can Work Wonders," *Oregonian*, March 10, 1991.

132. David T. Hardy, "Privacy and Public Funding: *Maher v. Roe* as the Interaction of *Roe v. Wade* and *Dandridge v. Williams*," *Arizona Law Review* 18 (1976): 915.

133. *Planned Parenthood of Southeast Pennsylvania v. Casey*, 112 Sup. Ct. 2791 (1992).

134. *Roe v. Wade*, 410 US 113 (1973).

135. Carole Joffe, "Reactions to Medical Abortion Among Providers of Surgical Abortion: An Early Snapshot," *Family Planning Perspectives* 31 (January–February 1999), 35–38.

136. Constance A. Nathanson makes this point in her excellent book, *Dangerous Passage: The Social Control of Sexuality in Women's Adolescence* (Philadelphia: Temple University Press, 1991), 211. Nathanson connects these changing "questions of guilt and innocence" directly to changing attitudes about young women as choicemakers: "There is substantial continuity . . . between the situation of a sexually unorthodox young woman in the nineteenth century ejected from a Florence Crittenton Home for her failure to repent and that of the similiarly unorthodox young woman of today whose second pregnancy causes her to be dropped from a program for teenage mothers. Wherever the line between deviance and conformity is drawn, a single crossing may be excused as involuntary; crossings that are repeated or unrepented are likely to be regarded as the outcome of deliberate choice. And whether the choice is characterized as sin or as irresponsible, the response it evokes is one of punishment rather than treatment and care." 212.

137. Sharon Gold-Steinberg and Abigail J. Stewart, "Psychologies of Abortion: Implications of a Changing Context," in Solinger, ed., *Abortion Wars*, 354.

138. Ibid., 369.

2: JUSTIFYING CHOICE

1. Brett Harvey, *The Fifties* (New York: HarperCollins, 1993), 24.
2. Patricia Miller, *The Worst of Times: Illegal Abortion—Survivors, Practitioners, Coroners, Cops, and Children of Women Who Died Talk About Its Horrors* (New York: HarperCollins, 1993), 195.
3. Bob Herbert, "In America: Bush v. Blackmun," *New York Times*, March 14, 1999, IV, 15.
4. Nancy Howell Lee, *The Search for an Abortionist* (Chicago: University of Chicago Press, 1969), 77.
5. Miller, *The Worst of Times*, 235–36.
6. Lee, *The Search for an Abortionist*, 102.
7. Mary S. Calderone, ed., *Abortion in the United States: A Conference Sponsored by the Planned Parenthood Federation of America, Inc. at Arden House and the New York Academy of Medicine* (New York: Harper, 1958), 162.
8. Carlson Wade, *Butchers in Waiting: The Shocking Story of Abortion in the USA* (n.p.: Chariot Book, 1960), 101.
9. John Bartlow Martin, "Abortion, Part 2," *Saturday Evening Post*, May 27, 1961, 52.
10. Harvey, *The Fifties*, 27; Angela Bonavoglia, *The Choices We Made: Twenty-Five Women and Men Speak Out About Abortion* (New York: Random House, 1991), 74.
11. Miller, *The Worst of Times*, 15, 75, 151, 297.
12. Ellen Messer and Kathryn E. May, *Back Rooms: An Oral History of the Illegal Abortion Era* (New York: Touchstone, 1989), 97.
13. Bonavoglia, *The Choices We Made*, 97, 113.
14. See Rickie Solinger, "Extreme Danger: Women Abortionists and Their Clients before *Roe v. Wade*," in Joanne Meyerowitz, ed., *Not June Cleaver: Women and Gender in Postwar America, 1945–1960* (Philadelphia: Temple University Press, 1994), 335–57, for a discussion of the scope of these dangers and for citations referencing trial transcripts in which such situations were at issue.
15. "A New Abortion Law," *New York Times*, February 13, 1965, 20; Bonavoglia, *The Choices We Made*, 73.
16. Lee, *The Search for an Abortionist*, 101.
17. Edwin Schur, *Crimes Without Victims: Deviant Behavior and Public Policy* (Englewood Cliffs, N.J.: Prentice-Hall, 1965), 50.
18. Leslie J. Reagan, *When Abortion Was a Crime: Women, Medicine and the Law in the United States, 1867–1973* (Berkeley: University of California Press, 1997), 164; also see Rickie Solinger, *The Abortionist: A Woman Against the Law* (New York: Free Press, 1994), and Solinger, "Extreme Danger," for extended descriptions of police raids and the terror they inflicted on women.
19. Reagan, *When Abortion Was a Crime*, 154, 169.
20. *People of the State of California v. Laura Miner, Nedra Montana Cordon, and*

Josephine M. Page (1949), 368 (transcript in California State Archives, Sacramento).

21. *State of California v. Lena Califro and Andrew Mareck* (1952), 800 (transcript in California State Archives, Sacramento).

22. Nanette Davis, *From Crime to Choice: The Transformation of Abortion in America* (Westport, Conn.: Greenwood, 1985), 84–85, 78.

23. Arthur J. Mandy, "Reflections of a Gynecologist," in Harold Rosen, ed., *Therapeutic Abortion: Medical, Psychiatric, Legal, Anthropological, and Religious Considerations in the Prevention of Conception and the Interruption of Pregnancy* (New York: Julian Press, 1954), 292.

24. Charles C. Dahlberg, "Abortion," in Ralph Slovenko, ed., *Sexual Behavior and the Law* (Springfield, Ill.: Charles Thomas, 1965), 383.

25. Myrna Loth and H. Close Hesseltime, "Therapeutic Abortion at the Chicago Lying-In Hospital," *American Journal of Obstetrics and Gynecology* 72 (August 1956): 304–11.

26. Davis, *From Crime to Choice*, 77.

27. Bonavoglia, *The Choices We Made*, 99.

28. See Rickie Solinger, *Wake Up Little Susie: Single Pregnancy and Race before Roe v. Wade* (New York: Routledge, 1992).

29. Jerome E. Bates and Edward S. Zawadzki, *Criminal Abortion: A Study in Medical Sociology* (Springfield, Ill.: Charles C. Thomas, 1964), 81.

30. Messer and May, *Back Rooms*, xvi. See also Chapters 3 and 4 of this volume.

31. Carole Joffe, *Doctors of Conscience: The Struggle to Provide Abortion before and after Roe v. Wade* (Boston: Beacon Press, 1995), ch. 1.

32. Miller, *The Worst of Times*, 111–13.

33. Alex Barno, "Criminal Abortion Deaths, Illegitimate Pregnancy, and Suicide in Pregnancy: Minnesota 1950–1965," *American Journal of Obstetrics and Gynecology* 98 (June 1967): 262.

34. Jack Star, "The Growing Tragedy of Illegal Abortion," *Look*, October 19, 1965, 156.

35. See generally Christopher Tietze, "Abortion as a Cause of Death," *American Journal of Public Health* 38 (October 1948): 1434–41.

36. Barno, "Criminal Abortion Deaths," 364.

37. Lee, *The Search for an Abortionist*, 167.

38. *The Abortion Problem: Proceedings of the Conference Held under the Auspices of the National Committee on Maternal Health* (Baltimore: Williams and Wilkins for the National Committee on Maternal Health, 1944), 110.

39. Messer and May, *Back Rooms*, 166–69.

40. "The Abortion Menace," *Ebony*, January 1951, 26.

41. Martin, "Abortion, Part 2," 52; also see Bates and Zawadzki, *Criminal Abortion*, for this typical description of the motivations of female practitioners: "Our experience with professional non-medical abortionists tends to confirm . . . that the untrained female abortionist is reacting, in large part, to an unconscious

need to reject children or to deny them to others of her sex by reason of certain emotional deprivations in her own background." 125–26.

42. Harvey, *The Fifties*, 24.
43. Miller, *The Worst of Times*, 108.
44. Wade, *Butchers in Waiting*, 36.
45. Frederick J. Taussig, "Effects of Abortion on the General Health and Reproductive Function of the Individual," in *The Abortion Problem*, 125.
46. Wade, *Butchers in Waiting*, 36–37.
47. Miller, *The Worst of Times*, 97, 99, 114.
48. "Suggests Doctors Relax 'Hypocrisy,' " *New York Times*, January 31, 1942, 1.
49. Miller, *The Worst of Times*, 313.
50. See Rickie Solinger, " 'A Complete Disaster': Abortion and the Politics of Hospital Abortion Committees, 1950–1970," *Feminist Studies* (summer 1993): 241–59.
51. Miller, *The Worst of Times*, 117, 192–93, 285.
52. See Joffe, *Doctors of Conscience*, ch. 3, especially 59–61.
53. Quoted in Dorothy Fadiman, "From Back Alley to the Supreme Court and Beyond," audiotape, Women's International NewsGathering Service, n.d.
54. See Christopher Tietze, "Introduction to the Statistics of Abortion," in *Pregnancy Wastage*, ed. E. T. Engle (Springfield, Ill.: Charles C. Thomas, 1953).
55. Calderone, ed., *Abortion in the United States*, 55.
56. "The Abortion Menace," 21.
57. Frederick J. Taussig, *Abortion, Spontaneous and Induced: Medical and Social Aspects* (St. Louis: Mosby, 1936), 387–88.
58. Tietze, "Abortion as a Cause of Death," 1434–35.
59. Bates and Zawadzki, *Criminal Abortion*, 96.
60. Miller, *The Worst of Times*, 327.
61. Barno, "Criminal Abortion Deaths," 356–67.
62. Harvey, *The Fifties*, 24.
63. Calderone, ed., *Abortion in the United States*, 57, 63.
64. See Dr. X as told to Lucy Freeman, *The Abortionist* (Garden City, N.Y.: Doubleday, 1962); Miller, *The Worst of Times*; Ed Keemer, *Confessions of a Pro-Life Abortionist* (Detroit: Vinco Press, 1980); Solinger, *The Abortionist*; and Joffe, *Doctors of Conscience*.
65. Myer S. Tulkoff, "Legal and Social Control of Abortion," *Kentucky Law Review* 40 (May 1952): 415.
66. Miller, *The Worst of Times*, 145.
67. Lee, *The Search for an Abortionist*, 7.
68. *The Abortion Problem*, 135.
69. Taussig, *Abortion, Spontaneous and Induced*, 402.
70. Calderone, ed., *Abortion in the United States*, 36–40.
71. Russell S. Fisher, "Criminal Abortion," *Journal of Criminal Law and Criminology* 42 (July–August 1951): 242–49.

72. Morton Sontheimer, "Abortion in America Today," *Women's Home Companion*, October 1955, 100.
73. Miller, *The Worst of Times*, 262–63.
74. See generally Laura Kaplan, *The Story of Jane: The Legendary Underground Feminist Abortion Service* (New York: Pantheon, 1995).
75. Rosalind Pollack Petchesky, *Abortion and Women's Choice: The State, Sexuality, and Reproductive Freedom*, rev. ed. (Boston: Northeastern University Press, 1990), 129.
76. Regine K. Stix, "A Study of Pregnancy Wastage," *Milbank Memorial Fund Quarterly* 13 (October, 1935): 351–52; also see Reagan, *When Abortion Was a Crime*, 138 and 307 n. 27.
77. Taussig, *Abortion*, 352.
78. Calderone, ed., *Abortion in the United States*, 57, 65.
79. Dorothy Fadiman, "From Danger to Dignity," audiotape, Women's International NewsGathering Service, n.d.
80. Miller, *The Worst of Times*, 12–13.
81. Until the early 1960s, newspapers rarely used the term "abortion" at all; it had such frightful, intimate, sexual connotations. The preferred term was "illegal operation."
82. Petchesky, *Abortion and Women's Choice*, 73.
83. Taussig, *Abortion*, 390.
84. Reagan, *When Abortion Was a Crime*, ch. 5, 161.
85. Solinger, *The Abortionist*, 35.
86. See Reagan, *When Abortion Was a Crime*, 147.
87. Zad Leavy and Jerome M. Krummer, "Let's Talk About Abortions," *Police* (July–August 1961): 15–16.
88. Lee, *The Search for an Abortionist*, 97.
89. Miller, *The Worst of Times*, 11.
90. Dr. X as told to Lucy Freeman, *The Abortionist*, 42–43.
91. Messer and May, *Back Rooms*, 232.
92. Quoted in Garrett Hardin, "Abortion—Or Compulsory Pregnancy," *Journal of Marriage and the Family* 30 (May 1968): 248.
93. Joffe, *Doctors of Conscience*.
94. Bonavoglia, *The Choices We Made*, 13, 18, 76.
95. Miller, *The Worst of Times*, 21–24, 182–84, 252.
96. Messer and May, *Back Rooms*, 27.
97. John Bartlow Martin, "Abortion, Part I," *Saturday Evening Post*, May 20, 1961, 21.
98. Miller, *The Worst of Times*, 206.
99. Fadiman, "From Danger to Dignity."
100. Bonavoglia, *The Choices We Made*, 6.
101. Miller, *The Worst of Times*, 70.
102. Bonavoglia, *The Choices We Made*, 60.

103. See, for example, Flanders Dunbar, *Psychiatry in the Medical Professions* (New York: McGraw-Hill, 1959), 279–81; Flanders Dunbar, "Abortion and the Abortion Habit," in Rosen, *Therapeutic Abortion*, 27; Hans Lehfeldt, "Willfull Exposure to Unwanted Pregnancy: Psychological Explanations for Patient Failures in Contraception," *American Journal of Obstetrics and Gynecology* 78 (September 1959): 661–65.

104. See the (Portland) *Oregon Journal*, July 13, 1951, 4, for a statement issued by the Oregon State Board of Medical Examiners the day after many abortion practitioners were arrested in Portland. This is an excellent example of how doctors distanced themselves from the criminal abortion arena.

105. Quoted in Star, "The Growing Tragedy of Illegal Abortion," 153.

106. Carole Joffe has argued that estimates of death from illegal abortion have been highly contested, with the anti-abortion movement, in particular, accusing the pro-choice movement of inflating the figures. *Doctors of Conscience*, 216.

107. Joffe, *Doctors of Conscience*, 153, 160.

108. Warren Hern, M.D., "Life On the Front Line," in Rickie Solinger, ed., *Abortion Wars: A Half-Century of Struggle, 1950–2000* (Berkeley: University of California Press, 1998), 316.

3: CLAIMING RIGHTS IN THE ERA OF CHOICE (I)

1. Kathleen Leahy Koch, letter to the author, October 20, 1997.

2. Rickie Solinger, *Wake Up Little Susie: Single Pregnancy and Race before Roe v. Wade* (New York: Routledge, 1992, 2000).

3. I have had countless conversations—far more than a hundred—over the past eight years with women who lost their "illegitimate" babies to adoption in the postwar decades. I have received autobiographical letters of considerable length describing the experience from more than fifty women. I taped extensive interviews with approximately twenty such women. To write these chapters, I also relied on published and unpublished memoirs, newspaper articles, organizational pamphlets, and newsletters.

4. Ann Hege Hughes, letter to author, August 31, 1997.

5. Pollie Robinson, letter to author, October 23, 1997.

6. Karen Kottmeier, letter to author, 1997 (no date).

7. Elizabeth Avens, letter to author, June 9, 1997.

8. Anonymous, letter to author, CUB conference, Beaumont, CA, October 11, 1997.

9. Eleanor Whitmore, letter to author, June 20, 1997.

10. Ellen Simmons, letter to author, March 24, 1998.

11. Whitmore, letter to author.

12. Cindy Bhimani, e-mail to author, January 3, 1998.

13. Janice Fruland, letter to author, November 4, 1997.

14. Barbara Anderson-Keri, letter to author, August 10, 1997.

15. "Understanding the Birthmother," pamphlet published by Concerned United Birthparents, 1977, in possession of author.
16. Koch, letter to author.
17. Kottmeier, letter to author.
18. "Love, Emily," by Jane O'Reilly, New York Newsday, November 27, 1991, 52, 95.
19. Sue Tavela, e-mail to author, October 13, 1997.
20. Robinson, letter to author.
21. Kay Ball, letter to author, 1997 (no date).
22. "Julie," letter to author, 1997 (no date).
23. Darst, letter to author.
24. Carole Anderson, interview with author, Grand Island, NB, March 1–3, 1997.
25. Quoted in Sandra Kay Musser, I Would Have Searched Forever: A Birthmother's Search for the Child She Surrendered (Coral Gables, Fla.: Adoption Awareness Press, 1979), 94.
26. Anderson-Keri, letter to author.
27. Whitmore, letter to author; Leslie Noxon, letter to author, September 20, 1997.
28. Alison Ward, letter to author, September 25, 1997.
29. Quoted in Betty Jean Lifton, Lost and Found, rev. ed. (New York: Harper and Row, 1988), 223.
30. Quoted in "Understanding the Birthparent," pamphlet published by Concerned United Birthparents, 1982, in possession of author.
31. Anderson interview.
32. See Laura Kaplan, The Story of Jane: The Legendary Underground Feminist Abortion Service (New York: Pantheon, 1996); Carole Joffe, Doctors of Conscience: The Struggle to Provide Abortion Rights before and after Roe v. Wade (Boston: Beacon Press, 1995); and Rickie Solinger, The Abortionist: A Woman Against the Law (New York: Free Press, 1994).
33. Cited in "Proceedings, Institute on Services to Unmarried Parents" (Washington, D.C.: National Conference of Catholic Charities, 1974), 5.
34. Becky, letter to author, 1997 (no date).
35. Robinson, letter to author.
36. Randa Phillips, letter to author, October 5, 1997.
37. Lee Campbell, "Hello Again," unpublished manuscript, in possession of Lee Campbell.
38. Whitmore, letter to author.
39. "Angie," letter to author.
40. Anderson-Keri, letter to author.
41. Whitmore, letter to author.
42. Hughes, letter to author.
43. "Kathy," letter to author, 1997 (no date).
44. "Elizabeth," letter to author, 1997 (no date).

45. Ward, letter to author.

46. Whitmore, letter to author.

47. Carole Whitehead, letter to author, October 28, 1997.

48. Lynn Kopatich, letter to author, October 28, 1997.

49. "Angie," letter to author.

50. Quoted in Musser, *I Would Have Searched*, 125–26.

51. Patricia Taylor, interview with author, Grand Island, NB, March 1–3, 1997.

52. Patricia E. Taylor, *Shadow Train: A Journey Between Relinquishment and Reunion* (Baltimore, Md.: Gateway Press, 1995), 215, 220.

53. Carol Schaefer, *The Other Mother* (New York: Soho Press, 1991), 166–68.

54. *CUB Communicator*, January 1978, in author's possession.

55. Janice Chalifaux, interview with author, Andover, MA, March 21, 1998.

56. Betty Jean Lifton, *Lost and Found*, 13.

57. Susan Darke, interview with the author, Andover, MA, March 21, 1998.

58. Lynn Lilliston, "Who am I? Adoptees Seek Right to Know," *Los Angeles Times*, July 22, 1973, 1, 14–15.

59. Fred and Tabitha Powledge, "The Adopted Seek Out Real Parents—Just to Know," *New York Times*, January 30, 1977, IV, 8.

60. Quoted in Annette Baran, Reuben Pannor, Arthur D. Sorosky, *The Adoption Triangle: The Effects of the Sealed Record on Adoptees, Birth Parents, Adoptive Parents* (New York: Anchor Press, 1978), 121, 136.

61. See, for example, Enid Nemy, "Adopted Children Who Wonder, 'What Was Mother Like?'" *New York Times*, July 25, 1972, 22.

62. See, for example, D. W. Winnicott, *Collected Papers* (London: Tavistock, 1958); R. A. Spitz, "Anxiety in Infancy: A Study of Its Manifestations in the First Year of Life," *International Journal of Psycho-Analysis* 31 (1950): 138–43; Melanie Klein, "On the Theory of Anxiety and Guilt," *International Journal of Psycho-Analysis* 29 (1948); Anna Freud, *Normality and Pathology in Children: Assessments of Development* (New York: International Universities Press, 1965); John Bowlby, *Attachment and Loss, Vol. II, Separation: Anxiety and Anger* (New York: Basic Books, 1973).

63. René Spitz, "The Role of Ecological Factors in Emotional Development in Infancy," *Child Development* 20 (1949): 145–55.

64. See, for example, "Unwed Mother's Key Decision: To Give Up or Keep Her Child," *New York Times*, April 11, 1971, 57; Sandra Gardner, "Adoption: Should Records Be Opened?" *New York Times*, June 13, 1982, XI, 1; J. T. Freeman, "Who Am I? Where Did I Come From? A Girl's Search for Her Real Mother," *Ladies' Home Journal*, March 1970, 74, 132–36; E. J. LeShan, "Should Adoptees Search for Their 'Real' Parents?" *Woman's Day*, March 1977, 40, 214, 218.

65. Jeanie Kasindorf, "Who Are My Real Parents?" *McCall's*, May 1974, 53.

66. See Pearl Buck, *Matthew, Mark, Luke and John* (New York: John Day, 1967); Jeannette Eyerly, *A Girl Like Me* (New York: Lippincott, 1966); H. M. Ryberg, "Are You My Real Parents?" *Parents*, February 1974, 56, 87–88.

67. Mary Howard, "I Take After Somebody; I Have Real Relatives; I Possess a Real Name," *Psychology Today*, December 1975, 33, 35–37.

68. See, for example, "Adult Adoptees as Children Pressing Hunt for Parents," *New York Times*, July 13, 1980, XI, 2.

69. Alfonso A. Narvaez, "State High Court Backs Mother in 'Baby Lenore' Adoption Case," *New York Times*, April 8, 1971, 37.

70. "DeMartinos Seeking Reversal on Child," *New York Times*, April 9, 1971, 26.

71. "Petitions Support Family in Brooklyn in Adoption Battle," *New York Times*, February 3, 1971, 33.

72. Edward Olsen, letter to *New York Times*, February 12, 1971, 36.

73. Florence Fisher, *The Search for Anna Fisher* (New York: A. Fields Books, 1973), 226–27, 238, 246.

74. Gardner, "Adoption: Should Records Be Opened?"

75. Reported in the *CUB Communicator*, July 1977, in author's possession.

76. Darke interview with author.

77. Campbell, "Hello Again," 308–9, 319.

78. Musser, *I Could Have Searched*, 32–33.

79. Janet Fenton, interview with author, Grand Island, NB, March 1–3, 1997.

80. Anderson, interview with author.

81. Anderson-Keri, letter to author.

82. Whitmore, letter to author.

83. Noxon, letter to author.

84. Darst, letter to author.

85. Mary Redenius, interview with author.

86. Taylor, interview with author.

87. Peggy Matthews-Nilsen, letter to author, November 20, 1997.

88. Noxon, letter to author.

89. Fenton, interview with author.

90. Carole Anderson, typescript, "CUB History," October 19, 1996, in possession of author.

91. Merrill Clarke Hunn, e-mail to author, July 26, 1997.

92. Quoted in Betty Jean Lifton, *Lost and Found: The Adoption Experience* (New York: Dial Press, 1979), 208.

93. Anderson, interview with author.

94. Bonnie Bis, interview with author, Grand Island, NB, March 1–3, 1997.

95. Delores Teller, letter to author, October 15, 1997; state statistics reported in "Proceedings, Institute on Services to Unmarried Parents," 4.

96. "Proceedings, Institute on Services to Unmarried Parents," 4.

97. Darke, interview with author.

98. Taylor, interview with author.

99. Chalifaux, interview with author.

100. Maris A. Vinovskis, "An Epidemic of Adolescent Pregnancy? Some Historical Consideration," *Journal of Family History* (summer 1981), 221.

101. See Guida West, *The National Welfare Rights Movment: The Social Protest of Poor Women* (New York: Praeger, 1981).

102. I am thinking of groups like the National Center for Lesbian Rights (founded in 1977), Lavender Families Resource Network (1974), National Council for Single Adoptive Parents (1973), Custody Action for Lesbian Mothers (1974), Gay and Lesbian Parents Coalition International (1979), and Unwed Parents Anonymous (1979).

103. Nadine Brozan, "Single Mothers Sharing a Difficult Time," *New York Times*, May 14, 1979, 16.

104. See Martha Fineman, "Images of Mothers in Poverty Discourse," *Duke Law Journal* 2 (1991): 274–95, for a discussion of issues embedded in the term "single mother."

105. *New York Times*, August 12, 1978, 12.

106. Carole Klein, *The Single Parent Experience* (New York: Walker, 1973), 113.

107. Barbara Haring, "Adoption Trends, 1971–1974," *Child Welfare* 54 (1975), 524–25.

108. Lynn McTaggert, *The Baby Brokers* (New York: Doubleday, 1983), 5.

109. Jacqueline Honor Plumez, "Adoption: Where Have All the Babies Gone?" *New York Times*, April 13, 1980, VI, 34.

110. Lester David, "I Refused to Give Up My Baby," *Seventeen*, June 1977, 162–63.

111. Hearings before the Subcommittee on Children and Youth of the Committee on Labor and Public Welfare, U.S. Senate, 94th Congress, 1st sess., on Examination and Exploration of Existing and Proposed Federal Policies Affecting the Adoption of Children and Their Placement in the Foster Care System, Baby Selling, April 28 and 29, Adoption of Children with Special Needs, July 14 and 15, 1975 (Washington, D.C.: U.S. Government Printing Office, 1975), 208–9.

112. Hearings before the Subcommittee on Criminal Justice of the Committee on the Judiciary, House of Representatives, 95th Congress, 1st sess., on the Sale of Children in Interstate and Foreign Commerce, March 21 and April 25, 1977 (Washington, D.C.: U.S. Government Printing Office), 8.

113. See, for example, Julia Wyatt Martin, "School-Age Mothers Go To Classes," *Educational Digest* 36 (January 1971), 44–45.

114. M. K. Benet, *The Politics of Adoption* (New York: Free Press, 1976), 152.

115. "Proceedings, Institute on Services to Unmarried Parents," 13–14.

116. Martha Dawson (pseudonym), "To Be An Unmarried Mother: The Most Important Decision I Ever Made," *Redbook*, February 1974, 33–34.

117. Karol Hope, "So You Want to Be a Single Mother . . . ," *Mademoiselle*, January 1975, 110–12.

118. David, "I Refused to Give Up My Baby," 162–63. Actually, *Seventeen* began to publish articles in this vein even earlier. In January 1973 the magazine featured "Having a Baby is a Very Alone Thing," by Cokie and Steven V. Roberts, about teen sex, pregnancy, unwed mothers, abortion, and the "trend" among

unmarried mothers to keep their babies; 74, 112, 114. Thanks to Naomi Kirsten for directing me to this article.

119. Klein, *The Single Parent Experience*, 76.
120. Libbi Campbell, interview with the author, Andover, MA, March 21, 1998.
121. Sheila Ganz, letter to author, 1997 (no date).
122. *CUB Communicator*, September 1977, in possession of author.
123. Marsha Riben, "Adoption: A Circle of Love," *Mothering*, winter 1983, 21.
124. Steven M. Spender, "The Birth Control Revolution," *Saturday Evening Post*, January 15, 1966, 66.
125. Hearings on Baby Selling, U.S. Senate, 1975, 62.
126. *Philadelphia*, February 1975, 78.
127. "Single Motherhood," *Time*, September 6, 1971, 48.
128. "The New Face of Adoption," *Newsweek*, August 13, 1971, 67.
129. Quoted in *CUB Communicator*, April 1978, in possession of author.
130. Kenneth Groves, letter to *New York Times*, May 28, 1977, 18.
131. Tom Wicker discussed this proposal in a *New York Times* editorial, May 8, 1977, IV, 19. A Catholic Charities report noted in 1974 "the reaction and seeming hostility of persons to girls keeping their babies, particularly those on welfare, when so many worthy couples wish to adopt and no babies are available." "Proceedings, Institute on Services to Unmarried Parents," 12.
132. Brendan Jones, "Counseling for People Who Plan to Adopt," *New York Times*, July 20, 1981, II, 4.

4: CLAIMING RIGHTS IN THE ERA OF CHOICE (II)

1. Lee Campbell, "Hello Again," unpublished manuscript, in possession of Lee Campbell, 336, 338, 350.
2. Carole Anderson, interview with author, Grand Island, Nebr., March 1–3, 1997.
3. Campbell, "Hello Again," 350.
4. Carole Anderson, "CUB History," typescript, October 19, 1996, in possession of author.
5. Campbell, "Hello Again," 339, 350.
6. Anderson, CUB History.
7. *CUB Communicator*, October 1979, reports that CUB received more than 4,000 letters after Lee Campbell's first appearance on *Donohue*. In possession of author; also see Campbell, "Hello Again," 368.
8. Susan Darke, interview with author, Andover, Mass., March 21, 1998.
9. *CUB Communicator*, November 1977, in possession of author.
10. Annette Baran, Reuben Pannor, and Arthur D. Sorosky, *The Adoption Triangle: The Effects of the Sealed Record on Adoptees, Birth Parents, Adoptive Parents* (New York: Anchor Press, 1978), 58.
11. Lee Campbell, "Beyond the Shadows: A Study of the Birthparent," CUB paper, 1982, in possession of author.

12. Sheila Ganz, letter to the author, 1997 (no date).

13. Campbell, "Hello Again," 440–41.

14. *CUB Communicator*, July 1978, in possession of author.

15. Libbi Campbell, interview with author, Andover, Mass., March 21, 1998.

16. Pauline A. Evans, *Search for Paul David* (Salt Lake City: Northwest, 1994), 75; Laura Watkins Lewis, "In Search of Daniel," *Washington Post*, Health Section, February 13, 1990, 15.

17. Carol Schaefer, *The Other Mother* (New York: Soho Press, 1991), 184.

18. Evans, *Search for Paul David*, 37.

19. Patricia E. Taylor, *Shadow Train: A Journey Between Relinquishment and Reunion* (Baltimore, Md.: Gateway, 1995), 222.

20. Campbell, "Hello Again," 356.

21. *CUB Communicator*, November 1976, in possession of author.

22. *CUB Communicator*, October 1976, in possession of author.

23. *CUB Communicator*, August 1977, in possession of author; Anderson, "CUB History."

24. *CUB Communicator*, March 1977, in possession of author.

25. *CUB Communicator*, July 1978, in possession of author.

26. *CUB Communicator*, May 1977, in possession of author.

27. Campbell, "Hello Again," 353.

28. Anderson, "CUB History."

29. *CUB Communicator*, May 1978.

30. Anderson, interview with author.

31. Sandra Kay Musser, *I Would Have Searched Forever: A Birthmother's Search for the Child She Surrendered* (Cape Coral, Fla.: Adoption Awareness Press, 1979), 112.

32. "Understanding the Birthparent," pamphlet issued by Concerned United Birthparents, 1982, in possession of author.

33. Darke, interview with author.

34. Libbi Campbell, interview with author.

35. *CUB Communicator*, October 1979.

36. Kristin Luker, *Dubious Conceptions: The Politics of Teenage Pregnancy* (Cambridge, Mass.: Harvard University Press, 1997), 71–72.

37. Taylor, *Shadow Train*, 224.

38. Carole Anderson with Lee Campbell and Mary Anne Cohen, "Eternal Punishment of Women: Adoption Abuse: An Appeal to Feminists," CUB position paper, 1981, in possession of author.

39. Musser, *I Would Have Searched Forever*, 115.

40. Campbell, "Hello Again," 358.

41. Barbara Shaw, written communication to author, CUB conference, Beaumont, Calif., October 11, 1997.

42. Ann Hege Hughes, written communication to author, CUB conference, Beaumont, Calif., October 11, 1997.

43. Pat Taylor, interview with author, Grand Island, Nebr., March 1–3, 1997.
44. Mary Anne Cohen, fax to author, July 21, 1997.
45. Elizabeth Avens, letter to author, July 9, 1997.
46. See Lauri Umansky, *Motherhood Reconceived: Feminism and the Legacies of the Sixties* (New York: New York University Press, 1996), for a discussion of motherhood discourse among early second wave feminists.
47. Anderson, interview with author.
48. Ibid. Birthmother Karen Kottmeier called Denver NOW in the early 1970s, soon after the *Roe v. Wade* decision. She told the woman who answered the phone that she had been forced to surrender her child when she had wanted to keep him. Karen said to the NOW member, "I'd like to know what NOW is doing about matters like these, what you're doing to help women." She remembered, "I even made it clear that I could have had an abortion but chose not to. The NOW woman thought for a minute and then she said, 'That's why we have to make abortion safe and legal.' She hadn't heard me at all." Telephone interview with author, March 5, 1998.
49. Libbi Campbell, telephone interview with author, January 21, 1998.
50. Carole Anderson, e-mail to author, December 15, 1997. See "Linking Adoption and Abortion in One Crusade," *New York Times*, May 16, 1986, 16, in which Alice Gee, a NARAL spokesperson, is quoted as saying, "We support a woman's right to choose, whether it be abortion or adoption or any other option, so of course we would favor adoption efforts."
51. Anderson, Campbell, and Cohen, "Eternal Punishment of Women."
52. The Boston group of CUB founders have, however, always felt successful in having an impact on the content of the adoption section of *Our Bodies, Ourselves*, according to Libbi Campbell.
53. Randa Phillips, letter to author, October 5, 1997.
54. Anderson, Campbell, and Cohen, "Eternal Punishment of Women."
55. Quoted in Baran, Pannor, and Sorosky, *The Adoption Triangle*, 58.
56. Anderson, CUB History.
57. See Lee H. Campbell, "The Birthparent's Right to Know," *Public Welfare* 37 (summer 1979): 22–27; and *CUB Communicator*, October 1979.
58. Judy Klemesrud, "Mothers Find the Children They Gave Up," *New York Times*, August 29, 1983, II, 5.
59. Avens, letter to author.
60. Merrill Hunn, e-mail to author, July 26, 1997.
61. Peggy Matthews-Nilsen, e-mail to author, July 20, 1997.
62. Sue Tavela, letter to author, October 13, 1997.
63. Lynn Kopatich, letter to author, October 28, 1997.
64. Anderson, interview with author.
65. Ann Hege Hughes, letter to author, October 17, 1997.
66. Janet Fenton, interview with author, Grand Island, Nebr., March 1–3, 1997.
67. Betty Jean Lifton described the awakening this way: "In the past, of course,

birthmothers could never hope to see their children again, no matter what tragic circumstances befell them. Now, in an age when women's rights are being emphasized, they are able to speak out against what they consider a cruel injustice." Betty Jean Lifton, *Lost and Found*, rev. ed. (New York: Harper and Row, 1988), 232.

68. Taylor, *Shadow Train*, 226.

69. Campbell, "Hello Again"; also see Marsha Riben, *Shedding Light on the Dark Side of Adoption* (Detroit: Harlo Press, 1988), 77.

70. "National CUB Takes a Stand," CUB pamphlet, 1983, in possession of author.

71. Barbara Joe, *Public Policies Toward Adoption* (Washington, D.C.: Urban Center, 1979), 2.

72. Sheila Rule, "Couples Taking Unusual Paths for Adoptions," *New York Times*, July 26, 1984, 1.

73. Diane Cole, "The Cost of Entering the Baby Chase," *New York Times*, August 9, 1987, III, 9; Julie Johnson, "Baby Brokering: Desperate Girl's Case Reveals Shadowy World," *New York Times*, October 29, 1987, II, 1.

74. "Babies: Three Thousand Dollars a Pound," *Moneysworth*, May 17, 1973; Hearings before the Subcommittee on Children and Youth of the Committee on Labor and Public Welfare, U.S. Senate, 94th Congress, 1st sess., On Examination and Exploration of Existing and Proposed Federal Policies Affecting the Adoption of Children and Their Placement in the Foster Care System, Baby Selling, April 28 and 29, Adoption of Children with Special Needs, July 14 and 15, 1975 (Washington, D.C.: U.S. Government Printing Office, 1975), 52.

75. The interests of the baby were probably the most popular concern. Senator Robert Taft expressed his concern this way: "To me, the most important person in this situation must be the child itself. It is the best interest of the child that has to be the dominating consideration, and the minute you get away from that, I think you run into difficulty." U.S. Senate Adoption Hearings, 1975, 46.

76. Rule, "Couples Taking Unusual Paths."

77. U.S. Senate Adoption Hearings, 1975, 115.

78. Ibid., 117.

79. Johnson, "Baby Brokering."

80. Robert Lindsey, "Adoption Market: Big Demand, Tight Supply," *New York Times*, April 5, 1987, 1.

81. The Black social workers' statement, issued in April 1972, is quoted in Benet, *The Politics of Adoption*, 140; see Wendell Rawls, Jr., "Adoption Abroad Brings Heartache to Some Couples," *New York Times*, June 24, 1978, 1. Also see David Andelman, "Tale of Unwanted Babies in Thailand, and a Happy Landing on Long Island," *New York Times*, February 24, 1976, 37, which quotes prices paid for Thai babies after the Americans left Thailand and explains that "many of the women who in the past might have tried to keep their child find it financially impossible [now] . . . [as] the babies are merely an added disadvantage in survival." Also articles about the burgeoning foreign adoption market can be found in the *New York Times*: "Judge Upholds Adoptions that He

Had Ruled Illegal," July 26, 1977, 16; Andrew H. Malcolm, "South Korea Seeks to End Flow of Orphans to Families Abroad," August 10, 1977, 2; Robert Lindsey, "Childless Couples Adopt in Mexico, Often Illegally," November 13, 1978, 18.

82. See "Adoption Rulings," *New York Times*, July 3, 1979, II, 2; and Abigail McCarthy, review of *Lost and Found* by Betty Jean Lifton, July 15, 1979, VII, 11.

83. Lindsey, "Childless Couples Adopt in Mexico," which, in addition to discussing this case, reports that in 1977 a San Diego adoption agency fielded 652 inquiries for only 38 babies, whereas this agency formerly had between 200 and 225 babies to place.

84. "Two Held in Baby-Smuggling Ring," *New York Times*, August 30, 1985, 14.

85. Warren Hoge, "Ring in Columbia Kidnaps Children for Sale Abroad," *New York Times*, August 16, 1981, 12.

86. Quoted in ElisaMB@aol.com, *Confessions of a Lost Mother* (Baltimore: Gateway Press, 1996), 118.

87. Achtenberg is quoted in Amy Jane Cheney, "The Adoptees' History," *Coming Up!*, October 1987, 1.

88. Amy Jane Cheney, "To Lesbian Parents, Time to Come Out of the Adoption Closet"; and Celeste Newbrough, "Adoption Doesn't Just Happen Once," *Coming Up!*, October 1987.

89. Phillips, letter to the author.

90. Randa Phillips, "The Need to Know Does Not Go Away," *Coming Up!*, October 1987, 2.

91. Velma L. Jordan and William F. Little, "Early Comments on Single Parent Adoptive Homes," *Child Welfare* 45 (1966): 536–38.

92. *Single Parent Adoption*, U.S. Department of Health and Human Services, Office of Human Development Services, Administration for Children, Youth, and Families, Children's Bureau, DHHS Publication Number 81-30306, 1, April 1981.

93. Joe, *Public Policies Toward Adoption*, 33. Additional early considerations of adoption by single persons include Alfred Kadushin, "Single Parent Adoptions: An Overview and Some Relevant Research," *Social Service Review* 44 (September 1970): 263–74; Joan Shireman and Penny Johnson, "Single Persons as Adoptive Parents," *Social Service Review* 50 (March 1976): 103–16; L. B. Coctin, "Adoption of Children by Single Parents," *Child Adoption*, no. 59, 31–33.

94. Amanda Richards, "On Becoming a Single Parent," *Adoption Report*, 1980; reprinted in *Single Parent Adoption*.

95. Klein, *The Single Parent Experience*, 109.

96. Maris A. Vinovskis, "An Epidemic of Adolescent Pregnancy? Some Historical Considerations," *Journal of Family History* (summer 1981): 205–30; also see Kristin Luker, *Dubious Conceptions*.

97. Vinovskis, "An Epidemic"; Catherine S. Chilman, "Social and Psychological

Research Concerning Adolescent Childbearing, 1970–1980," *Journal of Marriage and the Family* (November 1980): 783–805. Baran, Pannor, and Sorosky, *The Adoption Triangle*, note that by 1977, of the 600,000 teenage girls giving birth annually, 94 percent were keeping their babies.

98. Martha C. Ward, "Early Childbearing: What Is the Problem and Who Owns It?" in Faye D. Ginsburg and Rayna Rapp, eds., *Conceiving the New World Order: The Global Politics of Reproduction* (Berkeley: University of California Press, 1995), 140–58.

99. Benet, *The Politics of Adoption*, 175.

100. See Carol Sanger, "M is for the Many Things," *Southern California Review of Law and Women's Studies* 1 (1992): 44–45.

101. *CUB Communicator*, August 1977.

102. Hearings before the Subcommittee on Criminal Justice of the Committee on the Judiciary, House of Representatives, 95th Congress, 1st sess., on Sale of Children in Interstate and Foreign Commerce, March 21 and April 25, 1977 (Washington, D.C.: U.S. Government Printing Office, 1977), 85.

103. "U.S. Abortion Panel Disbanded by Chief," *New York Times*, November 27, 1977, 1.

104. See, for example, "Reagan Names Adoption Group," *New York Times*, August 25, 1987, 13.

105. U.S. Senate Adoption Hearings, 1975, 673.

106. Anderson, Campbell, and Cohen, "Eternal Punishment of Women."

107. Musser, *I Would Have Searched Forever*, 116.

108. "One-Parent Families Rose 79% in Decade, U.S. Report Indicates," *New York Times*, August 17, 1980, 29; "Women-Led Families Rise," *New York Times*, December 3, 1980, III, 15.

109. " 'Broken Homes' Found to Hurt Schoolwork," *New York Times*, July 29, 1980, III, 4; also see Fred Hechinger, "Is One-Parent Household a Handicap for Pupils?" *New York Times*, September 30, 1980, III, 1.

110. Campbell, "Hello Again," 439.

111. Fruland, letter to author.

112. Chalifaux, interview with author.

113. Bhimani, e-mail to author.

114. *CUB Communicator*, October 1979.

115. Taylor, interview with author.

116. Anderson, interview with author.

5: CONSTRAINING CHOICE

1. Dian Wilkins, testifying in 1972 on "Problems in Administration of Public Welfare Programs," Hearings before the Subcommittee on Fiscal Policy on the Joint Economic Committee, Congress of the United States, 92d Congress, 2d sess., May 1972 (Washington, D.C.: U.S. Government Printing Office, 1973), Part 2, 819.

2. Al Sheahen, "The Real Welfare Chiselers," *Commonweal*, February 13, 1976, 106.

3. Quoted in Michael Weiler, Anne Edwards, and Early Reagan, "The Reagan Attack on Welfare," in Michael Weiler and W. Barnett Pearce, eds., *Reagan and Public Discourse in America* (New York: William Morrow, 1987), 230.

4. Margaret Orelup, "Private Values, Public Policy, and Poverty in America, 1890–1940," unpublished dissertation, University of Massachusetts, 1995, 197, 147–48.

5. Wayne McMullen, "Client 'Fraud' in Chicago," *Social Service Review* 14 (March 1940), 36.

6. See, for example, A. H. Raskin, "Newburgh's Lessons for the Nation," *New York Times Magazine*, December 17, 1961, 7; Joseph T. Ritz, *The Despised Poor: Newburgh's War on Welfare* (Boston: Beacon Press, 1966); "The Meaning of Newburgh," *Nation*, July 29, 1961, 42; Meg Greenfield, "The 'Welfare Chiselers' of Newburgh, NY," *Reporter*, August 17, 1961, 39.

7. See, for example, Michael K. Brown, "Race in the American Welfare System: The Ambiguities of the 'Universalistic' Social Policy since the New Deal," in Adolph Reed, Jr., ed., *Without Justice for All: The New Liberalism and Our Retreat from Racial Equality* (Boulder, Colo.: Westview Press, 1999), 93–122.

8. *Final Report*, prepared by the Select Committee on Population, U.S. House of Representatives, 95th Congress, 2d sess., January 1979 (Washington, D.C.: U.S. Government Printing Office, 1979), 48.

9. Paul Molloy, "The Relief Chiselers Are Stealing Us Blind," *Saturday Evening Post*, September 8, 1951, 32ff. Apparently this article contained many inaccuracies. A rejoinder was published in the *Oklahoma City Advertiser* a few months later: Leon Hatfield, "The Real McCoy," January 17, 1952. See Milda C. M. Arndt, "An Appraisal of What the Critics are Saying About Public Assistance," *Social Service Review* 26 (December 1952): 469. In her groundbreaking 1965 book *Aid to Dependent Children* (New York: Columbia University Press, 1965), Winifred Bell remarks on a midcentury fraud investigation in Detroit: "Certainly, the investigations produced no evidence that fraud was a large-scale problem in public welfare, but this fact did not alter press interpretation." Bell goes on, "as Harold Silver of Detroit noted in an address to the Family Service Association of America in March, 1950, 'the headlines and impressions created by the press were that from thirty to fifty percent of the . . . clientele were "frauds" and "chiselers," that millions of dollars of tax funds were being wasted through carelessness and negligence of administration.' In fact after exhaustive investigation of the Department of Public Welfare in Detroit, in 1948, only two warrants for fraud were issued, and neither resulted in conviction" (62). See, generally, pp. 60–62 and 87–92 in this book. A typical media treatment of these events is Rufus Jorman, "Detroit Cracks Down on Relief Chiselers," *Saturday Evening Post*, December 10, 1949, 17–19, 122, 125–26.

10. See William T. Patterson, *America's Struggle Against Poverty, 1900–1994*, rev. ed. (Cambridge, Mass.: Harvard University Press, 1994), 110.

11. See Mimi Abramovitz, *Regulating the Lives of Women: Social Welfare Policy from Colonial Times to the Present*, rev. ed. (Boston: South End Press, 1996), for a full discussion.

12. Jill Quadagno, *The Color of Welfare: How Racism Undermined the War on Poverty* (New York: Oxford University Press, 1994). In his study *Why Americans Hate Welfare: Race, Media, and the Politics of Antipoverty Policy* (Chicago: University of Chicago Press, 1999), Martin Gilens writes, "Gradual demographic changes in residential patterns and welfare receipt by African Americans laid the groundwork for the changes to come in how Americans viewed the poor. But the more immediate percipitating events were the shift in focus within the civil rights movement from the fight for legal equality to the battle for economic equality and the urban riots that rocked the country during the summers of 1964 through 1968" (107).

13. David J. Kallen and Dorothy Miller, "Public Attitudes Toward Welfare," *Social Work* 16 (July 1971): 89. Also see Jon P. Alston and K. Imogene Dean, "Socioeconomic Factors Associated with Attitudes Toward Welfare Recipients and the Causes of Poverty," *Social Services Review* 46 (March 1972): 13–23, which is based on 1964 Roper survey data.

14. Henry F. and Katharine Pringle, "The Case for Federal Relief," *Saturday Evening Post*, July 19, 1952, cited in Blanche Coll, *The Safety Net: Welfare and Social Security, 1929–1979* (New Brunswick, N.J.: Rutgers University Press, 1995), 221.

15. Gilens, *Why Americans Hate Welfare*, 105, 114, 129.

16. Julius Horowitz, "The Arithmetic of Delinquency," *New York Times Magazine*, January 31, 1965, 12ff.

17. In 1968, a University of Michigan economist, James N. Morgan, testified before Congress regarding Americans' general—if mistaken—belief that "natural mothers" were the best caretakers of their children. He said, "Our society has never had the courage to suggest that if children are not being properly raised, they ought to be separated from their parents . . . The [poor] mother has been used as a cheap source of taking care of her own children. I happen to think this may be a big mistake." Representative Martha Griffiths agreed, reminding the speaker: "But this is what the $600 million is in the welfare amendment for, setting up day care centers, trying to withdraw the children away from their homes as quickly as you can." "Income Maintenance Programs," Hearings before the Subcommittee on Fiscal Policy of the Joint Economic Committee, Congress of the United States, 90th Congress, 2d sess., June 1968 (Washington, D.C.: U.S. Government Printing Office, 1968), Vol. 1, 178–80.

18. Phillips Cutright and John Scanzoni, "Income Supplements and the American Family," in *The Family, Poverty, and Welfare Programs: Factors Influencing Family Stability*, Paper No. 12, Part I, A Volume of Studies Prepared for the Use of the Subcommittee on Fiscal Policy of the Joint Economic Committee, U.S. Congress, November 4, 1973 (Washington, D.C.: U.S. Government Printing Office: 1973), 91.

19. McMullen, "Client 'Fraud,' " 50.
20. See Martha Minow, "The Welfare of Single Mothers and Their Children," *Connecticut Law Review* (spring 1994): 817–42.
21. Frances Fox Piven and Richard Cloward, *Regulating the Poor*, 2d ed. (New York: Vintage, 1993), 396.
22. Gwendolyn Mink, *The Wages of Motherhood* (Ithaca, N.Y.: Cornell University Press, 1998), 142.
23. A 1968 Children's Bureau report noted the continuation of this trend: "Twice as many non-white than white mothers worked because they had to support their families; specifically 32% of the non-white compared with 17% of the white mothers were the mainstays of their families." The report also noted that "the chance of having a working mother was greater for the non-white than for the white child. One in four of the nation's non-white children under age fourteen—compared with one in five white children—had a mother who worked at least half a year in 1964." Seth Low and Pearl G. Spinder, "Child Care Arrangements of Working Mothers in the United States," Children's Bureau Publication number 461-1968 (Washington, D.C.: U.S. Government Printing Office, n.d.), 9, 18.
24. See, for example, Ralph H. Turner, "The Non-White Female in the Labor Force," *American Journal of Sociology* 56 (March 1951): 438–47.
25. Dorothy Roberts, "The Value of Black Mothers' Work," *Connecticut Law Review* 26 (spring 1994): 876. The most prominent spokesman for this claim was, of course, Daniel Patrick Moynihan, *The Negro Family: The Case for National Action* (Washington, D.C.: U.S. Department of Labor, 1965), especially 29–45.
26. A leading welfare policy analyst in the late 1960s, Sar Levitan, submitted a statement to Congress about these matters: "There is increasing evidence that providing free public education should start before the age of six. This seems to be particularly true in the case of children coming from impoverished homes who are frequently 'retarded' and comparatively disadvantaged when placed in the same classroom with children from more affluent homes." "Income Maintenance Programs," Hearings, Vol. 1, 214.
27. See, for example, Patricia Morton, *Disfigured Images: The Historical Assault on Afro-American Women* (Westport, Conn.: Praeger, 1991), 119.
28. "Administration of the AFDC Program: A Report to the Committee on Government Operation," Congressional Research Service of the Library of Congress, April 1977 (Washington, D.C.: U.S. Government Printing Office, 1977), 1.
29. Michael Katz, *In the Shadow of the Poorhouse: A Social History of Welfare in America*, 10th anniversary edition (New York: Basic Books, 1996), 275.
30. For example, *King v. Smith* 392 US 309, 20 L.Ed. 118, 88 S. Ct. 2128 (1968), denied Alabama's right to deny federally funded assistance to a mother who lived with a man who wasn't legally responsible for supporting her children; *Doe v. Shapiro* 396 US 488, 24 L.Ed. 2d 677, 90 S. Ct. 641 (1970), found that a mother's refusal to name the father of her "illegitimate" child did not disqual-

ify the child from receiving welfare payments; *Goldberg v. Kelly* 397 US 254, 25 L.Ed. 2d, 287, 90 S. Ct. 1011 (1970), determined that New York State's practice of terminating public assistance without a prior evidentiary hearing violated the due process rights of the recipient.

31. Sar Levitan, Martin Rein, and David Marwick, *Work and Welfare Go Together* (Baltimore: Johns Hopkins University Press, 1972), 12. Also see "Income Maintenance Programs," Hearings, Vol. 1, 57, regarding the steep rise of the acceptance rate.

32. Levitan, Rein, and Marwick, *Work and Welfare*, 14.

33. The U.S. Census Bureau reported in 1975 that poor families, white and Black, were increasingly headed by women. In 1959 18 percent of poor families were headed by women; in 1973 the proportion was 36 percent and one-half of all children in families headed by women lived in poverty. "More Poor Families Now Led by Women," *New York Times*, January 26, 1975, 48. Also see "Money Income and Poverty Status of Families and Persons in the United States," U.S. Bureau of the Census, Current Population Reports, Series P-60, No. 125 (Washington, D.C.: U.S. Government Printing Office, 1979).

34. James Patterson discusses reasons for the explosion of welfare rolls at this time in *America's Struggle Against Poverty*, 178–84.

35. Thomas Sugrue, *The Origins of the Urban Crisis: Race and Inequality in Postwar Detroit* (Princeton, N.J.: Princeton University Press, 1996), 126–27, 141–47.

36. *Final Report*, prepared by the Select House Committee on Population, January 1979, 45.

37. "Problems in Administration of Public Welfare Programs," Hearings, Part 2, 551.

38. See Eleanor Holmes Norton, "Restoring the Traditional Black Family," *New York Times Magazine*, June 2, 1985, 43.

39. Linda C. McClain, "Irresponsible Reproduction," *Hastings Law Journal* 47 (January 1996): 451.

40. Coll, *Safety Net*, 221. Perhaps not everyone knew that. The chair of the commission on social action of the National Association of Social Workers spoke for many in his profession when he noted, "We think the purpose of the aid to dependent children in 1935 is still valid today; namely, to afford mothers a choice, a choice based on all the counseling and all the help she can get, but a choice between deciding to devote herself to the upbringing of her children at home or a choice—provided adequate day care is available . . . [to] go to work. Our objection is to a situation where the choice disappears, and when they can only be coerced, 'You must go to work,' because it seems to me that those who created the Social Security Act were fully aware of the value of a mother's devotion to bringing up her own children." In contrast, the director of the Illinois Department of Public Aid advocated "compulsory training for mothers." He decried "this choice philosophy" that ignored "the detrimental conditions surrounding child-rearing in our urban centers." "Social Security Amendments

of 1967," Hearings before the Committee on Finance, U.S. Senate, 90th Congress, 1st sess., Part 2, September 1967 (Washington, D.C.: U.S. Government Printing Office, 1967), 937–38; Part 3, Appendix 148.

41. "Economic Problems of Women," Part 2, Hearings before the Joint Economic Committee, Congress of the United States, 93d Congress, 1st sess. (Washington, D.C.: U.S. Government Printing Office, 1973), 393.

42. In 1982, the number of children with mothers in the workforce was 30 million; the number with mothers at home was 27 million. "Economic Status of Women," Hearings before the Joint Economic Committee, U.S. Congress, 97th Congress, 2d sess., February 1982 (Washington, D.C.: Government Printing Office, 1982), 19.

43. See, for example, Myron L. Belfer, "Mothers of Children in Day Care," *Child Welfare* 53 (June 1974): 367. Elizabeth Wickenden, one of the leading welfare experts in the country, noted in the late 1960s that "men who would not wish their own wives to work outside the homes lest their children's development suffer seem to see in enforced work for other mothers an easy answer to the "welfare problem." Regarding the issue of the "value" of poor mothers, Wickenden noted, "It seems . . . that the public welfare agency and its already overburdened workers are to serve as judge, jury, and policeman in deciding which mothers are 'worthy' to be supported at home, and which must be goaded, deprived, humiliated, and threatened off the welfare rolls." "Social Security Amendments of 1967," Hearings, Part 3, 1940.

44. Levitan, Rein, and Marwick, *Work and Welfare*, 54.

45. Mimi Abramovitz, *Under Attack, Fighting Back: Women and Welfare in the United States* (New York: Monthly Review Press), 76.

46. Daniel Patrick Moynihan, "The Crises in Welfare," in *Coping: Essays in Practice of Government* (New York: Random House, 1973), 164.

47. Paul J. Placek and Gary E. Hendershot, "Public Welfare and Family Planning: An Empirical Study of the 'Brood Sow' Myth," *Social Problems* 21 (June 1974): 660.

48. Placek and Hendershot actually found—having interviewed 300 women collecting AFDC in Tennessee in June and July of 1972—that participating in the welfare program did not lead women to have more children but, in fact, led them to higher levels of participation in family planning programs. Ibid. For a discussion about the association of the pill and individual choice, see Elizabeth Siegel Watkins, *On the Pill: A Social History of Oral Contraceptives, 1950–1970* (Baltimore: Johns Hopkins University Press, 1998), 75.

49. Coll, *Safety Net*, 120.

50. *Handbook of Public Assistance*, Bureau of Public Assistance (Washington, D.C.: U.S. Department of Health, Education, and Welfare, 1946), Part IV, Sections 3401 and 3401.1. In 1950 the government opposed "any policy of denying or withdrawing aid to dependent children as a method of bringing pressure upon women with young children to accept employment." Mildred Rein,

Welfare or Work: Factors in the Choice for AFDC Mothers (New York: Praeger, 1974), 8.

51. Alvin L. Schorr, "Problems in the ADC Program," *Social Work* 5 (April 1960): 7–8.

52. Testimony of Mamie Blankley, "Problems in Administration of Public Welfare Programs," Hearings, Part 2, 733.

53. Levitan, Rein, and Marwick, *Work and Welfare*, 34.

54. For discussions from two different eras about the failure of WIN, see Joel F. Handler and Ellen Jane Hollingsworth, "Work, Welfare, and the Nixon Reform Proposals," *Stanford Law Review* 22 (1970); and Sonya Michel, "A Tale of Two States: Race, Gender and Public/Private Welfare Provision in Postwar America," *Yale Journal of Law and Feminism* 19 (1997): 123–56.

55. Levitan, Rein, and Marwick, *Work and Welfare*, 103.

56. Katz, *In the Shadow of the Poorhouse*, 287–88.

57. "Problems in Administration of Public Welfare Programs," Hearings, Part 1, 108, 69.

58. Ibid., Part 2, 411.

59. Ibid., Part 3, 1042.

60. Ibid., Part 1, 69, 107.

61. "Administration of the AFDC Program," Hearings before a Subcommittee of the Committee on Government Operations, House of Representatives, 95th Congress, 1st sess., July 1977 (Washington, D.C.: U.S. Government Printing Office, 1977), 576.

62. Leonard Goodwin, *Do the Poor Want to Work?* (Washington, D.C.: Brookings Institution, 1972).

63. Patterson, *America's Struggle Against Poverty*, 175.

64. "Welfare Block Grant/Fiscal Relief Program," Hearing before the Subcommittee on Public Assistance of the Committee on Finance, U.S. Senate, 95th Congress, 2d sess., September 12, 1978 (Washington, D.C.: U.S. Government Printing Office, 1978), 70.

65. "Problems in Administration of Public Welfare Programs," Hearings, Part 1, 93, 110.

66. Ibid., Part 2, 527.

67. Gwendolyn Mink, *Welfare's End* (Ithaca, NY: Cornell University Press, 1998), 49–50.

68. Welfare mothers were not alone in this era as they claimed "rights" for their kind. A number of prominent mainstream—establishment—reports and studies of the welfare system issued in the late 1960s insisted that welfare must be a right. See, for example, "Having the Power, We Have the Duty," the Report to the Secretary of Health, Education, and Welfare from the Advisory Council on Public Welfare (Washington, D.C.: U.S. Department of Health, Education, and Welfare, Welfare Administration, June 29, 1966), especially 67–74; and *Report of the National Advisory Commission on Civil Disorders* [the Kerner Re-

port] (New York: Bantam, 1968), 457–67. The growing public and political discussion at this time about the need to construct a national income maintenance system also reflected a sense that the poor had "the right" to a basic standard of living.

69. Deborah Grey White, *Too Heavy a Load: Black Women in Defense of Themselves, 1894–1994* (New York: Norton, 1999), 216.

70. See "Income Maintenance Programs," Hearings, 1968, Vol. I, 51–85; Vol. II, 538–74.

71. Susan Handley Hertz, *The Welfare Mothers' Movement: A Decade of Change for Poor Women?* (Lanham, Md.: University Press of America, 1981), 114. Some politicians also grew in relation to this idea of welfare rights. In 1978, Senator Moynihan referred to welfare rights organizations as a mark of "good fellowship [sic]," and noted that a welfare rights group "reflects a community of interest among the poor and brings attention to the problems and their possible improvement." Presumably signaling his respect for these kinds of groups, in 1978 Moynihan invited the Illinois and Chicago Welfare Rights Organizations to submit "Poor People's Suggestions on How to Improve the Emergency Assistance Provisions of . . . Various Welfare Reform Proposals to a Congressional Committee." "Welfare Reform Proposals," Hearings before the Subcommittee on Public Assistance of the Committee on Finance, U.S. Senate, 95th Congress, 2d sess., Part V, May 2 and 4, 1978 (Washington, D.C.: U.S. Government Printing Office, 1978), 1210, 1221–23.

72. Hertz, *The Welfare Mother's Movement*, 34–35, 114. For additional examples of the strength of welfare activists' voices, see "Examination of the War on Poverty," Hearings before the Subcommittee on Employment, Manpower, and Poverty of the Committee on Labor and Public Welfare, U.S. Senate, 90th Congress, 1st sess., Part 10, July 1967 (Washington, D.C.: U.S. Government Printing Office, 1967), 3369–80.

73. Patrick M. Horan and Patricia Lee Austin, "The Social Bases of Welfare Stigma," *Social Problems* 21 (June 1964): 656.

74. "Problems in Administration of Public Welfare Programs," Hearings, Part 1, 94–104.

75. Hertz, *The Welfare Mothers' Movement*, 145. See, for example, John Kifer, "Tell It Like It Is: Digalo Como Es, Welfare Sit-ins Netting Millions, Protest Unit Says City Aid Has Risen by $3 Million," *New York Times*, May 30, 1968.

76. John A. Gardiner and Theodore Lyman, *The Fraud Control Game: State Responses to Fraud and Abuse in AFDC and Medicare* (Bloomington: Indiana University Press, 1984), 1–2.

77. Mimi Abramovitz, *Regulating the Lives of Women*, 335.

78. Sheahen, "The Real Welfare Chiselers," 105. Also see Arthur H. Miller, "Will Public Attitudes Defeat Welfare Reform?" *Public Welfare* 36 (summer 1978): 48–50. Miller found that in the early 1970s, Americans were adding

negative attitudes toward recipients to their negative attitudes toward welfare programs.

79. John B. Williamson wrote, "[A]s the poor begin to take collective action on their own behalf with increasing frequency, it is likely that there will be a reduction in the prevalence of the belief that they are lazy and unmotivated." "Beliefs About the Welfare Poor," *Sociological and Social Research* 58 (January 1974): 174.

80. Gilens, *Why Americans Hate Welfare*, 140.

81. See generally Shanto Iyengar, *Is Anyone Responsible: How Television Frames Political Issues* (Chicago: University of Chicago Press, 1991).

82. Quoted in Quadagno, *The Color of Welfare*, 79.

83. James Warren, "Nixon on Tape Expounds on Welfare and Homosexuality," *Chicago Tribune*, November 7, 1999.

84. Susan Sheehan, "A Welfare Mother," *New Yorker*, September 29, 1975, 42–99. When this study appeared as a book, it won the Sidney Hillman Foundation Award. Sheehan revisited this subject in the same spirit in a book entitled *Life For Me Ain't Been No Crystal Stair* (New York: Pantheon, 1993). And the *New Yorker* has returned to the subject in Adrian Nicole LeBlanc, "A Reporter at Large, Landing from the Sky," April 24–May 1, 2000.

85. In 1995, another *New Yorker* writer, Michael Massing, reflected on the genre that Sheehan was pioneering in the 1970s and that had come into its own in the 1990s: "The very qualities that make today's journalism so compelling— the seamless narrative, the eye for detail, the blend of empathy and candor— serve also to highlight the behavior of the poor, making it seem the cause of their poverty rather than the other way around . . . The larger economic, political, and even cultural factors that lie beyond the ghetto and the behavior of its residents—in boardrooms, say, or in Washington—also lie beyond the scope of [such work]." Massing added, "The recent books on the poor seem less like clarion calls than like morality tales—political parables about the risks of illegitimacy, the dangers of drug abuse, the perils of irresponsible parenting." "Ghetto Blasting," *New Yorker*, January 16, 1995, 37. Also see Ruth Hamill, Timothy DeCamp Wilson, and Richard E. Nisbitt, "Insensitivity to Sample Bias: Generalizing from Atypical Cases," *Journal of Personality and Social Psychology* 39 (1980): 578–89, for a discussion of the power of lurid descriptions of a single welfare mother in shifting readers' attitudes about welfare recipients in a negative direction. Martin Gilens agrees that a story about a specific poor person is much more powerful in shaping ideas about "the poor" than statistical information, "even if the evidentiary value of the statistical information is far higher." Gilens also points out that the race of the poor person in the story matters much more than the "aggregate statistics about the racial composition of the poor that occasionally accompany [such] stories." *Why Americans Hate Welfare*, 135, 206.

86. Sheehan, "A Welfare Mother," 42, 62. For a recent review of sensational treat-

ments of the misbehavior of poor families see Micaela diLeonardo, *Exotics at Home: Anthropologies, Others, American Modernity* (Chicago: University of Chicago Press, 1998), 121–23.

87. Sheehan, "A Welfare Mother," 56, 72, 79.
88. Quoted in Johnnie Tillmon, "Welfare is a Women's Issue," Liberation News Service, No. 415, February 26, 1972; reprinted in Rosalyn Baxandall, Linda Gordon, and Susan Reverby, eds., *America's Working Women* (New York: Vintage, 1976), 357.
89. "Problems in Administration of Public Welfare Programs," Hearings, Part 3, 858.
90. See, for example, ibid., Part 1, 119.
91. Gardiner and Lyman, *The Fraud Control Game*, 3.
92. University of Wyoming, American Heritage Center Library, Women's History Resource Collection, Box 50, File 3, "Welfare 1969–1971," Newsletter, August 10, 1971, no further identification. According to legal scholar Thomas Ross, "The central theme of the [U.S. Supreme] Court's cases dealing with the food stamp program has been the assumption that poor people will cheat." Ross cites *Lyng v. Castillo* 477 U.S. 635 as an example. *Just Stories: How the Law Embodies Racism and Bias* (Boston: Beacon Press, 1996), 84.
93. "Workfare Versus Welfare," Hearings before the Subcommittee on Trade, Productivity, and Economic Growth of the Joint Economic Committee, Congress of the United States, 99th Congress, 2d sess., April 1986 (Washington, D.C.: U.S. Government Printing Office, 1986), 100.
94. James R. Storey, "Welfare in the 1970s: A National Study of Benefits Available in 100 Local Areas, A Staff Study Prepared for the Use of the Subcommittee on Fiscal Policy of the Joint Economic Committee," Studies in Public Welfare, Paper No. 15 (Washington, D.C.: U.S. Government Printing Office, 1974) 7.
95. "Economic Status of Women," 98.
96. "Administration of the AFDC Program," Hearings, 73.
97. Orelup, "Private Values, Public Policy, and Poverty in America," 151.
98. *New York Times*, December 26, 1981, 23.
99. Cutright and Scanzioni, "Income Supplements and the American Family," 56. Also see Martin Rein and Lee Rainwater, "Patterns of Welfare Use," *Social Service Review* 52 (December 1978): 511–34, which reports on a study showing little welfare fraud.
100. Cutright and Scanzoni, "Income Supplements and the American Family," 57.
101. Sharon Galm, "Welfare—An Administrative Nightmare," in *Studies in Public Welfare*, Paper No. 5, Part I, Issues in Welfare Administration, A Staff Study Prepared for the Use of the Subcommittee on Fiscal Policy of the Joint Economic Committee, U.S. Congress, December 13, 1972 (Washington, D.C.: U.S. Government Printing Office: 1972), 35. Also see pp. 35–41 for many other examples of twisted findings, reflections, and recommendations regarding welfare fraud.

102. Rein, *Welfare or Work*, 119.
103. "Welfare: America's No. 1 Problem," *U.S. News and World Report*, March 1, 1971, 38.
104. "Problems in Administration of Public Welfare Programs," Hearings, Part 2, 450. Martha Griffiths served in the House of Representatives from 1955 to 1974. From 1971 to 1974 she served as the chair of the Subcommittee on Fiscal Policy, which held hearings on aspects of public welfare in several cities, the transcripts of which are frequently cited in this chapter. Griffiths was an old-style "equal rights" feminist who was extremely instrumental in getting the Equal Rights Amendment through Congress in the early 1970s. She deeply believed that poor women should eschew dependency (and their children!) and get jobs like middle-class women. For a statement by Griffiths, see "Welfare Reform: Rationale, Criteria, and Choices," *Public Welfare* 32 (summer 1974), 33–38.
105. Weiler, Edwards, and Reagan make a similar point as part of a discussion of Reagan's coinage of "the welfare safety net" in 1981. See "The Reagan Attack on Welfare," 242. Also see "Welfare Cheating," Address of Hon. Russell B. Long, chairman, Committee on Finance, and Supporting Material, March 14, 1972 (Washington, D.C.: U.S. Government Printing Office, 1972).
106. J. Y. Smith, "District Welfare Seen Overpaying—Study Shows Others Are Underpayed," *Washington Post*, January 7, 1972.
107. "Income Maintenance Programs," Hearings, Vol. I, 56.
108. Linda Greenhouse, "Carey Asks $3.7 Million to Computerize Data on Relief Recipients," *New York Times*, May 30, 1976, 27.
109. See, for example, "Disposition of Public Assistance Cases Involving Questions of Fraud, Fiscal Year 1974," U.S. Department of Health, Education and Welfare, Social and Rehabilitative Service, Office of Information Systems, National Center for Social Statistics, 1975.
110. "Administration of the AFDC Program," Hearings, 252–53.
111. Mary Dedinsky, "The Role of the Media," *Public Welfare* 35 (winter 1977): 14–15.
112. "The Role of Computer Technology in Fraud Detection," Conference Proceedings, National Conference on Fraud, Abuse, and Error, Protecting the Taxpayer's Dollar, December 13, 1978, U.S. Department of Health, Education and Welfare, Office of the Secretary, Washington, D.C., July, 1979, 146.
113. Alphonso A. Narvaez, "Fraud in Welfare Program is Laid to City Laxity," *New York Times*, November 16, 1971, 57.
114. "Problems in Administration of Public Welfare Programs," Hearings, Part 2, 714.
115. "Workfare Versus Welfare," Hearings, 100.
116. See, for example, in the *New York Times*: "A Homeowner Commutes for City Welfare Check," February 17, 1976, 35; "18 Women with Jobs Held on Relief-

Fraud Charges," March 17, 1976, 38; "Carey Asks $3.7 Million to Computerize Data on Relief Recipients," May 30, 1976, 27; "Ineligibles on Welfare Decrease," June 12, 1976, 27. When Senator Moynihan asked the assistant secretary of labor for policy, evaluation, and research in 1977, "What proportion of AFDC families are headed by someone who is now working?" the assistant secretary answered, "About half the people on AFDC now work." "President's Statement on Principles of Welfare Reform," Hearings before the Subcommittee on Public Welfare of the Committee on Finance, U.S. Senate, 95th Congress, 1st sess., May 5 and 12, 1977 (Washington, D.C.: Government Printing Office, 1977), 68.

117. "Detroit Mom Charged with Cheating Welfare," *Jet*, March 4, 1985, 40. For a brilliant discussion of the survival strategies of poor mothers in the 1990, see K. Edin and L. Lein, *Making Ends Meet: How Single Mothers Survive Welfare and Low-Wage Work* (New York: Russell Sage Foundation, 1997).

118. In 1978, for example, with welfare rolls at a seven-year low in New York City, and a newly beefed-up 48 percent rejection rate (one study estimated that as many as half of those applicants may have been wrongly rejected), Mayor Koch announced a seven-point program aimed at reducing erroneous and fraudulent welfare payments in the city. See, in the *New York Times*: Glen Fowler, "Plan to Fight Fraud in Welfare Offered," February 12, 1978, 31; Peter Khiss, "Half of H.R.A. Welfare Rejections Are Found Incorrect in Sampling," April 19, 1978, II, 3.

119. "Administration of AFDC Programs," 1977, 255.

120. Dedinsky, "The Roll of the Media," 13, 14.

121. "Problems in Administration of Public Welfare Programs," Part 3, 848–49.

122. "Barriers to Self-Sufficiency for Single Female Heads of Families," Hearings Before a Subcommittee of the Committee on Government Operations, House of Representatives, 99th Congress, 1st sess., July 1985 (Washington, D.C.: U.S. Government Printing Office, 1985), 486. Margaret Orelup shows that this was an enduring problem: writing about the 1930s, she says, "Convinced fraud was rampant, Cleveland commissioned a commercial credit corporation to audit their relief program. The corporation report indicated that a total of two percent of the cases examined should not have received aid. The cost of the fraudulent two percent about equaled the cost of the audit. Cleveland's experience went unreported by the major news periodicals." "Private Values, Public Policy, and Poverty in America," 150–51.

123. "How Welfare Keeps Women From Working," *Business Week*, April 7, 1973, 51. Martin Gilens found that "overall, the sustained negative coverage of welfare during 1972 and 1973 was accompanied by the highest proportions of blacks in newsmagazine images of the poor at any point during the entire forty-three year period examined." *Why Americans Hate Welfare*, 123.

124. Melba Blanton, "What Ever Happened to Oklahoma's Welfare?" *Oklahoma Observer* 11, no. 36 (n.d.), University of Wyoming, American Heritage Center

Library, Women's History Resource Collection, Box 50, Folder 4, "Welfare, 1972–73."

125. White, *Too Heavy a Load*, 215. White also points out that "the survival of the [National] Council [of Negro Women] and the demise of the national feminist and welfare organizations are indicative of the kind of women Black people wanted as national representatives" (255).

126. At a 1978 conference on fraud, Mayor Richard G. Hatcher of Gary, Indiana, said, "We will have to find ways of changing the notion abroad in our land that welfare is somehow a rip-off of the rest of the nation by Black people . . ." "Conference Proceedings," National Conference on Fraud, Abuse, and Error, Protecting the Taxpayer's Dollar, December 13–14, 1978, 10, 8.

127. Bernard Weinraub, "Welfare Trims Expected to Affect 17% In Program," *New York Times*, June 30, 1981, IV, 21.

128. H.J. Res. 495, *Congressional Record*, 97th Congress, 2d sess., vol. 128, 1982.

129. See, for example, Arthur H. Miller, "Political Issues and Trust in Government: 1964–1970," *American Political Science Review* 68 (September, 1974): 951–72. Miller shows here that between 1958 and 1976, a significant majority of Americans came to believe that the government was wasting a lot of their tax money; during this period, the percentage who agreed with this proposition rose from 45 percent to 76 percent. Note that earlier in this chapter, I cited the following datum: between 1958 and 1977 government expenditures on aid to families with dependent children rose from $800 million a year to $11 billion.

130. "Problems in Administration of Public Welfare Programs," Hearings, Part 1, 68.

131. Dedinsky, "The Role of the Media," 15. See Daniel Reich, "The Needy Get Iciness," an assessment of the impact of "official fraud" by government welfare workers vs. fraud "by a small minority of clients," *New York Times*, September 29, 1977.

132. See Thomas Ross, "The Rhetoric of Poverty: Their Immorality, Our Helplessness," *Georgetown Law Journal* 79 (1991): 1499–1547.

133. Weiler, "The Reagan Attack on Welfare," 241, 232.

134. Dorothy Roberts, "Welfare and the Problems of Black Citizenship," *Yale Law Journal* 105 (1996): 1563–1602.

135. Hertz, *The Welfare Mother's Movement*, 107.

136. Eric Foner, *The Story of American Freedom* (New York: Norton, 1998), 40.

137. Hertz, *The Welfare Mothers' Movement*, 107.

138. "Administration of AFDC Program," 1977, 526.

139. For a powerful description of the female tradition of self-sacrifice, see Stephanie Golden, *Slaying the Mermaid* (New York: Harmony Books, 1998).

140. "Workfare Versus Welfare," Hearings, 67.

141. "Children, Youth, and Families: Beginning the Assessment," Hearings before the Select Committee on Children, Youth, and Families, House of Representa-

tives, 98th Congress, 1st sess., April 1983 (Washington, D.C.: Government Printing Office, 1983), 6.

142. Abramovitz, *Regulating the Lives of Women*, 327, 121.

143. This narrative device, "I was talking with a . . . ," was characteristic of Griffiths and also of Ronald Reagan, both of whom habitually "quoted" outraged, unnamed persons as sources of dramatic expert testimony.

144. "Problems in Administration of Public Welfare Programs," Part 3, 956–57.

145. Ibid., Part 2, 502.

146. Michael B. Katz, *The Undeserving Poor: From the War on Poverty to the War on Welfare* (New York: Pantheon, 1989), 49.

147. "Problems in Administration of Public Welfare Programs," Part 1, 203.

148. Ibid., Part 3, 1197.

149. Maris Vinovskis, *An "Epidemic" of Adolescent Pregnancy? Some Historical and Policy Considerations* (New York: Oxford University Press, 1988). Even by 1968 some people thought this charge that teen mothers were having babies for profit was old and tired. During AFDC hearings that year, Representative Martha Griffiths remarked, "The greatest criticism that I hear on ADC, and I might say I hear this from school superintendents, is that teenage girls graduate or drop out of school and there are no jobs available. But they have available to them an excellent source of income at once. All they have to do is have a baby." In response, Ellen Winston, former U.S. commissioner of welfare, retorted sharply, but to little effect: "Madame Chairman, I think that over the years we have tended to make too much of a relationship between the availability of AFDC and the illegitimacy rate. There are other forces in our society that are leading to the increase in the rate of births out of wedlock. We find these births in all income groups. We still conceal them a bit better in the higher income groups than we do in the lower income groups . . . So I think the first point we need to make is that we really have no evidence that there is this direct relationship, although I know it is in all the discussions about the effects of public assistance." "Income Maintenance Programs," Hearings, Vol. 1, 291.

150. "The Editorial Notebook: Poverty by Choice," Robert Curvin, *New York Times*, July 27, 1982, 22.

151. "Problems in Administration of Public Welfare Programs," Hearings, Part 3, 1281.

152. See, for example, Jean Y. Jones, "The American Family: Problems and Federal Policies," Congressional Research Service, Mary 16, 1977, Library of Congress (Washington, D.C.: Government Printing Office: 1977), 6. Jones cites a 1974 Rand Corporation study ("Non-Support of Legitimate Children by Affluent Fathers as a Cause of Poverty and Welfare Dependency," by Marion P. Winston and Truce Forsher) that found that "failure of fathers to pay child support has contributed to the generally low income of female-headed families. It is estimated that four out of ten divorced fathers are not paying any child support

one year after the divorce and that after ten years, only two out of ten make any payment." The study also found that nonpayment was "as prevalent among affluent and middle-class fathers as among low-income men."

153. "Welfare: American's No. One Problem," 40.
154. See Katz, *In the Shadow of the Poorhouse*, 284.
155. Ibid., 278.
156. Hertz, *The Welfare Mothers' Movement*, 66.
157. "Problems in Administration of Public Welfare," Hearings, Part 2, 750. A child welfare expert in New York City testified at a 1967 congressional hearing regarding these matters: "We find . . . that women who make between sixty and seventy dollars a week pay up to twenty dollars a week for a baby to be cared for by totally unsuitable persons. One person was found obviously not very sober and listening to TV and not caring for the children in her apartment at all." Dr. Trude Lash, Executive Director, Citizens' Committee for the Children of New York, "Social Security Amendments of 1967," Hearings, Part 3, 2020.
158. White, *Too Heavy a Load*, 263. A representative of the National Council of Black Women defined the work requirements of the 1967 Social Security Amendments as inconsistent with "the freedom to choose your own life work." Ruth Atkins (for Dorothy Height), "Social Security Amendments of 1967," Hearings, Part 2, 1503.
159. "Problems in Administration of Public Welfare," Hearings, Part 2, 764, 818.
160. Ibid., Part 3, 1079.
161. Peter Khiss, "Coalition Finds Errors Cause Food Problems for Welfare Families," *New York Times*, April 9, 1979, IV, 11.
162. "Problems in Administration of Public Welfare," Hearings, Part 3, 1027.
163. Ibid., Part 2, 772.
164. Stout, "Another Look at Welfare Fraud," 334.
165. "Women and Children in Poverty," Hearings before the Task Force on Entitlements, Uncontrollables and Indexing of the Committee on the Budget, House of Representatives, 98th Congress, 1st sess., October 1983 (Washington, D.C.: Government Printing Office, 1983), 11.
166. White, *Too Heavy a Load*, 237.
167. "American Families: Trends and Pressures," Hearings before the Subcommittee on Children and Youth of the Committee on Labor and Public Welfare, U.S. Senate, 93rd Congress, 1st sess., September 1973 (Washington, D.C.: Government Printing Office, 1974), 115.
168. "Problems in Administration of Public Welfare Programs," Hearings, Part 2, 608, 818.
169. "Women and Children in Poverty," Hearings, 7.
170. "Problems in Administration of Public Welfare Programs," Part 2, 735.
171. Leonard Goodwin, "Do the Poor Want to Work?" See also Leonard Goodwin, "How Suburban Families View the Work Orientation of the Welfare Poor: Problems in Social Stratification and Social Policy," *Social Problems* 19 (1972):

337–48. In part, the research in this article shows that the values of welfare recipients and their orientations toward work are similar to those of the general population.

172. William F. Farrell, "Welfare Reforms Near a Standstill," *New York Times*, January 18, 1976, 1.

173. "Women and Children in Poverty," Hearings, 8.

174. "Problems in Administration of Public Welfare Programs," Hearings, Part 2, 737.

175. "Social Security Amendments of 1967," Hearings, Part 3, 2020.

176. The speaker is Robert E. Jornlin, Social Welfare Director, Contra Costa County Welfare Department. "Administration of the AFDC Program," 381. Also see "Problems in Administration of Public Welfare Programs," Hearings, Part 3, 958.

177. "Problems in Administration of Public Welfare Programs," Hearings, Part 2, 775.

178. Lawrence M. Mead, "Expectations and Welfare Work: WIN in New York City," *Policy Studies Review* 2 (May 1983): 648–62, and "Expectations and Welfare Work in New York State," *Polity* 18 (winter 1985): 224–52.

179. "Problems in Administration of Public Welfare Programs," Hearings, Part 3, 958.

180. Ibid., Part 2, 826, 739.

181. Roberts, "The Value of Black Mothers," 872.

182. Robert E. Weems, "The Revolution Will be Marketed: American Corporations and Black Consumers During the 1960s," *Radical History Review* 59 (1994): 102. Weems shows how advertising revenue in *Ebony* rose from $3,630,804 in 1962 to $9,965,898 in 1969. Also see Robert E. Weems, *Desegregating the Dollar* (New York: New York University Press, 1998).

183. White, *Too Heavy a Load*, 228; also see Felicia Kornbluh, "To Fulfill Their 'Rightly Needs': Consumerism and the National Welfare Rights Movement," *Radical History Review* 69 (fall 1997): 76–113.

184. For an early example of this development, see "Economic Opportunity Act of 1964," Hearings before the Subcommittee on the War on Poverty Program of the Committee on Education and Labor, House of Representatives, 88th Congress, 2d sess., Part 3, April 1964 (Washington, D.C.: Government Printing Office, 1964), 1738–40, which includes the statement of J. Orrin Shipe, the managing director of the Credit Union National Association. Shipe reviews here "the credit union experience in the field of low-income persons."

185. "Examination of the War on Poverty," April 27, 28, May 2, 1967, Part IV (Washington, D.C.: U.S. Government Printing Office, 1967), 1515. Also see *Report of the National Advisory Commission on Civil Disorders*, 274–77, in which the Kerner Commission ascribes the urban rebellions of the late 1960s to "unfair commercial practices affecting Negro consumers" and "exploitative consumer practices." This section of the report is entitled "Exploitation of Dis-

advantaged Consumers by Retail Merchants." Beulah Saunders, a vice chairman of the National Welfare Rights Organization, made a series of strong
statements about the centrality of consumer status to poor women when she
testified before Congress in 1968. See "Income Maintenance Programs," Vol. 1,
66–71.
186. "Problems in the Administration of Public Welfare Programs," Hearings,
Part 2, 511.
187. Sheahen, "The Real Welfare Chiselers," 105.
188. Johnnie Tillmon, "Welfare Is a Women's Issue," in Baxandall, Gordon, and
Reverby, *America's Working Women*, 357.
189. Elaine Abelson, *When Ladies Go A-Thieving: Middle-Class Shoplifters in the Vic-
torian Department Store* (New York: Oxford University Press, 1989), 8.
190. Elaine Abelson cites this interesting photo essay in *When Ladies Go A-
Thieving*, 202: "One out of Sixty is a Shoplifter," *Life*, December 15, 1967,
66–73.

6: MOTHERHOOD AS CLASS PRIVILEGE IN AMERICA

1. A. Delafield Smith, "Public Assistance as a Social Obligation," Harvard Law
Review 63 (1949): 274.
2. *Kathleen Ramos et al. Kenneth F. Fare et al.*, U.S. District Court, Southern District of California, Memorandum of Points and Authorities in Support of
Motions for Temporary Restraining Orders, Preliminary Injunctions and
Certification of Necessity for Three-Judge District Court, September 2, 1969,
2, National Indian Law Library, Boulder, CO, File 001246-B.
3. "Petition to make Kathleen Ramos a Ward of the Court," Superior Court,
State of California, County of San Diego, Juvenile Department, April 22,
1969, Exhibit A, National Indian Law Library, File 001246.
4. *Ramos v. Fare*, U.S. District Court, Southern District of California, Complaint
for Three Judges, September 2, 1969, 4–5, National Indian Law Library, File
001246-A.
5. *Ramos v. Fare*, File 001246-B, 14, 2–3, 4.
6. Mrs. Mason is quoted in *Ramos v. Montgomery* 313 F. Supp. 1179 (1970).
Kathy Ramos's lawyers argued that "the higher aid payments to foster families
frustrates the express congressional purpose of . . . encouraging the care of dependent children in their own homes or in the homes of relatives." They also
pointed out in one of their pleadings that "according to the state's 'need' figures, a child such as Kathy Ramos needs $39.10 per month, or about $1.30 per
day, for food and clothing. She receives even less. An additional $1.90 . . . per
day would make a large difference (a 190% increase). To put it bluntly, plaintiffs cannot afford an adequate diet. Any increase in their income would help."
Ramos's lawyers were countering the defendants' claim that a difference of "less
than $2.00 a day" was hardly significant. *Ramos v. Montgomery*, American In-

dian Law Library, File 001246-C. The Ramos case followed the enactment of the 1967 Social Security Amendments. A spokeswoman for the National Council of Negro Women described the effect of the foster care provisions of these amendments: "[They] permit increased payments for foster care for children removed from their own homes, but [do] not increase the amount available to mothers to provide better care for their children at home, although this would cost far less financially and emotionally. The family as the basic social unit emerges badly bruised from this legislative mixing pot." "Social Security Amendments of 1967," Hearings before the Committee on Finance, U.S. Senate, 90th Congress, 1st sess., Part 3, September 1967 (Washington, D.C.: U.S. Government Printing Office, 1967), 1503; also see 1464.

7. Gerben DeJong, "Setting Foster Care Rates," *Public Welfare* 33 (fall 1975): 37.

8. Jenkins and, Sauber, "Paths to Child Placement: Family Situations Prior to Foster Care" (New York: Community Council of Greater New York, 1966), 7.

9. Robert H. Mnookin, "Foster Care—In Whose Best Interest?" *Harvard Education Review* 43 (November, 1973): 619. Of course poor mothers have been vulnerable to child removal for a long time. See, for example, Linda Gordon, "Single Mothers and Child Neglect, 1880–1920," in which Gordon shows that "only one variable other than single mother was a better predictor of court-ordered child removal: poverty." *American Quarterly* 37 (1985): 173. Also see Michael B. Katz, *In the Shadow of the Poorhouse: A Social History of Welfare in America* (New York: Basic Books, 1986), ch. 5. For examples of more recent child removal because of poverty, see Odeana R. Neal, "Myths and Moms: Images of Women and Termination of Parental Rights," *Kansas Journal of Law and Public Policy* (fall 1995): 61–76. Also see Amanda T. Perez, "Transracial Adoption and the Federal Adoption Subsidy," *Yale Law and Policy Review* 17 (1998): 201–47.

10. Justine Wise Polier, "The Invisible Legal Rights of the Poor," *Children* 12 (1965): 218.

11. Herma Hill Kay and Irving Phillips, "Poverty and the Law of Child Custody," *California Law Review* 54 (1966): 736. Ten years later, in 1976, "the average payment for an AFDC–foster care child in a foster family home was $260 dollars a month, and in an institution $601 per month . . . compare[d] to an average monthly payment of $72.35 per recipient in his or her own home under the regular AFDC program." Jean Y. Jones, *The American Family: Problems and Federal Policies* (Washington, D.C.: Congressional Research Service, Library of Congress, 1977), 26.

12. Harry D. Krause, "Child Welfare, Parental Responsibility, and the State," Studies In Public Welfare, Paper No. 12, Part II, The Family, Poverty, and Welfare Programs: Factors Influencing Family Stability, Prepared for the Use of the Subcommittee on Fiscal Policy of the Joint Economic Committee, Congress of the United States (Washington, D.C.: U.S. Government Printing Office, November 4, 1973), 267.

13. Mary Brady, "Prevention and Parenting: As These Issues Relate to the Minority Family," *Proceedings of the First National Conference on Child Abuse and Neglect*, January 4–7, 1976, DHEW Pub. No. OHD 77-30094, 60.

14. Mnookin, "Foster Care—In whose Best Interest?," 619–20, 629; Betty Reid Mandell, *Where Are the Children?: A Class Analysis of Foster Care and Adoption* (Lexington, Mass.: Lexington Books, 1973), 56–57; Sanford Katz, *When Parents Fail* (Boston: Beacon Press, 1971).

15. Mandell, *Where Are the Children?*, 59. The threats of Mayor Rudolph Giuliani of New York City in late 1999 to remove the children from families living in homeless shelters show how vibrant this attitude remains and how vulnerable poor parents remain. See, for example, Nina Bernstein, "City May Remove Children From Families in Shelters," *New York Times*, December 4, 1999, A13.

16. See Kay and Phillips, "Poverty and the Law of Child Custody"; and Katz, *When Parents Fail*. One family policy expert put it this way in the early 1970s: "While it remains a basic tenet of our family-centered society that it is in the best interests of the child to be with its parents even if the parents are less than perfect, the notion of parental right is fading. In custody matters generally, it has been argued of late that "the best interests of the child" should control over "parental rights." Krause, "Child Welfare, Parental Responsibility and the State," n. 44. In 1973, Robert Mnookin noted, regarding this new development, "One obvious objection to the best interests of the child test is that by its very terms it ignores the interests of the parents." "Foster Care—In Whose Best Interest?," 614. A director of the American Civil Liberties Union was direct in assessing these developments, as reflected in provisions of the 1967 Social Security Amendments: "The provision for foster homes to increase the removal of children in AFDC programs and place them in foster homes infringes on the right of a mother to raise her child. This should be a choice of hers and it is not a function of the State. When the State starts determining that children would be better off in foster homes, then it seems to me we have gone a long way toward a totalitarian society. The right of individuals to raise their children, even under very tough economic circumstances is still a right of the individual. This is certainly contrary to the whole concept of continuing the family unit." "Social Security Amendments of 1967," Hearings, Part 2, 1229.

17. Everett R. Holmes, "Outcry Holds Up California Bid to Deal with Illegitimate Births," *New York Times*, October 30, 1972, 20.

18. "State Urged to Take Illegitimate Children," *Oakland Tribune*, March 24, 1971, 1.

19. In 1977, 502,000 children were in foster care in the United States. "Federally Funded Child Welfare, Foster Care, and Adoption Assistance Programs," Hearings before the Subcommittee on Human Resources of the Committee on Ways and Means, 101st Congress, 2d sess., April 4–5, 1990 (Washington, D.C.: U.S. Government Printing Office, 1990), 6. A poor mother's situation in

this regard may not have improved since the late 1970s. An October 2000 letter from the executive director of the Child Welfare Organizing Project to the *New York Times* reports that "More than 85% of New York City's children in foster care are there not as a result of abuse, but of neglect allegations related to poverty, homelessness, addiction or domestic violence. Despite this, New York City child welfare practice remains lopsidedly focused on protective removal and placement. In effect, the city is telling families: We know what kind of help you need, but what we mostly have to offer is the involuntary removal of your children." October 20, 2000, A30.

20. Theodore J. Stein, "Early Intervention in Foster Care," *Public Welfare* 34 (spring 1976): 39; Alan R. Gruber, *Foster Home Care in Massachusetts: A Study of Foster Children and Their Biological and Foster Parents* (Boston: Governor's Commission on Adoption and Foster Care, 1973), 50–52.

21. Henry S. Maas and Richard E. Engler, Jr., *Children in Need of Parents* (New York: Columbia University Press, 1959), 390–91.

22. Dorothy A. Murphy, "A Program for Parents of Children in Foster Family Care," *Children Today*, November–December 1976, 39.

23. Ner Littner, "The Importance of the Natural Parents to the Child in Placement," *Child Welfare* 54 (March 1975): 175; Murphy, "A Program for Parents," 38.

24. Murphy, "A Program for Parents," 38–39.

25. *Kathleen Ramos et al. v. John C. Montgomery*, U.S. District Court, Southern District of California, Memorandum of Points and Authorities in Opposition to Defendants' Motion to Dismiss and in Support of Plaintiffs' Motion for Preliminary Injunction, File 001246-C, 29; *Kathleen Ramos v. John C. Montgomery*, Supreme Court of the United States, October Term, 1970, No. 5912, on appeal for the United States District Court for the Southern District of California, Jurisdictional Statement, September 21, 1970, File 001246-E, 15, American Indian Law Library.

26. *Ramos v. Montgomery*, File 001246-E, 3–4.

27. Ramos's lawyers quoted the following from an HEW-printed pamphlet: "The extent of neglect of AFDC children is relatively unknown. Findings from special studies and surveys in several states would indicate that the percentage of neglected children is low. However, many children served by this program are deprived and many live in great hardship because the assistance grants are inadequate. This diminishes the capacity of parents to look after their children satisfactorily and often leads to family breakdown." See *Ramos v. Montgomery*, File 0001246-C. Given these statements about the "low" incidence of neglect and the intense impact of poverty on child rearing, the District Court's argument in support of higher payments to foster parents seems a model of poor reasoning. The court's opinion was that "some children must of necessity be placed in foster homes due to the financial inability of the parents to provide a suitable home. If such parents were to receive the same aid per child as foster

parents receive there is no doubt that they could do a better job in supporting their children. Nevertheless, to give them that additional aid from appropriated funds would result in an over-all reduction in money available for foster home care. A reduction in foster home care aid would threaten the continued existence of the entire program and jeopardize the welfare of thousands of children." The core of the decision was that foster parents provide services to their foster children that they do not have a moral or legal obligation to perform, as biological parents have. Thus, they are entitled to higher subsidies. *Ramos v. Montgomery* 313 F. Supp. 1179 (1970). The Supreme Court affirmed this decision.

28. See Rickie Solinger, "Poisonous Choice," in Molly Ladd-Taylor and Lauri Umansky, eds., *Bad Mothers: The Politics of Blame in Twentieth-Century America* (New York: New York University Press, 1998), 381–402; and Rickie Solinger, "Dependency and Choice: The Two Faces of Eve," in Gwendolyn Mink, ed., *Whose Welfare?* (Ithaca, N.Y.: Cornell University Press, 1999), 7–35.

29. In the earlier, postwar, pre–*Roe v. Wade* period, resourceless women were not so readily marked. See, for example, the statement of Commissioner of Social Security Arthur Altmeyer in 1948, who insisted in an address to the National Social Work Assembly "that public funds . . . should not be accompanied by controls that limit choice or control conduct in ways different from those which apply to other members of the community." Quoted in Hilda M. Arndt, "An Appraisal of What the Critics are Saying About Public Assistance," *Social Service Review* 26 (December 1952): 465. A particularly brilliant discussion of the relationship between race, motherhood, and citizenship is Dorothy E. Roberts, "Welfare and the Problem of Black Citizenship," *Yale Law Journal* 105 (1996): 1563–1602.

30. See, for example, Krause, "Child Welfare, Parental Responsibility, and the State," 267–68. Krause quotes the text of several state laws that aim to disqualify women from motherhood because they have had a child while unmarried.

31. See Mimi Abramovitz, *Regulating the Lives of Women: Social Welfare Policy from Colonial Times to the Present*, rev. ed. (Boston: South End Press, 1996), 327, 338. UAW President Walter Reuther objected to welfare policies in the late 1960s that mixed the issues of illegitimacy, work requirements, foster care, and mothers' rights. He presented his views to Congress: "In the name presumably of encouraging participation in the work training programs, discouraging illegitimacy and having children brought up in more wholesome surroundings, [the 1967 Amendments provide] the states with incentives to remove a child from the care of a parent and place the child in foster care . . . [This] is intended to increase very substantially the number of children in foster care." "Social Security Amendments of 1967," Hearings, Part 3, 1688.

32. Louisiana Constitution, Article Sections 1 (5)(6).

33. This association was particularly strong in Louisiana. See Winifred Bell, *Aid to Dependent Children* (New York: Columbia University Press, 1965), ch. 9; also

Rickie Solinger, *Wake Up Little Susie: Single Pregnancy and Race before Roe v. Wade*, rev. ed. (New York: Routledge, 2000), 192–93.

34. See Marlene Gerber Fried and Loretta Ross, "Our Bodies, Our Lives, Our Right to Decide: The Struggle for Abortion Rights and Reproductive Freedom" (excerpt from *Open Magazine Pamphlet*, reprinted in *Radical America* 24 (April–June 1990, published July 1992): "[The government] locates the cause and the blame of poverty in women's individual choices—women are poor because they have too many children" (36).

35. In "Our Bodies, Our Lives," Fried and Ross note, "Individual freedom of choice is a privilege not enjoyed by those whose reproductive lives are shaped primarily by poverty and discrimination" (36).

36. See Teresa Amott and Julie Matthaei, *Race, Gender and Work: A Multicultural Economic History of Women in the United States* (Boston: South End Press, 1996), ch. 10.

37. Ibid., Table 9–6, 310.

38. Ibid., Appendix C, "Women's Labor Force Participation Rates, by Racial-Ethnic Group, 1900–1990, 412.

39. For a straightforward expression of this conviction, see the oral testimony of William Pierce, executive director of the National Committee for Adoption: "If we had an adoption system that worked in this country, we would have hundreds of thousands of babies that would be placed with capable couples. They wouldn't be raised by young, poorly educated, unemployed young women." U.S. Congress, "A Bill to Prohibit Certain Arrangements Commonly Called Surrogate Motherhood and for Other Purposes," October 15, 1987, 103.

40. See Winifred Bell's discussion of the principles guiding the mothers' pension programs at the 1909 White House Conference, *Aid to Dependent Children*, 5; also see Joanne L. Goodwin, *Gender and the Politics of Welfare Reform: Mothers' Pensions in Chicago, 1911–1929* (Chicago: University of Chicago Press, 1997); Linda Kerber, *Women of the Republic: Intellect and Ideology in Revolutionary America* (Chapel Hill: University of North Carolina Press, 1980); Linda Kerber, *No Constitutional Right to Be Ladies* (New York: Hill and Wang, 1999); and Gwendolyn Mink, *The Wages of Motherhood: Inequality in the Welfare State. 1917–1942* (Ithaca, N.Y.: Cornell University Press, 1995).

41. Mink, *The Wages of Motherhood*, 30.

42. See Krause, "Child Welfare, Parental Responsibility, and the State." Krause entitles a section of his essay "Inadequate Mothers." Also see Abramovitz, *Regulating the Lives of Women*, 339–40; and Joel F. Handler, "The Transformation of Aid to Families with Dependent Children: The Family Support Act in Historical Context," *New York University Review of Law and Social Change* 16 (October 1988): 457–533. Handler makes the excellent point in this essay that many Americans came to feel that poor mothers on welfare should be sent to work at about the same time that most mothers were going to work; but the fact is, he points out, poor mothers of color have always worked. See n. 41.

43. Testimony of Grace Ganz Blumberg, "Economic Problems of Women," Hearings before the Joint Economic Committee, U.S. Congress, 93rd Congress, 1st sess., Part II, July 1973 (Washington, D.C.: U.S. Government Printing Office, 1973), 240 (italics added). Also see "Roundup of Current Research," *Society*, March 1974, 12, for evidence that most Americans did not approve of day care for young children at this time. Institutions reinforced this bias against institutional care; see *U.S. v. Briggs*, 366 F. Supp. 1356 (N.D. Fla. 1973), in which the court found that a jury selection plan providing an automatic hardship excuse to mothers with children under ten years old was constitutionally permissible.

44. Krause, "Child Welfare, Parental Responsibility, and the State," 272.

45. Myron L. Belfer, "Mothers of Children in Day Care," *Child Welfare* 53 (June 1974): 367. Also see Ann D. Murray, "Maternal Employment Reconsidered: Effects on Infants," *Journal of Orthopsychiatry* 45 (October 1975): 773–90; and Laurie Johnson, "More U.S. Day-Care Aid is Proposed," *New York Times*, April 10, 1972, 22. The history of ideologies and attitudes shaping U.S. child care policy is surveyed in Sonya Michel, *Children's Interests/Mothers' Rights* (New Haven: Yale University Press, 1999).

46. Murray, "Maternal Employment Reconsidered," 780.

47. Sheila Kamerman, "Other People's Children," *Public Interest* 30 (winter 1973): 11–27. Union leader Walter Reuther remarked, "There is no moral justification in a free society for confronting a mother, for example, with a choice between being separated from her child and being forced into work and training that may be inappropriate or worse." "Social Security Amendments of 1967," Hearings, Part 3, 1688.

48. Edward C. Banfield, "The Cities: Babies for Sale," *New York Times*, October 13, 1970, 45.

49. Thomas Ross, "The Rhetoric of Poverty: Their Immorality, Our Helplessness," *Georgetown Law Journal* 79 (1991): 1523–24. Also see Barbara Katz Rothman, *Recreating Motherhood: Ideology and Technology in a Patriarchal Society* (New York: Norton, 1989), 188; Judith Blake Davis, "Are Babies Consumer Durables?" *Population Studies* 22 (March 1968): 24; Arthur A. Campbell, "The Role of Family Planning in the Reduction of Poverty," *Journal of Marriage and the Family* 30 (May 1968): 236–45; Martin Waldron, "Birth Control Urged to Cut Relief Costs," *New York Times*, March 11, 1979, XI, 1.

50. Susan Bordo makes an interesting related observation: "In the fathers' rights cases, every assertion of male feeling has been accompanied by a corresponding denial of *female* sensibility; every attempt to prove that men can be nurturers, too, has involved an attempted discreditation of the *woman's* nurturing capabilities—for instance, picturing her as lacking the qualities of caring selflessness, and so forth, that are required of a 'true parent.'" *Unbearable Weight: Feminism, Western Culture, and the Body* (Berkeley: University of California Press, 1993), 92.

51. Mink, *The Wages of Motherhood*, 10; Linda Kerber, *No Constitutional Right*, 244, 245, 134.

52. Gary L. Bauer, *The Family: Preserving America's Future* (Washington, D.C.: U.S. Department of Education, December 12, 1986), 1.

53. U.S. Civil Rights Commission, *A Growing Crisis: Disadvantaged Women and Their Children* (Washington, D.C.: U.S. Government Printing Office, May 1983); U.S. Department of Health and Human Services, "Aid to Families with Dependent Children, Characteristics and Financial Circumstances of AFDC Recipients," no. 42 (1992); Margaret L. Usbansky, "Single Motherhood: Stereotypes v. Statistics," *New York Times*, February 11, 1996, E4; David T. Ellwood and Lawrence H. Summers, "Is Welfare Really the Problem?" *Public Interest* 83 (spring 1986): 69; Gwendolyn Mink, "Welfare Reform in Historical Perspective," *Connecticut Law Review* (spring 1994): 890–92.

54. In 1975, the prospects looked good for poor women. Two policy analysts found that "overall, the picture is one of more favorable income and benefit status for female-headed families in many jurisdictions, and of increasing favor for those families as (1) welfare benefits grow faster than earnings, and (2) female-headed families continue to experience broader categorical eligibility for cash and in-kind programs, and lower tax rates in those programs than husband-wife families." Ross and Sawhill, *Time of Transition*, 101. Mimi Abramovitz notes that "between 1960 and 1970, the average earnings of workers rose by 48%, while the average AFDC benefits jumped 78%. In the early 1970s, the AFDC grant exceeded the minimum wage in many high-benefit states." *Under Attack, Fighting Back: Women and Welfare in the United States* (New York: Monthly Review Press, 1996), 76.

55. "Workfare vs. Welfare," Hearings before the Subcommittee on Trade, Productivity and Economic Growth of the Joint Economic Committee, U.S. Congress, 99th Congress, 2d sess., April 23, 1986 (Washington, D.C.: U.S. Government Printing Office, 1986), 98. Mead had a record of tarring the poor. For example, in 1982 he referred to "the lower class" as "unhinged." *Public Interest* 69 (fall 1982): 19.

56. "Workfare vs. Welfare," Hearings, 39.

57. Bauer, *The Family*, 24. For another example of casually perceived motivations, see Nathan Glazer, "The Social Policy of the Reagan Administration: A Review," *Public Interest* 75 (spring 1984): 87.

58. See, for example, Anthony Brandt, "The Right to be a Mother," *McCall's*, March 1984, 146.

59. Carol Pateman argues that paid employment has replaced military service as "the key to [male] citizenship." In the 1980s, employment—or economic solvency—was becoming key to female citizenship as well. "The Patriarchal Welfare State," in Amy Gutmann, ed., *Democracy and the Welfare State* (Princeton, N.J.: Princeton University Press, 1988), 237.

60. The U.S. Civil Rights Commission asserted in 1983 that "Poor women do par-

ticipate in the labor force . . . The problem is they are often unable to find work, must work part-time, or the jobs do not pay a wage adequate to support a family." *A Growing Crisis*, 15, 35.

61. "Problems of Working Women," Hearing before the Joint Economic Committee, Congress of the United States, 98th Congress, 2d sess., April 3, 1984 (Washington, D.C.: U.S. Government Printing Office, 1984), 97; "Barriers to Self-Sufficiency for Single Female Heads of Families," Hearings before a Subcommittee of the Committee on Government Operations, House of Representatives, 99th Congress, 1st sess., July 9, 10, 1985 (Washington, D.C.: U.S. Government Printing Office, 1985), 179.

62. "Poverty and Hunger in the Black Family," Hearings before the Select Committee on Hunger, House of Representatives, 99th Congress, 1st sess., September 26, 1985 (Washington, D.C.: U.S. Government Printing Office, 1985), 6.

63. "Barriers to Self-Sufficiency," Hearings, 509.

64. "Poverty and Hunger in the Black Family," Hearings, 15.

65. "Congress Study Finds Reagan Budget Curbs Put 557,000 People in Poverty," *New York Times*, July 26, 1984, A19.

66. "Sharp Rise is Seen in Poor Children," *New York Times*, April 29, 1983, A12.

67. "Sob Sisters," *New York Times*, March 3, 1982, A26.

68. See Mink, "Welfare Reform in Historical Perspective," 882.

69. "Federally Funded Child Welfare, Foster Care, and Adoption Assistance Programs," Hearings, 225.

70. "Changes in State Welfare Reform Programs," Hearings Before the Subcommittee on Social Security and Family Policy and Committee on Finance, U.S. Congress, 102d Congress, 2d sess., February 3, 1992 (Washington, D.C.: U.S. Government Printing Office, 1992), 29. Also see Martha F. Davis, "War on Poverty, War on Women," *New York Times*, August 2, 1991, A19, regarding how public policies were pressing coercively on poor mothers' lives.

71. See, for example, Isabel Wilkerson, "Wisconsin Welfare Plan: To Reward the Married," *New York Times*, February 12, 1991, A16. Also see Dorothy Roberts, *Killing the Black Body: Race, Reproduction, and the Meaning of Liberty* (New York: Pantheon, 1997), throughout, and especially ch. 4. At a congressional hearing in 1990, the president of the National Council of Juvenile and Family Court Judges talked about institutionalizing drug-abusing pregnant women. In response, Tom Downey, a representative from Long Island, cautioned the judge: "I am not anxious to see a program where we take lots of black women, put them in structured care, and close our eyes as people in the suburbs are merrily on their way to drinking themselves into oblivion." "Federally Funded Child Welfare, Foster Care, and Adoption Assistance Programs," Hearings, 245, 271.

72. "Federally Funded Child Welfare, Foster Care, and Adoption Assistance Programs," Hearings, 215. Like other such polemicists, Shaw provided no evidence for "the terrible thing."

73. "Federally Funded Child Welfare, Foster Care, and Adoption Assistance Programs," Hearings, 6.

74. Pro-adoption forces in the administration and elsewhere relied on such studies as Steven D. McLaughlin, Susan E. Pearce, Diane L. Manninen, and Linda D. Winges, "To Parent or Relinquish: Consequences for Adolescent Mothers," *Family Planning Perspectives* 20 (January–February, 1988): 25–32, which argued, fundamentally, that women who "chose adoption" would be likely "to live in higher income households" eventually. The authors acknowledged that "those who relinquished . . . were less satisfied with the decision than those who decided to parent." But the researchers discredited this finding: "It is unlikely," they wrote, "that a mother who chose to parent would report that she regrets her decision." It seems remarkable that the study's authors were willing to make such narrow and economistic claims, given how normative single motherhood had become by the mid-1980s and how outspoken single mother groups, and birthmother groups had become about their mother rights.

75. Gary Bauer, *The Family*, 33, 35. See Kristin Luker, *Dubious Conceptions: The Politics of Teenage Fertility* (Cambridge, Mass.: Harvard University Press, 1996), ch. 3.

76. Bill Lehman, U.S. representative from Florida, explained what was positive about adoptions in 1991: they "save the government money by removing the traditional dependency of these children—and their biological parents—on publicly funded services such as foster care and Medicaid." "Federal Adoption Program," Hearings before the Subcommittee on Human Resources of the Committee on Ways and Means, House of Representatives, 102th Congress, 1st sess., May 21, 1991 (Washington, D.C.: U.S. Government Printing Office, 1991), 138. For later samples of federal plans to beef up adoption opportunities, see "Federal Adoption Policy," Hearings before the Subcommittee on Human Resources of the Committee on Ways and Means, House of Representatives, 104th Congress, 1st sess., May 10, 1995 (Washington, D.C.: U.S. Government Printing Office, 1996); H.R. 867, "The Adoption Promotion Act of 1997," Hearings before the Subcommittee on Human Resources of the Committee on Ways and Means, House of Representatives, 105th Congress, 1st sess., April 8, 1997 (Washington, D.C.: U.S. Government Printing Office, 1997).

77. "The Adoption Promotion Hearings of 1997," Hearings, 4–6. Among the forms of federal support for adoption that Smith advocated were funding for maternity homes and for fellowships for graduate students doing work "on positive benefits for adopted children, families, and women who make adoption plans." Also see Carol Lawson, "Getting Congress to Support Adoption," *New York Times*, March 28, 1991, C1.

78. "Federal Adoption Policy," Hearings, 1991, 53.

79. "Barriers to Adoption," Hearings before the Subcommittee on Human Resources of the Committee on Ways and Means, House of Representatives, 104th Congress, 2d sess., June 27, 1996 (Washington, D.C.: U.S. Government Printing Office, 1997), 52–53.

80. Julie Johnson, "Insurance and the Cost of Infertility," *New York Times*, March 5, 1989, IV, 24.

81. "Federal Employee Family-Building Act of 1987," Hearings before the Subcommittee on Civil Service of the Committee on Post Office and Civil Service, House of Representatives, 100th Congress, 2d. sess., March 9, 1988 (Washington, D.C.: U.S. Government Printing Office, 1988), 1.

82. "Federal Employee Family-Building Act of 1987," Hearings before the Subcommittee on Civil Service of the Committee on Post Office and Civil Service, House of Representatives, 100th Congress, 1st sess., July 23, 1987 (Washington, D.C.: U.S. Government Printing Office, 1987), 17–26, 34–35, 62.

83. "Federal Employee Family-Building Act of 1987," Hearings, March 9, 1988, 2.

84. "Federal Employee Family-Building Act of 1987," Hearings, July 23, 1987, 2, 56.

85. "Contract With America—Welfare Reform," Hearings before the Subcommittee on Human Resources of the Committee on Ways and Means, House of Representatives, 104th Congress, 1st sess., Part I, January 1995 (Washington, D.C.: U.S. Government Printing Office, 1995), 69–70.

86. "Federal Employee Family-Building Act of 1987," Hearings, July 23, 1987, 52, 58.

87. "Federal Employee Family-Building Act of 1987," Hearings, March 9, 1988, 25. Reuben Pannor, former director of adoption services at Vista Del Mar, a large child welfare agency in the Los Angeles area, and still active in the field, reports that his current research is showing that today nearly every child placed for adoption is "retrieved by lawyers" from one of the many "pockets of poverty" in the United States. Telephone interview with the author, November 13, 1999.

88. "Adoption Figures," *Welfare in Review* 2(January 1964), 12; "Barriers to Adoption," Hearings, 23.

89. Representative Christopher Smith of New Jersey, a strong anti–abortion rights congressman, suggested the authority he would like to employ when he pointed out that if control over fertility could be regained from women, "a large number of [the] children [lost to abortion] . . . would be eligible for adoption." "Federal Adoption Program," Hearings, 1991, 13.

90. "Changes in State Welfare Reform Programs," Hearings, 46.

91. "Contract With America—Welfare Reform," Hearings, Part I, 544.

92. "Adoption Promotion Act of 1997," Hearings, 4.

93. Eric Schmitt, "House Endorses Break on Taxes for Adoption," *New York Times*, May 11, 1996, A1, 7.

94. Congress first became involved in the issue of infertility in 1978 when it recognized "the problem of infertility and the urgent need for infertility services for about a million American couples who are unable to achieve their family size goals." *Final Report*, prepared by the Select Committee on Population, House of Representatives, 95th Congress, 2d sess., January 1979 (Washington, D.C.:

U.S. Government Printing Office, 1979), 15. For 1988–89 developments, see Julie Johnson, "Insurance and the Cost of Infertility," *New York Times*, May 5, 1989, IV, 24; also see "50% Success Rate in $1 Billion Infertility Fight," *New York Times*, May 18, 1988, A25; Office of Technology Assessment, *Infertility: Social and Medical Choices* (Washington, D.C.: U.S. Government Printing Office, 1988), 161. A study by the National Center for Health Statistics in 1990 cast "doubt on much-discussed infertility epidemic, finding no change in overall rate of infertility since 1965." Philip J. Hilts, "New Study Challenges Estimates on Odds of Adopting a Child," *New York Times*, December 10, 1990, B10.

95. "Federal Employee Family-Building Act of 1987," Hearings, July 23, 1987, 1, 10, 21, 22–23.

96. "Federal Employee Family-Building Act of 1987," Hearings, March 9, 1988, 117; also see Office of Technology Assessment, *Infertility*, 144.

97. See "50% Success Rate"; and Office of Technology Assessment, *Infertility*, 161.

98. Mary Thom, "Dilemmas of the New Birth Technologies," *Ms.*, May 1988, 71; also see *Infertility Services in the United States: Need, Accessibility and Utilization* (New York: Alan Guttmacher Institute, 1985).

99. "Medical and Social Choices for Infertile Couples and the Federal Role in Prevention and Treatment," Hearings before a Subcommittee of the Committee on Government Operations, House of Representatives, 100th Congress, 2d sess., July 14, 1988 (Washington, D.C.: U.S. Government Printing Office, 1989), 28. Also see Office of Technology Assessment, *Infertility*, 156; and John A. Robertson, "Embryos, Families, and Procreative Liberty: The Legal Status of the New Reproduction," *Southern California Law Review* 59 (1986): 939.

100. Office of Technology Assessment, *Infertility*, 156, 149, 153, 149–50, 156; also see Johnson, "Insurance and the Cost of Infertility."

101. Dorothy K. Seavey and Beth M. Miller, "Getting to the Big Picture: Anti-Welfare Fertility Politics in Context," *Society* 33 (July–August 1996): 35.

102. Thomas G. Wiggan, president of Serono Laboratories, was the speaker. "Federal Employee Family-Building Act of 1987," Hearings, March 9, 1988, 67.

103. Carol Sanger, "M is for the Many Things," 63.

104. "Federal Employee Family-Building Act of 1987," Hearings, March 9, 1988, 24.

105. Reflecting and supporting the continued vulnerability of fertile women, U.S. Representative Dick Armey of Texas and five of his colleagues suggested in 1989 that the infertility problems of middle-class couples should be solved by canceling all women's abortion rights and transferring "1.5 million pre-born children each year . . . to infertile couples . . . This is a match which deserves much more attention . . . [It's] a genuine solution." "Infertility in America: Why Is the Federal Government Ignoring a Major Health Problem?" Eighth Report by the Committee on Government Operations together with Dissenting and Additional Views, 101st Congress, 1st sess., House Report 101-389,

December 1, 1989 (Washington, D.C.: U.S. Government Printing Office, 1989), 34.

106. Seth Mydans, "U.S. Food Program Tightens Its Belt and Millions on Welfare Feel Pinch," *New York Times*, June 2, 1990, A10.

107. Bell, *Aid to Dependent Children*, 70.

108. "Illegitimacy and Its Impact on the Aid to Dependent Children Program: Implications for Federal and State Administrators," Bureau of Public Assistance, Social Security Administration, U.S. Department of Health, Education, and Welfare (Washington, D.C.: U.S. Government Printing Office, 1960), 47.

109. *Dandridge v. Williams* 397 US 471 (1970).

110. Thomas Ross, *Just Stories: How the Law Embodies Racism and Bias* (Boston: Beacon Press, 1996), 72.

111. Thomas Ross, "The Rhetoric of Poverty: Their Immorality, Our Helplessness," *Georgetown Law Journal* 79 (1991): 1520.

112. For *New York Times* coverage of these events, see, for example, Peter Kerr, "Trenton Legislator Proposes Overhaul of Welfare System," April 9, 1991, B4; Jason DeParle, "As Funds For Welfare Shrink, Ideas Flourish," May 12, 1991, IV, 5; Wayne King, "Maverick Democrat Confronts Trenton's Welfare Rules," September 4, 1991, B1; Wayne King, "Trenton Panel Supports Plan for Welfare," December 6, 1991, B1.

113. "Changes in State Welfare Reform Programs," Hearings, 7, 28.

114. For example, see Andrew Rosenthal, "Bush Backs Wisconsin Attempt at Welfare Reform," *New York Times*, April 9, 1992, D20, for a description of Wisconsin's family cap plans; and Jason DeParle, "California Plan to Cut Welfare May Prompt Others to Follow," December 18, 1991, A1, for a description of California's.

115. Gwen Ifill, "Clinton Backs New Jersey's Changes in Welfare System," *New York Times*, May 23, 1992, 8.

116. Linda C. McClain, "Irresponsible Reproduction," *Hastings Law Journal* 47 (January 1996): 398–99.

117. *C.K. v. Shalala*, 883 F. Supp. 991, 1014.

118. McClain, "Irresponsible Reproduction," 403. Welfare policy analyst Richard Nathan observed in 1992 that "New Jersey politicians have been kicked for a tax increase. They want something to kick back. In this case it is welfare babies. For a largely symbolic move, it is just not worth it. It sends the wrong message to people who have been down long enough—in some cases, all their lives." "Changes in State Welfare Reform Programs," Hearings, 94.

119. "Changes in State Welfare Reform Programs," Hearings, 28.

120. "Contract With America—Welfare Reform," Hearings before the Subcommittee on Human Resources of the Committee on Ways and Means, House of Representatives, 104th Congress, 1st sess., Part II, February 2, 1995 (Washington, D.C.: U.S. Government Printing Office, 1995), 1153.

121. Heather MacDonald, "The Ideology of 'Family Preservation,'" *Public Interest*

115 (September 1994): 45; "Contract With America—Welfare Reform," Hearings, Part I, 677.

122. Jason DeParle, "The 1994 Election: Momentum Builds for Cutting Back Welfare System," *New York Times*, November 13, 1994, A1. Eleanor Holmes Norton called the orphanage proposal "Murray's orphanage idea," and indicated that this type of child removal was "meant as a punishment and a deterrent for out-of-wedlock child-bearing." "Contract With America—Welfare Reform," Hearings, Part I, 584.

123. U.S. Representative Christopher Shay of Connecticut explained how the legislation ending AFDC would create block grants which "may be used to establish orphanages." Sheila Jackson Lee, a representative from Texas, pointed out how silly the orphanage plan was: "Under this [welfare reform plan], of the 541,000 children who are currently receiving AFDC in Texas, 288,000 would be denied benefits and only 310 federal orphanage slots would be funded." "Contract With America—Welfare Reform," Hearings, Part I, 735, 642.

124. Elizabeth Drew, *Showdown: The Battle between the Gingrich Congress and the Clinton White House* (New York: Simon and Schuster, 1996), 46.

125. See "Contract With America—Welfare Reform," Hearings, Part II, 841.

126. Ross D. London, "The 1994 Orphanage Debate: A Study in the Politics of Annihilation," in Richard B. McKenzie, ed., *Rethinking Orphanages for the 21st Century* (Thousand Oaks, Calif.: Sage, 1999), 98.

127. Christopher Jencks and Kathryn Edin, "Do Poor Women Have a Right to Bear Children?" *American Prospect* 20 (winter 1995): 47.

128. Eleanor Holmes Norton, "Contract With America—Welfare Reform," Hearings, Part II, 584.

129. Dorothy Roberts: "The Only Good Poor Woman: Unconstitutional Conditions and Welfare," *Denver University Law Review* 72 (1995): 931–48; "Irrationality and Sacrifice in the Welfare Reform Consensus," *Virginia Law Review* 81 (1995): 2607–22; "The Value of Black Mothers' Work," *Connecticut Law Review* 26 (1994): 871–78; "Welfare's Ban on Poor Motherhood," in Gwendolyn Mink, ed., *Whose Welfare?* (Ithaca, N.Y.: Cornell University Press, 1999), 152–67; and *Killing the Black Body*, throughout.

130. Katha Pollitt, "Subject to Debate," *Nation*, December 12, 1994, 717.

131. "Contract With America—Welfare Reform," Hearings, Part II, 1344.

132. This motto comes from "A National Strategy to Prevent Teen Pregnancy," Annual Report, 1997–98, U.S. Department of Health and Human Services, June 1998, 1.

133. Kate Shatzkin, "A Better Message on Teen Pregnancy," *Baltimore Sun*, November 8, 1999, 1.

134. Jencks and Edin, "Do Poor Women Have a Right to Bear Children?" 45.

135. See, generally, "Equal Pay for Working Families" (Washington, D.C.: Institute for Women's Policy Research, 1999).

136. Jencks and Edin, "Do Poor Women Have a Right to Bear Children?" 47.
137. "Equal Pay for Working Families." Also see Abramovitz, *Under Attack, Fighting Back*.
138. Examples of presentations and reports targeting politicians and policy makers with this kind of information over time are: economist Nancy S. Barrett's testimony at "Economic Status of Women," Hearings before the Joint Economic Committee, Congress of the United States, 97th Congress, 2d sess., February 3, 1982 (Washington, D.C.: U.S. Government Printing Office, 1982), 85–86; "Mother-Only Families: Low Earnings Will Keep Many Children in Poverty" (GAO/HRD-91-62, April 2, 1991); "Testimony of the Child Welfare League of America," submitted to the Economic and Educational Opportunities Subcommittee on Early Childhood, Youth and Families on the Child Care and Development Block Grant and the Child and Adult Care Food Program, January 31, 1995, in "Contract With America: Child Welfare and Childcare," Hearings before the Subcommittee on Early Childhood, Youth and Families of the Committee on Economic and Educational Opportunities, House of Representatives, 104th Congress, 1st sess., January 31, 1995 (Washington, D.C.: U.S. Government Printing Office, 1995), 204–13.
139. "Millions in State Child Care Funds Going Unspent in New York," *New York Times*, October 25, 1999, A29. The article indicated that "the state has no detailed plan for getting the new money into the hands of low- and moderate-income parents."
140. Kathryn Edin and Laura Lein, *Making Ends Meet: How Single Mothers Survive Welfare and Low-Wage Work* (New York: Russell Sage Foundation, 1997), 220.
141. Charles Murray, "Symposium: Illegitimacy and Welfare, Keeping Priorities Straight on Welfare Reform," *Society* 33 (July–August 1996): 10–12.
142. See Richard P. Nathan, "Is It Necessary to Be Brutal?" *Society* 33 (July–August 1996): 15–16; and, Seavey and Miller, "Getting to the Big Picture," *Society* 33 (July–August 1996): 33–36.
143. Lawrence Mead, "Welfare Reform at Work," *Society* 33 (July–August 1966): 37–40.
144. Walter E. Williams, "The Welfare Debate," *Society* 33 (July–August 1966): 13–14.
145. "Contract With America—Welfare Reform," Hearings, Part I, 170.
146. "Welfare Booby Traps," *Newsweek*, December 12, 1994, 35.
147. "Contract With America—Welfare Reform," Hearings, Part I, 695, 191.
148. Robert Rector's comments in "Caring for America's Children—A Congressional Symposium on Child Care and Parenting," Hearings before the Subcommittee on Children and Families of the Committee on Labor and Human Resources, U.S. Senate, 105th Congress, 2d sess., February 23, 1998 (Washington, D.C.: U.S. Government Printing Office, 1998), 90. In 1995, at hearings on welfare reform, Katherine McFate of the Joint Center for Political and Economic Studies, cited a study by the Child Welfare League of America that

NOTES TO PAGES 215-16 / 281

found that "child abuse or neglect charges have been brought against less than 4% of all AFDC mothers." She referred to this evidence to refute "recent rhetoric around the welfare issue [that] seems to suggest that a high proportion of mothers on AFDC are inadequate parents." McFate also referred to research showing that, for poor children, "being institutionalized at an early age or trapped in the foster care system . . . [causes] children [to] have much higher rates of school failure, substance abuse, criminal activity, and psychological problems." "Contract With America—Welfare Reform," Hearings, Part II, 1094.

149. Handler, "The Transformation of Aid to Dependent Children," 487. For example, Cleveland exempted mothers from waged work if they had children under six months, Miami under three months. See Janet Quint et al., "Big Cities and Welfare Reform: Early Implementation and Ethnographic Findings from the Project on Devolution and Urban Change," Manpower Demonstration Research Corporation, April 1999, 6.

150. Edin and Lein, *Making Ends Meet*, 76.

151. William M. Epstein, "Passing into Proverbs," *Society* 33 (July–August 1996): 22.

152. Sanford M. Dornbusch, Melissa R. Herman, and I-Chun Lin, "Single Parenthood," *Society* 33 (July–August 1996): 31.

153. See, for example, Kristin Moore et al., "The JOBS Evaluation: How Well Are They Faring?" Manpower Demonstration Research Corporation, February 1996, 1.

154. Katherine S. Newman, "Tyesha's Dilemma: Anthropological Ruminations on the Consequences of Welfare Reform," Kennedy School of Government, Harvard University, May 1998, 15.

155. Richard F. Wertheimer, "Working Poor Families with Children," Childtrends (Web site), February 1999, 6. Wertheimer observes, "Although having one or more working parent reduces the likelihood that children will live in poverty, it does not provide a guarantee of escaping poverty. Thus, if welfare reform succeeds in moving more parents into the labor market, more working poor families may be a consequence." Also see S. Jody Heymann and Alison Earle, "The Work-Family Balance: What Hurdles are Parents Leaving Welfare Likely to Confront?" *Journal of Political Analysis and Management* 17 (1998): 313–21.

156. Seavey and Miller, "Getting to the Big Picture," 35; Quint et al., "Big Cities and Welfare Reform," 5; Edin and Lein, *Making Ends Meet*, 221.

157. S. Jody Heymann and Alison Earle, "The Impact of Welfare Reform on Parents' Ability to Care for the Children's Health," *American Journal of Public Health* 89 (April 1999): 502–5. Also see comments by Ellen Galinsky of the Family and Work Institute, showing that 63 percent of single parents of young children "do not have access to paid time off to care for their [sick] children." "Caring for America's Children," 58.

158. Martha J. Zaslow and Carolyn A. Eldred, eds., "Parenting Behavior in a Sam-

ple of Young Mothers in Poverty: Results of the New Chance Observational Study," Manpower Demonstration Research Corporation, April 1998, 7; also see Handler, "The Transformation of Aid to Dependent Children," 517.

159. Thomas Ross makes a related point in *Just Stories*, 86. Gwendolyn Mink compares the "opprobrium we foist on welfare mothers with the recent celebration of heterosexual, married domesticity surrounding the introduction of federal legislation to permit independent retirement account tax deductions for housewives." *Welfare's End* (Ithaca, N.Y.: Cornell University Press, 1999), 181. Legal scholar Linda C. McClain explains, "the notion that government should not subsidize 'irresponsible' procreation by providing welfare benefits ignores the extent to which government already subsidizes reproduction, chiefly to the benefit of middle income and wealthy families, through a taxation scheme allowing deductions for dependent children, child care, and mortgages, as well as through programs supporting public higher education." "Irresponsible Reproduction," 415.

160. "Caring for America's Children," Hearings, 65; also see Danielle Crittenden, *What Our Mothers Didn't Tell Us: Why Happiness Eludes the Modern Woman* (New York: Simon and Schuster, 1999).

161. "Caring for America's Children," Hearings, 36, 38.

162. James Q. Wilson's comment in 1995 illustrates how financial resources separate mothers, especially in the view of policy makers and policy analysts: "Only at the highest income level, that is to say, mothers earning over $50,000 a year, the Murphy Brown income, if you will, is the child immunized from the consequences of being raised with a single parent." "Contract With America—Welfare Reform," Hearings, Part I, 151.

163. "Caring for America's Children," Hearings, 44.

164. See Celia W. Dugger, "Researchers Find a Diverse Face on New York's Poverty," reporting on a study "challenging the stereotype of the poor as single mothers on welfare." Instead, the study, "Poverty and Public Spending Related to Poverty in New York City," issued by the Citizens Budget Commission, found that "only one in four poor households in New York City is headed by a single parent." *New York Times*, August 8, 1994, B10.

165. "Caring for America's Children," Hearings, 40–41, 67–68, 4; also see the comments of Darcy Olsen of the Cato Institute, 90.

166. "Contract With America—Welfare Reform," Hearings, Part I, 665.

167. Ibid., Part II, 1410.

168. See "Roundup of Current Research," *Society*, March 1974, 6–7, 10, 12; one finding reported here was that "in spite of the increase in approval, work carries little positive value for women. 68% of the women surveyed in a 1970 poll felt that 'taking care of a home and raising a family' is more interesting than having a job." Also see Nadine Brozan, "American Family: At the Crossroads," *New York Times*, April 21, 1977, III, 1, which reports that the "vast majority" of both "traditionalists" and "the new breed" of parents "disapprove of mothers of

young children working." A 1981 study conducted for the National Committee for Citizens in Education, a parents' rights group, found that there was a "tremendous amount of negative stereotyping" of single parent families. Glenn Collins, "Schools Stereotype Children with One Parent," *New York Times*, February 2, 1981, 16. As "motherhood" was fracturing in American society, President Ford made an attempt to honor the traditional mother "for holding families and nation together," including by doing dinner and the wash. See *New York Times*, May 9, 1976, III, 2.

169. Quoted in "American Women Workers in a Full Employment Economy," Hearings before the Subcommittee on Economic Growth and Stabilization of the Joint Economic Committee, U.S. Congress, 95th Congress, 1st sess., September 16, 1977 (Washington, D.C.: U.S. Government Printing Office, 1978), 29–31.

170. C. Christian Beels, "The Case of the Vanishing Mommy," *New York Times*, July 4, 1976, VI, 28.

171. See Solinger, "Dependency and Choice: The Two Faces of Eve."

172. Linda Kerber has written about the negative association of women and choice making in the years following the establishment of the United States: "A taste for literature—like a taste for dissipation—drew women's attention away from domestic work. In this context, reading of any sort was self-indulgent, it was an assertion of individual choice." *Women of the Republic*, 253.

173. "*Roe v. Wade*, The 1973 Supreme Court Decision on State Abortion Laws," in Robert M. Baird and Stuart E. Rosenbaum, eds., *The Ethics of Abortion: Pro-Life! vs Pro-Choice!* (Buffalo, N.Y.: Prometheus Books, 1993), 41–43.

174. Ruth Hubbard, *The Politics of Women's Biology* (New Brunswick, N.J.: Rutgers University Press, 1990), 145.

175. A remarkable example of the cultural incompatibility of motherhood and choice is the case of a married woman who applied for a bank mortgage in the early 1970s. She was told by the banker reviewing her case that she could only count her own income for the purposes of calculating the mortgage figures *if* she could produce medical papers proving that she'd had a hysterectomy. This case was described by Carol DeSarem, vice president of Manhattan NOW, at a government hearing, "Economic Problems of Women," Part IV, Hearings before the Joint Economic Committee, Congress of the United States, 93rd Congress, 2d sess., June 17, 1974 (Washington, D.C.: U.S. Government Printing Office, 1976), 619.

176. "Contract With America—Welfare Reform," Hearings, Part II, 1498.

177. "Welfare Booby Traps," *Newsweek*, December 12, 1994, 33.

178. Kerber, *No Constitutional Right*, 241.

179. Kerber, *Women of the Republic*, 11, 283–84; also see Mink, *The Wages of Motherhood*; Marybeth Norton, *Liberty's Daughters: The Revolutionary Experience of American Women, 1750–1800* (New York: Little, Brown, 1980).

180. See Roberts, "Welfare and the Problem of Black Citizenship."

181. Kerber, *Women of the Republic*, 287.

INDEX